Culture of Fear Revisited

Culture of Fear Revisited

Risk-taking and the Morality of Low Expectation

Fourth Edition

FRANK FUREDI

continuum

CONTINUUM

The Tower Building,   80 Maiden Lane,
11 York Road,   New York,
London,   NY 10038
SE1 7NX

www.continuumbooks.com

First edition published 1997 by Cassell
Revised editions published 2002, 2005 by Continuum
This edition published 2006

British Library Cataloguing-in-Publication Data
A catalogue record for this book is available from the British Library.

ISBN 0-8264-9394-7 (hardback)
      0-8264-9395-5 (paperback)

Designed and typeset by Ben Cracknell Studios
Printed and bound in Great Britain by
Cromwell Press Ltd, Trowbridge, Wiltshire

Contents

Preface   vii

Chapter 1   What is Distinct About the Way We Fear?   1

Chapter 2   The Explosion of Risks   23

Chapter 3   Why Do We Panic?   53

Chapter 4   The Culture of Abuse   79

Chapter 5   A World of Risky Strangers   113

Chapter 6   Who Can You Trust?   133

Chapter 7   The New Etiquette   153

Chapter 8   Conclusions – The Politics of Fear   175

Bibliography   201

Index   205

Preface
Culture of Fear Revisited

Back in 1997, when the original version of this book was published, the term 'culture of fear' meant little to most people. Unfortunately, today it resonates all too well with people's experience and it has become a widely used idiom. People frequently talk about the culture of fear as a tangible reality that shapes their daily life. To give a few current examples: The producer of a CBS television show *Conspiracy of Silence* claims that a culture of fear discourages people to talk about criminals in their neighbourhood.[1] A review of the Seattle-based rock band, Pearl Jam, observes that its lyricist is concerned with the 'culture of fear' propagated by the Bush administration.[2] A Canadian opponent of the war in Iraq notes that 'the world has gone crazy', before adding, 'haven't we learned that we're only feeding a culture of fear?'[3] An Australian whistleblower warns that there is 'a culture of fear' within the ambulance service that he works for.[4] 'There is a culture of fear around space travel' notes a report on this subject.[5] A report into the running of the Southern Baptist Convention complains that one of its officials had created a 'culture of fear' among the employees of its domestic mission force.[6] 'What I hadn't counted on was the incredible culture of fear', exclaims the director of a documentary on the retail giant Wal-Mart.[7] In everyday conversation, individuals blame one another for creating a culture of fear in the office or in school. The usage or even over-usage of the term indicates that fear is not simply a reaction to a specific danger, but a cultural metaphor for interpreting life.

It is not hope but fear that excites and shapes the cultural imagination of the early twenty-first century. And indeed, fear is fast becoming a caricature of itself. It is no longer simply an emotion, or a response to the perception of threat. It has become a cultural idiom through which we signal a sense of growing unease about our place in the world. Popular culture continually encourages an expansive alarmist imagination through providing the public with a steady diet of fearful programmes about impending calamities – man-made and natural. Alarmist television programmes about old and impending disasters, and films like *The Day After Tomorrow* self-consciously erode the line between fact and fiction. In May 2006, an ABC television disaster movie about a fictional bird-flu pandemic, *Fatal Contact: Bird Flu in America*, actually created a stir among health professionals, who were worried that its scary storyline would create unease and panic among viewers who would interpret it as fact. The programme, which transmits scenes of terrified people panicking, concludes with a scene where most of the inhabitants die as a result of the dreaded plague. In anticipation of an anxious public reaction to this work of fiction, The Health and Human Services Department published 'talking points' to health professionals to reassure worried viewers. Its briefing stated that 'while the movie serves to raise awareness about avian and pandemic flu, we hope it will inspire preparation – not panic'.[8] This incident involving public health officials, television scriptwriters and the media illustrates how fact becomes fiction and fiction turns into an object of policy deliberation.

Some experts and health professionals are quite happy to deploy alarmist fiction to promote their cause. Some of these fear entrepreneurs actually embraced *Fatal Contact* because of the publicity that this sensationalist show would provoke. Raising awareness through the promotion of fear is frequently justified by zealous crusaders. One climatologist, David Viner, acknowledged that the film *The Day After Tomorrow* 'got a lot of details wrong'. But hey, so what! He argues that anything that 'raises awareness about climate change must be a good thing'.[9]

Even so-called high culture can not resist the temptation of promoting the fear theme. The perils of modern living was the theme of an exhibition in the Museum of Modern Art in New York in 2005. Fear is also the motif that dominated the Eighth Contemporary Art Biennial of Lyon in the same year. Natasha Edwards wrote about the 'art of fear' that haunts this important exhibition of contemporary European Art. The artistic celebration of the theme of fear indicates that it has become a cultural metaphor for interpreting and representing the world around us. Indeed in some circles, fear is used as a form of affectation to signify a sensitivity to the many hidden perils facing people. To acknowledge fear is to demonstrate awareness. This self-conscious affectation does not mean that people are necessarily more scared than previously. It merely signals the idea that they *ought to be*. That is why public health professionals often sound as if they are rehearsing a script for a disaster movie. 'It is like a combination of global warming and HIV Aids', noted Dr David Nabarro, before predicting that up to 150 million people could be killed by a bird-flu pandemic. Nabarro, who is the UN health official charged with coordinating national responses to this pandemic, had no inhibitions about using artistic licence to spice up his official statement.[10]

It is not necessary for our imagination of fear to correspond to our experience of life. Compared with the past, people living in Western societies have less familiarity with pain, suffering debilitating diseases and death than ever before. We are far better placed to deal with the outbreak of new disease than was the case in the past. Recent outbreaks of Ebola, SARS and West Nilus virus have been contained with relatively small loss of lives. In 2006, Thailand and Vietnam were able to report that the bird flu had been contained even though they were at the epicentre of the epidemic a year previously.[11] Yet despite our growing capacity to deal with the problems facing humanity, we believe that we are likely to be overwhelmed by the disasters that loom ahead.

Every culture has something distinct to say about fear. In ancient societies, people were instructed to fear their gods or ancestors. In medieval times, communities were incited to fear witches and other malevolent supernatural forces. Some cultures fear death, others are concerned about unemployment. Until recent times, Western cultures were preoccupied with the threat of nuclear war. Today we are simply encouraged to regard fear as our default response to life itself. As Christophe Lambert observed in his study of French society, *The Fearful Society*, his compatriots are haunted by 'fear of the future, fear of losing, fear of others, fear of taking a risk, fear of solitude, fear of growing old'.[12]

Often fears are a sensible response to the circumstances facing people. As individuals, fear often helps us to concentrate the mind when we engage with unexpected and unpredictable circumstances. There are many experiences that we should rightly fear. My mother's fear of war and violent conflict is based on her experience of living through the Second World War and having to deal with the death and suffering of friends and family members. Our personal experiences shape the imagination and our fears. However, today, many of our fears are not based on personal experience. They are often shaped by television programmes such as *Fatal Contact*, or by alarmist media accounts of avian flu in Asia, the Ebola virus in Africa, or of desperate Middle Eastern terrorists plotting our downfall. These are threats that do not necessarily emerge out of our immediate personal experience. We can neither fight them nor flee from them. They are about dangers that we cannot directly confront, but simply fear passively.

The growing divergence of our sensibility of fear from our direct daily routine indicates that we are not talking about simply an emotional response to our experience. What is at issue is a more general cultural perspective on how we make sense of our lives. One of the principal features of our culture of fear is the belief that humanity is confronted by powerful destructive forces that threaten our existence. With so much at stake how can responsible people fail to raise the alarm? That is why it has become so easy for television producers to blur the line that used to divide reality from science fiction. That is also why officialdom appears to be in the business of transmitting scare stories to the public. Politicians and officials take the view that if they warn us to be afraid about some impending catastrophe, they will protect themselves from accusations of irresponsibility. This calculation motivated Michael Leavitt, secretary of the Department of Health and Human Services, who advised Americans to prepare for a possible flu pandemic by hoarding food, water and medicine at home.[13]

In public discourse, themes traditionally associated with science fiction have become politicized. According to professional asteroid-watchers it is imperative that governments take action to develop technology that can protect the planet from collisions with near-Earth objects (NEOs). The US Congress has charged NASA with responsibility to 'detect, track, catalogue and characterize' NEOs.[14] Asteroid-watchers regularly issue warnings about potentially menacing NEOs. In May 2006 the prestigious publication the *New Scientist* issued a warning about a 'newly discovered asteroid', which is 'now the biggest thing known with a possibility of hitting the Earth'. Although the article was titled 'Big New Asteroid Has Slim Chance of Hitting Earth' – apparently a risk of one in six million – some readers are likely to conclude that this is one more potential catastrophe waiting to happen.[15] But how do you calculate the risk of a Killer-Asteroid destroying human civilization? Where do you get the figure of a risk of one in six million? Primarily through the exercise of our cultural imagination! Distinguished astronomer and former president of the British Association for the Advancement of Science, Martin Rees, contends that we have reached the final century of human civilization. He also believes that more than one million people will be killed through a single act of bioterrorism or bio-error by 2020.[16] Cautionary fairy-tales are no longer written only for children. The language of science is frequently used to give grown-ups a good old scare.

Increasingly, the meaning of risk has expanded and has become a rhetorical idiom through which people imagine worst-case scenarios. Speculative risks are not the same as theoretical risks. Faced with uncertainty, theoretical risks are oriented towards exploring the probabilities and impact of hitherto unknown hazards, such as that posed by nanotechnology. Speculation is not so much the theoretical exploration of the unknown, as an exercise of the imagination. This was the procedure adopted by US defense secretary Donald Rumsfeld, at a press briefing on 12 February 2002, when he declared that:

> *As we know, there are known knowns; there are things we know we know. We also know there are known unknowns; that is to say we know there are some things we do not know. But there are also unknown unknowns – the ones we don't know we don't know.*[17]

Rumsfeld's reflections on 'unknown unknowns' were treated with derision by sections of the press. However, as Bill Durodie notes, this grotesque formulation has been widely used by environmentalists since the eighties.[18]

Speculation about the ones 'we don't know we don't know' is informed by moral disorientation, rather than information gained through scientific research. It invariably begins with the question of 'what if' and concludes with apocalyptic warnings about human survival. Speculation about risk has little to do with the real problems facing humanity. It is sustained by a worldview that is deeply pessimistic about prospects for the future. The pessimism is paralleled by an unprecedented mood of misanthropy. In popular and high culture and in the media, human beings are characteristically represented as a danger to themselves, to others and above all to the planet. From this perspective, humanity cannot be expected to creatively engage with risks. Instead of playing the role of problem solvers, people are the problem. Misanthropy has gained unprecedented influence in Western societies. It is the fear of ourselves as human beings that underpins the normalization of fear in contemporary society.

The downsizing of the status of the human species has as its corollary the inflation of the dangers it faces. Instead of human progress, children are warned to beware of calamities to come. Natural disasters such a tsunami, hurricane or flood are no longer regarded as just that – natural.

Adopting the perspective of medieval superstition, acts of misfortune are endowed with meaning. They are either signs of God's wrath, evidence of climate change or proof of the destructive power of humanity and of its essential malevolence. Scientists warn of impending flu pandemics, new super-bugs, a new European ice age, the disintegration of the Arctic ice shelf, more hurricanes and depletion of resources. But, as we argue in this book, it is not so much human survival, but the survival of our faith in humanity which is at issue.

The fear of ourselves

Increasingly, deliberations about the future focus on the issue of human survival. According to James Lovelock, 'before this century is over billions of us will die and the few breeding pairs of people that survive will be kept in the Arctic where the climate remains tolerable'.[19] Books with titles like James Howard Kunstler's *The Long Emergency; Surviving The Converging Catastrophes Of The Twenty-First Century*, or Jared Diamond's *Collapse: How Societies Choose to Fail or Survive*, or Eugene Linden's *The Winds of Change; Weather and the Destruction of Civilizations* project a scenario of unavoidable global catastrophe. 'This is a much darker time than 1938, the eve of World War II', warns Kunstler.[20] Alarming stories are circulated about an impending die-off and cities engulfed by rising oceans as the inexorable outcome of climate change. Today we don't just have Four Horsemen of the Apocalypse, but a cavalry regiment of doom-mongers. What we have is a secular version of St John's revelations. But one where the apocalypse has no future and where, instead of being redeemed, human beings disappear without a trace.

Anxieties about human survival go back to the beginning of human history. Through catastrophes like the Deluge or Sodom and Gomorrah, the religious imagination fantasized about the end of the world. With the passing of time apocalyptic ideas which were rooted in magic and theology have been recast into allegedly scientific statements about human destructiveness and irresponsibility. Elbowing aside the mystical St John, Lovelock assumes the mantle of the prophet scientist when he states that, 'I take my profession seriously, and now I, too, have to bring bad news'.[21] Today, human consumption, technological development or 'man playing God' is blamed for placing the future of the earth in jeopardy. And instead of Original Sin leading to the Fall of Man, we fear the degradation of Nature by a malevolent human species. The various Doomsday scenarios that surround discussions of the millennium bug, oil depletion, global warming, the avian flu and the destruction

PREFACE

of bio-diversity stress the theme of human culpability. They have as their premise the human species' destructiveness and moral bankruptcy. 'With breathtaking insolence', warns Lovelock in his *The Revenge of Gaia*, 'humans have taken the stores of carbon that Gaia buried to keep oxygen at its proper level and burnt them'.

Fear has acquired a powerful cultural validation and is constantly encouraged by the unprecedented level of suspicion towards the human species that prevails in the early twenty-first century. Human activity is continually blamed for threatening the existence of the earth. Scare stories about the scale of human destruction are regularly transmitted by the media, and promoted by advocacy groups and politicians. For example, it was claimed that human activity has reduced the number of surviving birds and fish species by 35 per cent during the past thirty years. This story, which was circulated by the environmentalist news service *Planet Ark* and picked up by the mainstream media, drew a direct correlation between human action and ecological destruction. The engagement of human beings with nature is frequently represented as *ecocide*, the heedless and deliberate destruction of the environment. Such a highly charged representation of humanity's attempt to domesticate nature turns this experience into a process akin to genocide or the Holocaust. The title of Broswimmer's polemic *Ecocide: A Short History of the Mass Extinction of Species* captures this sense of loathing towards the human. This point is also echoed by Jared Diamond, who argues that 'ecocide has now come to overshadow nuclear war and emerging diseases as the threat to global civilisations'.[22]

Increasingly, the term 'human impact' is associated with pollution, wanton destruction and the stripping bare of the earth's assets. It is a malevolent force to be feared. Former American Vice President Al Gore is concerned that the 'power of technologies now at our disposal vastly magnifies the impact each individual can have on the natural world', and therefore you get a 'violent destructive collision between our civilization and the Earth'.[23] Throughout the past four centuries the human impact on the world, leading to the humanization of nature, was positively affirmed by Western culture. These days human ingenuity is regarded ambiguously, since it assists the capacity of people to make an impact on the world. And the very idea of civilization is frequently presented as a force for ecological destruction. 'Civilizations have been destroying the living systems of the earth for at least 5,000 years', according to one misanthropic account.[24] Is it any surprise that the very meaning of human activity has acquired sinister connotations? According to some environmentalists, humans are a 'foreign negative element', even a 'cancer on the environment'.[25] For radical environmentalists the degradation of nature is due our species' belief in the unique qualities of the human. Such beliefs dubbed anthropocentrism are denounced for endangering the planet. Deep ecologists claim that humanity has degraded the planet because of its human-centred ideology that views nature from the perspective of its utility for people. The denigration of humanity often assumes a vitriolic form. The tendency to represent humans as parasites is not confined to a tiny circle of cultural pessimists. Michael Meacher, the former UK New Labour Minister for the Environment, referred to humans as 'the virus' infecting the earth's body.

The tendency to perceive human activity through a narrative that emphasizes its selfish, destructive and toxic behaviour underpins our culture of fear. Humanity is not simply indicted for the damage it inflicts on the planet in the here and now, but also for what it has done since the beginning of time. Increasingly, history is being rewritten in a form where it is difficult to detect any positive human contribution to the well-being of our planet. The past is reduced to a sordid story about the devastation inflicted on the earth by humans. According to a recently published UN report, *Global Diversity Outlook 2*, humans are responsible for the worst cycle of extinctions since the dinosaurs were wiped out 65 million years ago. According to this bleak account, the growth of the human population is destroying the environment for thousands of other species.[26] From this perspective the biblical story of the fall of man has been rewritten as an ecological cautionary tale about a perfidious species that refuses to recognize its own limits. There is now little point in fearing God, for in this moral drama our emotions are directed at the dreadful consequences of human behaviour.

Misanthropy

Although our declining faith in humanity is most visibly associated with apocalyptic thinking about the environment, it has a pervasive presence in everyday life. Increasingly, human relations come with a health-warning. We don't simply pollute the environment but also one another. We talk about 'toxic relationships', 'toxic parents' and 'toxic families'. Indeed, the many scares about the risks involved in human relationships have the same structure and dynamic that prevail in discussions of the environment or technology. Scare stories about the destruction of the environment are conveyed through misanthropic cultural idioms that are used just as much to pathologize human relationships.

The author of a best-selling self-help book represents childrearing as a form of 'toxic' parenting. From this perspective parents become the carriers of polluting agents who infect their unsuspecting children. Since the publication of *Toxic Parents* there has been a veritable genre of literature that dwells of the prevalence of poisonous human relationships. Virtually every possible relationship is associated with the metaphor of toxicity. *Toxic Bachelors, Toxic People: 10 Ways of Dealing with People Who Make your Life Miserable, Toxic Relationships And How To Change Them, Toxic Friends, Toxic Coworkers: How To Deal With Dysfunctional People On The Job*, and *Toxic Stress* transmit the kind of misanthropic message about relationships that are circulated by Neo-Malthusians about population and the environment. Nor is this metaphor confined to relationships. The institutions of public life also come with the toxic label. Books titled *Toxic Churches; Restoration from Spiritual Abuse, Toxic Work, The Allure of Toxic Leaders* or *Toxic Psychiatry* are testimony to an imagination that effortlessly associates forms of human experience with degradation.

Misanthropy has had a profound influence on public policy and political debate. Back in the 1950s, sociological research found that there was a clear correlation between how society viewed people and political attitudes. One study of an individual's orientation toward human nature indicated that it had a strong relationship to political attitude in general.[27] Attitude towards the democratic ideal of free speech is directly influenced by whether or not we believe that people are capable of making an intelligent choice between competing views and whether we fear them or not. 'The advocate of freedom of speech is likely to believe that most men are not easily deceived, are not swayed by uncontrolled emotions, and are capable of sound judgement', noted the author of this study. Such an approach implies a high level of faith in humanity. In contrast, 'the individual with low faith in people tends to believe in suppression of weak, deviant, or dangerous groups'. The study concluded that the 'individual's view of human nature would appear to have significant implications for the doctrine of political liberty'.[28] People who possess a positive valuation of human nature tend to have a tolerant attitude towards free speech and social experimentation. Those who fear human nature tend to opt for a risk-averse and illiberal approach.

Those who believe that people are driven by narrow self-interest, greed and other destructive passions are inclined to support measures that curb and restrain human freedom. The growth of censorship, the criminalization of thought through the enactment of so-called hate crimes and speech codes, and the powerful cultural stigma directed against the right to offend individuals and groups, is underpinned by the belief that people should not be able to make up their minds on where they stand on controversial subjects. Our censorious imperative is driven by a paternalistic and negative view of human nature and a lack of faith in the capacity of people to discriminate between right and wrong. That is why the culture of fear strives to displace individual freedoms and democratic rights with regulation and censorship.

In the early twenty-first century it is not simply isolated individuals or marginal interest groups that appear to possess a low level of faith in people. Not since the Dark Ages has there been so much concern about the malevolent passions that afflict humanity. Fear and suspicion towards human motives has acquired and expansive dimension. Small panics about Satanic Abuse have erupted on both sides of the Atlantic. Throughout the Western world there is a morbid expectation that just about every home contains a potential abuser. The belief that predatory monsters routinely prey upon their victims has imprinted itself on the everyday imagination. People regard others with the kind of suspicion that would have been rare just a few decades ago. Parents wonder whether the day-care-centre workers looking after their children can be trusted. In schools, children with bruises are apt to arouse the suspicion of teachers about what their parents have been doing. For their part, parents wonder whether any physical contact between their child and their teacher is permissible. In the UK, any adult employee that may come in contact with children has to undergo a police check. Sections of the UK child protection industry believe that police vetting should be extended into the university sector.

Obsession with abuse is not confined to the relationship between adult and child. Any interaction that touches on the emotions, physicality and sexuality can be potentially labelled as abusive. There are claims that 'peer abuse' is the key problem of our time. Others demand that action be taken against 'elder abuse'. And for good measure, alarms have been raised about 'pet abuse' and 'chicken abuse'.

Faith in people
How we view humanity really matters. If we insist on seeing humans as morally degraded parasites, then every significant technical problem from the millennium bug to the avian flu will be feared as a potential catastrophe beyond human control. Today's intellectual pessimism and

cultural disorientation serves to distract the human imagination from confronting the challenges that lie ahead. Alarmist accounts about human survival expresses a crisis of belief in humanity. That is why the real question at stake is not whether humanity will survive, but whether or not our belief in humanity can survive the twenty-first century. The scary stories that we continually transmit to one another indicate that society feels uncomfortable with itself and has little faith in people. Many of these stories have the character of a health warning. 'Be careful' dominates our cultural outlook.

This book is about society's reluctance to engage positively with risks. The original aim of the text was to try to explain why society was continually in the throes of panic about some food or drug, or some technological process. In the course of trying to answer this question, it became clear that the many panics about the environment or technology had a very similar structure to society's fears about more mundane matters, such as risky relations between people. Concern with safety is just as intense in the area of personal relations as it is in that of environmental issues. This book argues that our paranoia regarding the safety of children is driven by cultural forces that are very similar to the ones that make us apprehensive about climate change, ecocide or the food we eat.[29]

The world of killer-asteroids and climate change appears to be a million miles away from the sex deviant lurking in the background. Yet, they are all the constructions of a culture that continually inflates the risks facing people. Characteristically, exceptional events such as the abduction of a child are turned into a normal risk. The outbreak of a disease is immediately transformed into an epidemic. The language we use reflects this trend. Terms like 'risk' or 'at risk' are used in association with just about any routine event. The language we use reflects our unprecedented preoccupation with risk. Take the term 'at risk'. A search of UK newspapers indicates that it was used 2,037 times in 1994. Six years later, in 2000, its usage had increased almost nine-fold (*see next page*).

The growing usage of the term 'at risk' expresses attitudes towards everyday life. It is symptomatic of a tendency to regard a growing range of phenomena as threatening and dangerous. Even a highly desired experience such as falling in love can be represented as a risky enterprise. A group of US academics argue that counsellors should warn university students of the 'potential downside of being in love'. Why? Because they have discovered that 'in the name of love', young people tend to engage in 'risky behaviour'.[30]

The use of the term 'at risk' in UK newspapers[31]

1994	2037 mentions
1995	4288
1996	6442
1997	7955
1998	11234
1999	14327
2000	18003

When *Culture of Fear* was first published, I was mainly concerned with the way that society encouraged a panic-like reaction to issues of health, the environment, technology, new products and crime. In recent years it has become evident that probably the most damaging consequence of this process is the way in which risk aversion influences interpersonal behaviour. One of the most unattractive outcomes of the culture of fear is the way it subjects the domain of personal relations to the calculus of risk. It has created a troublesome legacy where people approach their relationship through a heightened sense of risk. An important study on the sociology of romantic attachments in the USA indicates that individuals are 'increasingly motivated by the need to alleviate expanding levels of perceived risks associated with interpersonal love relationships and mate selection'. As a result they are 'altering their relationship patterns' to minimize the risk to themselves. It argues that the 'response to these risks has been the application of rational management principles that have themselves become ritualized and have transformed the public risks associated with relationships into personal risks of self-fulfilment'.[32] The authors point out that one of the paradoxes of this instrumental orientation towards romantic attachments is to actually increase the risk of failure. The expectation of problems becomes a self-fulfilling prophecy.

One way that people are encouraged to manage the risks attached to emotional involvement is through what some sociologists call 'cultural cooling'. Numerous experts and self-help books advise people to lower their expectations and not get carried away by love. Books such as *Women Who Love Too Much*, *When Parents Love Too Much* or *For People*

Who Love Their Cats Too Much advise people not to trust the language of the heart. Although most people actively crave intimate relations and romantic attachments, the association of these experiences with danger has taken its toll. It is now common for people to approach their private relations with a heightened sense of emotional risk. One strategy for dealing with risks to the emotions is to distance oneself from potential sources of disappointment. Detachment from others appears to offer a measure of protection from emotional pain. At the very least, men and women are encouraged to manage the expanding levels of perceived risks associated with intimate relationships. A variety of tactics – from prenuptial agreements to cultivating the virtues of solo living – are used to manage the risks associated with emotional involvement.

The distancing of human beings from one another is not always a voluntary act – often there is an implicit element of coercion forcing people to become estranged from one another. For example, in Anglo-American societies, the risk of adults touching children has encouraged an informal ban on physical contact between the generations. Research carried out by Heather Piper at Manchester Metropolitan University reports cases in which teachers avoid putting a plaster on a child's leg wound, nursery workers are reluctant to help infants go to the toilet, and a male gym teacher leaves a girl injured in the hall while waiting for someone to get a female colleague. She notes that some schools have adopted 'touching guidelines' which insist that teachers cannot put a plaster on a child without parental consent. In one school, staff are obliged to log every 'touching incident'. Piper notes that anxiety about touching children has become 'mainstream'.[33] A society that pathologizes the act of touching a child transmits the very clear message that it has little faith in people. Is it surprising that there is a growing demand to keep children at a distance from grown-ups. Signs in play areas in the UK and the US warn that adults who are not accompanied by a child should stay out! This representation of adults as a risk to children highlights the premise of misanthropy on which the culture of fear is based.

But does it matter?
In slow and often imperceptible ways, our life is being transformed by the prevailing culture of fear. Children are the first to suffer. As far as they are concerned, the outside world has become a no-go area. They face constant adult supervision and are discouraged from taking risks in their lives. When I started working at my university all my students

used to hitchhike to get into town or travel further afield. I would frequently see queues of 20–25 animated students waiting for a ride. Today, none of them hitches a ride. The idea of getting into a car with a stranger has become stigmatized. Instead of regarding the act of offering a ride as a sociable, even altruistic, gesture it is now interpreted as a prelude to a crime. Sadly an opportunity for an exercise in civic responsibility has been lost.

My 10-year-old son loves his football. But I do not have a photograph of him playing with his mates. Before every training session a club official warns parents that they can not take pictures 'in case they fall into the wrong hands'. In numerous sports clubs and schools, people have been banned from taking a snapshot of their children performing in a play or running around the sports-field. That is how low we have sunk. Recently an inquest into the tragic death of a 2-year-old girl heard how a bricklayer drove past the infant as she walked through her village. He did not stop, he explained, because he feared that people would think that he was trying to abduct her. 'She wasn't walking in a straight line', he noted before adding that 'she was tottering and I kept thinking "should I go back"'. Minutes later she drowned in her garden pool.[34]

The culture of fear estranges people from one another. It also distracts people from facing up to the challenges confronting society. This book is motivated by a desire to counter our loss of faith in humanity. Contrary to the misanthropic dogma of our times – people are the solution and not the problem. Today's sad attempt to pathologise risk-taking has the effect of undermining the spirit of exploration and experimentation. Yet it is precisely these qualities that ensure that we can deal with the big problems of our time. Throughout history people have shown that they can find cures for deadly diseases and deal with the destructive consequences of catastrophes.

Despite the prevailing culture of fear, individuals possess an unprecedented potential for influencing the way they live their lives. It is only now that the promise of choice and control has acquired meaning for significant sections of the public. Autonomy and self-determination are still little more than ideals that can inspire. But we have moved away from the Stone Age of ideologies to a time when the transformative potential of people has acquired a remarkable force. We have also learnt that history does not issue any guarantees. Purposeful change is indeed a risky enterprise. But whether we like it or not, the taking of risks in order to transform our lives and to transform ourselves is one of our most distinct human qualities. That is why instead of worrying about our 'ecological footprints' we should take all the steps necessary for moving forward into the future.

Misanthropy threatens to envelop us in a new Dark Age of prejudice where we literally become scared of ourselves. In these conditions we have two choices. We can renounce the distinct human qualities that have helped to transform and humanize the world, and resign ourselves to the culture of fatalism that prevails today. Or we can do the opposite. Instead of abandoning faith in the unique moral qualities of the human, we can turn our creative energies towards assuming a measure of control over our future and embrace the values of experimentation and exploration. Human beings are not angels, and on a bad day we are capable of evil deeds. But the very fact we can designate some acts as evil indicates that we are capable of rectifying acts of injustice. And on balance, we aspire to do good. The aspiration to improve the conditions of life – the most basic motive of people throughout the ages – is one that has driven humanity from the Stone Age to the twenty-first century. That is why it is so important to rebel against our culture of fear.

Notes

1. 'From Out There…To On The Air: "Conspiracy of Silence"', *Public Eye*; 3 May 2006.

2. 'Pearl jam takes on the issues of the day', *Buffalo News*; 2 May 2006.

3. '9-11 Movie Released Too Soon', *Winnipeg Sun*, 9 May 2006.

4. 'Whistleblower says over 100 air RAV worries', *ABC Central Victoria*; 1 May 2006.

5. 'The think tank; It's time we reached for the stars again', *Herald*; 12 May 2006.

6. 'Evangelism Exec Exits', *Christianity Today*; 26 April 2006.

7. 'The $100 billion shop of horrors', *Daily Telegraph*; 12 May 2006.

8. 'It's a hell of a town', *Guardian*; 19 May 2005.

9. 'It's a hell of a town', *Guardian*; 19 May 2005.

10. Cited in 'Bird Flu Prophets of Doom Spread Nothing But Needless Alarm', *Daily Express*; 18 October 2005.

11. 'Avian Flu Wanes in Asian nations it First Hit Hard', *New York Times*; 14 May 2006.

12. See 'The Frightened European', *Chicago Tribune*; 25 April 2006.

13. See Gregg Easterbrook, 'The Mutant Chickens Are Coming!', *Slate*; 8 May 2006.

14. 'Asteroid-watchers worry about cosmic Katrina', MSNBC.com; 6 May 2006.

15. 'Big New Asteroid Has Slim Chance of Hitting Earth', *New Scientist*; 2 May 2006.

16. See 'The time of fear – apocalyptic scenarios of pop culture reflect ambiguity as to the promises of science and technology', *New Statesman*; 21 July 2003.

17. Cited in 'Rumsfeld's unknown unknows', *Guardian*; 1 December 2003.

18. Bill Durodie, 'An Apology For Capitalism' paper given at conference of The Scientific Alliance; 24 September 2004.

19. James Lovelock, 'The Earth Is About To Catch A Morbid Fever That May Last As Long As 1000 Years', *Independent*; 16 January 2006.

20. James Howard Kunstler (2005) *The Long Emergency; Surviving The Converging Catastrophes Of The Twenty-First Century*, Atlantic Books: London, p. 61.

21. James Lovelock, 'The Earth Is About To Catch A Morbid Fever That May Last As Long As 1000 Years', *Independent*; 16 January 2006.

22. Jared Diamond (2004) *Collapse: How Societies Choose to Fail or Survive*, Allan Lane: London.

23. Al Gore, 'The time to act is now – The climate crisis and the need for leadership', www.mi2g.net; 5 March 2006.

24. Thomas Lough, 'Energy, Agriculture, Patriarchy and Ecocide', *Human Ecology Review*, vol. 6, no. 2 1999.

25. See Einarrson, N. (1993) 'All animals are equal but some are cetaceans', in Milton, K. (1993) *Environmentalism: The View from Anthropology*, Routledge: London.

26. See David Adam, 'UN warns of worst mass extinctions for 65m years', *Guardian*; 21 March 2006.

27. Morris Rosenberg, 'Misanthropy and Political Ideology', *American Sociological Review*, vol. 21, no. 6, 1956.

28. Ibid. p. 694.

29. The impact of the culture of fear in relation to children is explored in F. Furedi (2001) *Paranoid Parenting*, London; Allen Lane.

30. Knox, D. and Zusman, M. (1998) 'What I did for Love; Risky Behaviour and College Students in Love', *College Student Journal*, vol. 32, no. 2, p. 203.

31. These figures are based on a search of Reuters' database.

32. Bulcroft, R., Bulcroft, K., Bradely, K. and Simpson, C. (2000) 'The Management and Production of Risk in Romantic Relationships: A Postmodern Paradox', *Journal of Family History*, vol. 25, no.1, p. 63.

33. ESRC funded research project RES-000-22-0815, 'Touchlines: the Problematics of Touching Between Children and Professionals', 2006.

34. 'Mum's Agony As She Finds Tot Of 2 Under Water', *Mirror*; 22 March 2006.

CHAPTER 1

What is Distinct About the Way We Fear?

Different cultures have different ways of fearing. The meaning a society attaches to the fear of God or the fear of Hell is not quite the same as the fear of pollution or of cancer. Matters are also complicated by the fact that the words and expressions used to describe fear are also culturally and historically specific. The language we use today represents fear through idioms that are unspecific, diffuse and therapeutic. Anxieties about being 'at risk' or feeling 'stressed' or 'traumatised' or 'vulnerable' indicate that we have internalized an individualized psychological vocabulary that influences out sensibility of fear. One of the distinguishing features of fear today is that it appears to have an independent existence. It is frequently cited as a problem that exists in its own right disassociated from any specific object. Classically societies associate fear with a clearly formulated threat – the fear of death or the fear of hunger. In such formulations, the threat was defined as the object of such fears. The problem was death, illness or hunger. Today we frequently represent the act of fearing as a threat itself. A striking illustration of this development is the fear of crime as a problem in its own right.

When fear itself becomes the problem

Today crime has become a highly politicized issue. Survey after survey indicates that the public takes the problem of crime very seriously. The debate that surrounds this issue seems to be one of the constants of political life. That is why it is easy to overlook the fact that not so long ago, crime was not a significant party political issue. Throughout most of the post-Second World War era, crime was rarely a subject of political debate. It was perceived as a discrete problem that was confined to a relatively small number of marginal communities. Officials and experts appeared confident that it was a challenge that could be contained, and even solved. It was in the 1970s that crime emerged as an important focus for public debate. Since that time it has succeeded in occupying a central position in political life.

The normalization of the issue of crime during the past 35 years is conveyed through the idea that it is a problem for everyone in society. The title of the Labour Party's 1995 policy statement, *Everyone's a Victim*, summed up the idea that crime had become a routine and normal fact of life. We are victims even if we have not directly experienced crime since we are all aware of it as a threat and some of us live in fear of it. Most surveys confirm that the fear of crime is widespread. In the UK, Home Office figures suggest that of those surveyed 15 per cent were very worried and 26 per cent were fairly worried about crime. Such fears are particularly pronounced amongst the elderly. A survey carried out by Age Concern in May 2003 claimed that 37 per cent of over 50s and 47 per cent of those over 75 stated that they were too afraid to leave their house at night. Since surveys also indicate that public alarm is often disproportionate to the incidence of crime – the fear of this phenomenon has acquired such a momentum that it is perceived as a problem in its own right. Indeed it appears that often it is the fear of crime rather than the breaking of a law that constitutes the focus of public attention. So back in April 2005 when the Lib Dem leader announced that an extra 10,000 police on the streets would help stamp out the fear of crime he was addressing the demand of perception management rather than the challenge of tackling real criminals.

In the UK and the US, the project of reducing the fear of crime as opposed to the level of crime is actively pursued by central and local institutions. So-called quality-of-life policing – visible policing, use of CCTV Cameras, campaigns of reassurance – aims to reassure the public and reduce fear levels. Reassuring the public is also the aim of antisocial behaviour orders. Numerous teenagers have been served with such an order, not because they committed a crime but because they had contributed to creating a 'climate of fear' in their neighbourhood! The Neighbourhood Watch's campaign 'Tackling Fear of Crime in Community' also has a similar mission – it seeks to 'encourage individuals and groups to get involved in reducing fear of crime'.

It is now widely accepted that the fear is often unconnected to the incidence of crime. Numerous surveys have indicated that often those who are most apprehensive about becoming victimized are the ones least likely to experience it. The absence of a clear relationship between crime trends and levels of fear suggests that anxieties about victimization may be subject to wider cultural influences. The criminologist David Garland describes these influences as a 'crime complex'.[1] This complex encompasses a cluster of attitudes that are shaped by the belief that high crime rates are a normal part of life. These attitudes are expressed through a consciousness of crime that is moulded by popular culture and institutionalized in the organization of everyday life. The consciousness of crime that is embedded in our culture encourages people to adopt private and highly individualized defensive routines. Although we are not always aware of it, crime-avoidance behaviour has become a daily dimension of our lives and integral to how we manage our affairs. This trend is particularly striking in the lives of the elderly. But it has also become one of the organizing principles of childhood. 'You can't let your children out on their own' is a frequent comment made by parents. Virtually every institution – bars, universities, doctors' surgeries, sport, public transportation – takes security very seriously. Burglar alarms, outdoor lights, panic buttons, CCTV cameras and an army of private security personnel are testimony to a flourishing market in fear.

Yet the emergence of the fear of crime as a distinct problem in its own right cannot be understood as simply a response to the influence of the crime complex or to the breakdown of law and order. It is important to note that fear as a discrete stand-alone problem is not confined to the problem of crime. Throughout society, fear is experienced as a problem in its own right. For example, fear about the health effects of mobile phones has been interpreted as a risk in itself. The Independent Expert Group on Mobile Phones, which was set up in 1999 by the then Health Minister Tessa Jowell, concluded that public anxiety itself could lead to ill health. The report of this committee noted that such anxieties 'can in themselves affect' the public's well-being.[2] In the same way, anxiety about health risks is now considered to be a material consideration in determining planning application. In other words, fear as such is treated as an independent variable by public bodies. The legal system has also internalized this trend and in the US there is a discernible tendency on the part of courts to compensate fear, even in the absence of a perceptible physical threat. This marks an important departure from the practices of the past, when 'fright', i.e. a reaction to an actual event, was compensated whereas now the fear that something negative would happen is also seen as grounds for making a claim. Frequently, public anxiety and concern are represented as a material factor that can have a significant impact on people's health. Contemporary medical culture contends that stress and fear are likely to increase the risk of heart disease, cancer and chronic lung disease. Some health professionals blame men's fear of cancer as a distinct cause of their death. According to a survey carried out by the UK's Institute of Cancer Research, 'ignorance and fear is stopping men from getting early help for cancer symptoms and the delay could prove deadly'.[3]

The tendency to treat fear as its very own pathology is one of the distinctive features of contemporary society. It is important to note that how we fear is subject to historical and cultural variations. Until recently fear was focused on a variety of socially stigmatized hazards. These were fears that were informed by prevailing social conventions and embedded in informal taken-for-granted folk knowledge about threats facing the community. The fear of unemployment, the fear of polio or the fear of divine retribution was transmitted through a shared cultural script. This script gave fear a tangible quality and a very clear focus. In contrast, today fear has an unpredictable and free-floating character. One day we fear gun-crime, a week later our attention is drawn to car-jacking, only to be distracted next month by the epidemic of happy slapping. In contemporary times, fear migrates freely from one problem to the next without there being a necessity for causal or logical connection.

When the Southern Baptist leader Reverend Jerry Vines declared in June 2002 that Mohammed was a 'demon possessed paedophile', and that Allah leads Muslims to terrorism, he was simply taking advantage of the logical leaps permitted by the free-floating character of our fear narratives.[4] This arbitrary association of terrorism and paedophilia can have the effect of amplifying the fear of both. The same procedure is adopted when environmental pollution is associated with the metaphor of the Holocaust or when an unexpected destructive storm is represented as a harbinger of global warming.

Fear today has a free-floating dynamic and can attach itself to a wide variety of phenomena. The fear of terrorism illustrates this trend. Since 11 September 2001, this fear floats into an ever-expanding territory. Deliberations on this subject have acquired a fantasy-like character. 'Corporations must re-examine their definition of risk and take seriously the possibility of scenarios that only science fiction writers could have imagined possible one year ago' argues a leading economist.[5] Fear floats into new territory because since 9/11 normal hazards can be turned into exceptional threats by associating them with the action of terrorists. As a result we do not simply worry about the hazard posed by a nuclear power station we also fear that it may turn into a terrorist target. The fact that an ever-expanding phenomenon can be perceived as a target is less an outcome of an increase in the capabilities of terrorists than of the free-floating fear dynamic. The free-floating dynamic of fear is promoted by a culture that communicates hesitancy and anxiety towards uncertainty and continually anticipates the worse possible outcome. This culture of fear encourages society to approach human experience as a potential risk to our safety. Consequently every conceivable experience has been transformed into a risk to be managed. The idea that *Everyone's a Victim* is not confined to the domain of crime. The anticipation of victimization is refracted through one of the most distinctive idioms of contemporary culture, which is that of being *at risk*. Anyone labelled as at risk is by definition a potential victim.

The emergence of the 'at risk' concept ruptures the traditional relationship between individual action and the probability of some hazard. To be at risk is no longer only about what you do, or the probability of some hazard impacting on your life – it is also about who you are. It becomes a fixed attribute of the individual, like the size of a person's feet or hands. Being at risk also implies the autonomy of the dangers that people face. Those who are at risk face hazards that are independent of them. If risk is autonomous, it suggests that it exists independently of any act or individual. Like the Greek gods, risk factors exist in a world of their own. But unlike the gods, whose acts conveyed a message with a meaning, the risk factors do not talk to us. Living with risk becomes our fate, encouraging a disposition towards a fatalistic perspective towards uncertainty. This sense of fatalism continually counsels us to avoid risks, to take measures that can promote safety.

So what does it mean to fear crime?

So how can we understand the fear of crime as a distinct cultural phenomenon? Throughout history numerous societies have confronted the challenge of lawlessness and threats to individual security without necessarily experiencing a high level of fearing crime. The fear of crime is a distinctive feature of a society where the influence of informal relations and taken-for-granted norms has diminished in influence. It is anxieties about the uncertainties of day-to-day existence that people echo in discussions about the subject of crime. Insecurity towards expected forms of behaviour and suspicion about the motives of others provide a fertile terrain where perceptions of threats can flourish. These perceptions are intensified in circumstances where social isolation has become pervasive. In such circumstances, fear in general and not just in relation to crime can acquire its own inner dynamic.

In May 2005, a survey carried out in England found that less than half of the 1,000 people interviewed knew their neighbours well enough to ask for help in an emergency. In effect, many of us live in neighbourhoods without neighbours. In such communities people live next to each other and are close spatially but remain isolated from one another in other respects. If you do not know very much about those living near you it is difficult to feel any affinity towards them. In such circumstances people often lack a mutually accepted convention for resolving tension and conflict. Frequently, such communities lack a web of informal rules through which people negotiate their day-to-day affairs. For some – especially the elderly – lack of clarity on this score represents an existential crisis. 'Can I count on respect and support of the younger generations or will they treat me with derision and scorn?', is the question facing many old people as they negotiate a street culture that is increasingly alien to them. But even the younger generations feel threatened by a lack of clarity about the rules of behaviour. For many, avoiding conflict has become part of their routine.

The experience of fearing crime is inextricably linked to a situation where the system of formal and, more importantly, of informal understanding about what people can expect from each other exists in a feeble form. Yet the unspoken code of everyday conduct influences behaviour and reminds us of the boundaries that should not be transgressed. That is why there can even be 'honour among thieves'. Such informal rules provide the foundation for relations of trust and help clarify the terms on which people relate to one another. Throughout history, such informal rules have served to contain antisocial behaviour. Such rules provide adults with the authority to intervene and stop young people from misbehaving. Unspoken assumptions about the inappropriate use of foul language, or intolerance towards threatening behaviour, pushed criminal activities to the margins. These rules also transmitted expectations of mutual solidarity and support. Individuals who when threatened can draw upon a network of support, fear very differently to those who are forced to deal with such problems on their own. The expectation of support assists people to deal with the threats that confront them. A robust system of informal relations not only helps contain acts of crime, but also helps to restrain our fears. How this system functions has a decisive influence on the very experience of crime and our reaction to it.

Contrary to received wisdom it is not formal policing but informally enforced rules that contain crime and other forms of antisocial behaviour. Peer pressure is a far more powerful influence on individual behaviour than the workings of formal institutions. The precondition for the high rates of crime that have kicked in since the 1970s has been the diminishing influence of such informal codes. Unfortunately, government policies, even when they seek to expand community policing, are focused on formal forms of crime prevention. However, the fear of crime cannot be minimized through measures that are intended to reassure the public but do not encourage the cultivation of informal life. Technological quick-fix solutions like CCTV cameras or visible policing only provide short-term and transient reassurance. It does little to create the kind of informal support necessary for significantly restraining the public fear of crime. Encouraging the revitalization of informal networks is likely to prove to be the most effective way of tackling the public fear of crime.

Our culture of fear

How we react in general and how we fear in particular is subject to historical and cultural variations. Work by Stearns and Haggerty provides interesting insights into the changing way that fear in relation to children has been conceptualized in the US. They point out that with the passing of time children's engagement with fear was increasingly interpreted through the prism of terror. One consequence of this perception of childhood has been the tendency towards getting rid of terror from children's books.[6] The other is to conceptualize children as 'vulnerable' and therefore unlikely to be able to cope with adverse circumstances. Equating fear with terror is one possible orientation towards a particular object of anxiety. However, historically fear has not always had negative connotations. The sixteenth-century English philosopher Thomas Hobbes regarded fear as essential for the realization of the individual and of a civilized society. For Hobbes and others, fear constituted a dimension of a reasonable response to new events. Nor does fear always signify a negative emotional response. As David Parkin argues, as late as the nineteenth century the sentiment of fear was frequently associated with an expression of 'respect' and 'reverence', or 'veneration'.[7] From this standpoint, the act of 'fearing the Lord' could have connotations that were culturally valued and affirmed. In contrast today, the act of fearing God is far less consistent with cultural norms. One important reason for this shift is that fearing has tended to become disassociated from any positive attributes. This change in attitude is conceptualized by Parkin as a shift from a concept of fear that 'encompassed that of respect' to what he calls 'raw fear'. The former is described as an 'institutionally controlled fear' whereas 'raw fear' has more of a free-floating and unpredictable character.

'Respectful' and 'raw' fear express very different relations to human experience. Parkin claims that respectful fear assumes 'predictable response to behaviour'. It is a form of 'knowable fear'. It is knowable because it is embedded in informal taken-for-granted and culturally sanctioned formal relations. In contrast 'raw fear' has as its premise 'an unpredictable aspect sustained by the victim'.[8] This is a fear that is not rooted in folk culture, and not guided by a generally accepted narrative of meaning. Hence its unpredictability.

The unpredictable character of fear points to its free-floating and dynamic character. Its volatility is enhanced by its unstable and unfocused trajectory. In contemporary times, fear migrates freely from one problem to the next without there being a necessity for causal or logical connection. The free-floating dynamic of fear is promoted by a culture that communicates hesitancy and anxiety towards uncertainty and continually anticipates the worse possible outcome. The culture encourages society to approach human experience as a potential risk to our safety. Consequently every conceivable experience has been transformed into a risk to be managed. One leading criminologist, David Garland, writes of the 'Rise of Risk' – the explosion in the growth of risk talk and risk literature. He notes that little connects this literature, other than the use of the word 'risk'.[9] However, the very fact that risk is used to frame a variety of otherwise unconnected experiences reflects confusion and uncertainty towards human experience. In contemporary society, little can be taken for granted other than an apprehensive response towards uncertainty. The French social theorist François Ewald believes that the ascendancy of this precautionary sensibility is underwritten by a cultural mood that assumes the uncertainty of causality between action and effect. This sensibility endows fear with a privileged status. Ewald suggests that the institutionalization of precaution 'invites one to consider the worst hypothesis (defined as the "serious and irreversible" consequence) in any business decision'.[10] The tendency to engage with uncertainty through the prism of fear, and therefore anticipate the worst possible outcome, can be understood as a crisis of causality.

The question of causation is inextricably bound up with the way communities attempt to make sense of acts of misfortune. The way people interpret such events – an accident or a catastrophe – is processed through the prevailing system of meaning. Questions like 'was it God?', 'was it nature?', or 'was it an act of human error?' have important implications in how we understand acts of misfortune. Today, such questions are complicated by the fact that Western societies possess a weak sense of shared meaning and therefore often lack a consensus about how to attribute blame and responsibility. The absence of consensus means that the link between cause and negative outcome is continually contested. Confusion about causation encourages speculation, rumours and mistrust. As a result, events often appear as incomprehensible and beyond human control.

The difficulty that society has in making sense of uncertainty is what gives contemporary fear its raw character. The distinction that Parkin made between the predictability of respectful fear and the uncontrolled character of raw fear can be understood as an expression of the growing tendency to contest the meaning of misfortune. Increasingly the questions of what we should fear and who to blame have become subjects of acrimonious debate. Lack of consensus over the meaning of misfortune bequeaths fearing a private, individuated and even arbitrary character. Disagreement about the meaning of misfortune is not new. As Russell Dynes points out, the debate surrounding the meaning of the 1755 Lisbon earthquake led to a confrontation between rival views of the world.[11] But past debates about the causes of disasters involved a clash of competing systems of meaning. Today, the protagonists in such a debate lack such moral and intellectual support and engage in the controversy as isolated individuals. Instead of a consensus forged around a society's fear, the way we respond to threat often tends to isolate us. 'Cancer and crime, pain and pollution: these fears isolate us', notes Bourke.[12] In the absence of a master-narrative that endows the threats we face with shared meaning, people's response has acquired an increasingly private and personalized character. Our perception of the threat of crime is only the most tangible expression of the privatization of our fears.

Avoiding risk

Our culture of fear discourages people from taking risks. It is a culture that continually promotes precaution as a virtue and fosters a climate where risk-taking is equated with irresponsible behaviour. In public life this attitude towards experience is frequently represented as the *politics of fear*.[13] It is in the writings of Thomas Hobbes that we first encounter a perspective that promotes the politics of fear in association with the project of rejecting risk-taking. Hobbes valued the public's fear of the state because it restrained them from risk-taking. 'The less they dare', he wrote, 'the better it is both for commonwealth and for themselves'. In the early twenty-first century, *not daring* has come to exercise a powerful influence on public policy and interpersonal relations. The act of daring is frequently associated with negative character traits. And those who dare to radically extend the frontiers of science are often castigated for their arrogance. 'Tampering with nature', 'Letting the genie out of the bottle', 'Opening Pandora's Box', 'scientists playing God', 'Science running ahead of ethics', 'Promethean Arrogance' are some of the metaphors used to indict those who dare. In everyday usage the words 'experiment' and 'experimentation' have acquired negative, if not sinister, connotations. To explain why risk aversion has acquired such widespread resonance, it is necessary to gain an overview of some of the principal features of the culture of fear.

1. Shift in moral reaction to harm

Contemporary society finds it difficult to make sense of misfortune and adversity. The harms that befall people are increasingly interpreted as the outcome of irresponsible or malevolent behaviour. We live in a world that finds it hard to accept the fact that occasionally bad things can happen to us. Safety experts and health promotion advocates dislike the word 'accident'. Public health officials often claim that most injuries suffered by people are preventable, and that to attribute such an event to an accident is irresponsible. The US emergency medicine establishment has been in the forefront of the campaign to remove the word 'accident' from its vocabulary. The *British Medical Journal* has also signed up to the crusade against the 'A' word. It has declared that it has decided to ban the word accident from its pages.[14] It argued that since 'most injuries and their precipitating events are predictable and preventable', the word accident should not be used to refer to 'injuries or the events that produce them'. The editorial reluctantly acknowledges that some injury-producing events may possibly be attributable to bad luck or acts of God. However, it claims that even in such cases – earthquakes or avalanches – prediction is often possible and therefore 'preventive steps can be taken by avoiding dangerous places at times of risk'. So the injuries caused by flying debris during a hurricane are caused not by an accident, but by the failure to adopt the correct precautionary strategy.

The BMJ's attitude towards accidents harks back to the way that misfortune and disaster were conceptualized in pre-modern times. Often perceived as acts of God – a form of divine retribution – disasters were frequently depicted as punishment for human transgression. Throughout medieval times, accidents and acts of misfortune were often invested with some hidden meaning. People searched for some nefarious agent to blame for such acts. Communities who burned witches for causing misfortune to people also did not believe that there was such a thing as an accident. It wasn't till the rise of secularism that societies began to change the way they made sense of acts of misfortune. The development of science as the new source of knowledge altered people's perception of disasters. They were increasingly defined as acts of nature. Though science could explain why and how it occurred, a natural disaster was divested of any inner meaning. However, in recent times we appear to be embracing the prejudices of medieval times. In the aftermath of rail crash or a disaster, the finger of blame invariably points towards another person. Government officials, big business or careless operatives are held responsible for the misfortune caused. We find it difficult to accept that accidents or disasters are natural. When a train crashes or a mine is flooded, we spontaneously ask the question 'who is there to blame?'

A culture that finds it difficult to accept that misfortune is part of the human condition, inadvertently reveals a desperate desire to find meaning in life. We explore our illnesses and injuries to discover their inner meaning. People wear their illness on their sleeves – they are incited to write books about it and explore its meaning on television. When someone is afflicted with a terrible injury or dies tragically, we search for some lessons that help illuminate the experience. The phrase 'this must not be allowed to happen again' expresses the conviction that if we can learn the real meaning of a tragedy, then similar adverse events can be avoided. Family members issue messages that outline the hope that something 'good' will come out of their relative's tragic fate. Even a single unexpected accident is sufficient to provoke calls for more regulations and preventative measures. Doing something, even if it is merely the holding of an official inquiry, helps give significance to what is often actually a meaningless act of misfortune. Contemporary culture rejects the idea that death has no intrinsic meaning. The notion that the person we love just happened to be in the wrong place at the wrong time is antithetical to an ethos that needs to endow every misadventure with an inner purpose.

Since religion can rarely excite the imagination of many of us, misfortune can no longer be attributed to a morally purposeful act of god. So how do we assign meanings to acts that were once attributed to chance? Usually, by blaming somebody or some institution for our predicament. It is worth recalling that although more than 20 million people died as a result of the influenza pandemic of 1918, there was little finger-pointing or blame. Today, even a small flu epidemic would lead to an outcry against irresponsible officials, politicians or health professionals. Cleansing the term 'accident' from our cultural narrative inexorably leads to a relentless search for someone to blame. This is where the legal professional takes over and provides the injured with an obvious target for a compensation claim. 'IT WAS JUST AN ACCIDENT…OR WAS IT? is the title of a leaflet published by Accident Line, a UK-based organization devoted to encouraging the injured to claim compensation. The leaflet boasts that 'many people who believed at first that their accident could not be blamed on anyone but themselves have gone on to make a successful claim'. Moreover, it assures the injured that 'sometimes you don't even realise that someone or something else is to blame'. Educating people to discover that what they thought was their fault can actually be blamed on someone else seems to be part of the project of purging the idea of an accident from the English language. Like the BMJ censors, this legal firm believes that behind every injury lurks an act of negligence.

Human beings have always required a vocabulary that helped them make sense of unexpected events, particularly those that caused pain and suffering. Today, this demand for an explanation almost always contains the implication that someone ought to be blamed. It is not selfishness or cynicism but our inability to make sense of uncertainty and misfortune which acts as the main driver of the litigation revolution. It has helped foster a climate where adverse experience is readily blamed on someone else's negligence. The corollary of this blame-game is a feeble sense of personal responsibility for one's predicament. The statement 'It wasn't my fault' conveys a refusal to take responsibility for the disagreeable experiences that afflict our lives. That is why people who trip and fall on the pavement feel that they are entitled to sue their local authority for compensation. As the BMJ editorial argues – this was not an accident.

2. Safety as an end in itself
No one likes accidental injuries. In every area of life people are continually confronted with the need to weigh up the benefits associated

with a particular activity against the likelihood of negative outcomes. Someone involved in contact sports knows that the excitement and enjoyment of this activity can be compromised by a painful injury. So the issue facing a skier or a football player is how to manage the risks encountered in their sport. The BMJ's one-sided advocacy of prevention represents a profound sense of hostility towards the taking of risks. It seeks to avoid rather than manage risks. The project of expunging the word 'accident' from the dictionary of medicine is motivated by the conviction that risks ought to be prevented and not taken, and certainly not enjoyed. The cultural script that informs the attitudes of the BMJ censors advocates a moral outlook that defines prevention as a virtue. The same script tends to frame risk-taking in negative terms.

The crusade against the 'A' word is justified on the grounds that it raises awareness about the preventable nature of injuries. It believes that such awareness will 'help reduce the incidence and severity of injuries'. Preventing injuries is, of course, a worthwhile objective. But not all injuries can be prevented. Nor should we seek to employ all measures available to prevent all injuries that are preventable. For example, there is a perfectly effective way of preventing skiing injuries altogether – ban people from putting on their skiing booths and taking to the mountains. We can prevent injuries suffered by people out bicycling, by forbidding them to ride a bike. An enlightened society recognizes that human beings need to take risks and that in doing so they will sometimes experience an adverse outcome. Risk is part of life, and a society that adopts the view that preventing injury is an end in itself will have to ban a variety of creative and challenging activities. Banning the word accident will do little to reduce physical injury. However, it will reinforce the current climate of intolerance towards risk-taking and experimentation. Safety-at-any price is a symptom of compulsive behaviour rather the product of enlightened thinking.

Western societies are obsessed with safety. Passions that were once devoted to a struggle to change the world (or to keep it the same) are now invested in trying to ensure that we are safe. The label 'safe' gives new meaning to a wide range of human activities, endowing them with unspoken qualities that are meant to merit our automatic approval. 'Safe sex' is not just sex practised 'healthily' – it implies an entire attitude towards life. And safer sex is only the most high profile of the safety issues today. Advocates demand the creation of 'safe spaces' in a zealous and religious search for sanctuaries from normal life. Public and private institutions continually declare that their main objective is to secure the safety of their customers and stakeholders. When I commute to London, my railway company continually reassures me about their commitment to passenger safety. They have far less to say about running trains on time or about ensuring their cleanliness. When we moved house and looked for a school for my son, teachers constantly reminded us about how much they cared about their pupils' safety. They appeared less animated or concerned about telling us about the quality of education that my child would receive.

Personal safety is a growth industry. In a trend which took off in the US but has swiftly crossed the Atlantic to Britain, hardly a week now passes without some new risk to the individual being reported, and another safety measure proposed. A wide network of charities and organizations has grown up with a view to offering advice on every aspect of personal safety, and the same concerns are echoed in the programme of every major political party.

Every public and private place is now assessed from a safety perspective. Hospital security has emerged as a central concern of health professionals. Concern for protecting newborn babies from potential kidnappers indicates that a preoccupation with safety can never begin too soon. In the USA, a scare about violent babysitters has led to a massive expansion of the nursery security business. Crawford Kindergarten in London was the first nursery in the UK to allow parents to monitor their children from home or office through closed circuit television. In the USA, an Orwellian-sounding Parentwatch Inc. has set up a website that allows parents to monitor the activities of their toddlers at home or in the nursery. A manual for US parents, entitled *Perfectly Safe*, offers information about how to create 'the perfectly safe home'. Expectant parents can also rely on a small industry of consultants who are in the business of redesigning homes to make them safe for babies and toddlers.

In UK and US schools, safety is a big issue. The comprehensive range of cameras, swipe cards and other security measures that are now routine make many schools look more like minimum security prisons. Meanwhile, car phones are sold as safety devices to protect women who fear violent attacks on their vehicles, and the electronics industry speculates that it is only a matter of time before CCTVs become a standard household item.

Economic life is clearly oriented towards the promotion of safety. The inexorable rise of health spending in the Western world is conventionally explained as an outcome of the high cost of new medical breakthroughs. However, it is not new medical technology but a concern with minimizing risks that has transformed the health industry into one of the most profitable sectors in the USA and the UK. The growing market for alternative treatments and medicines indicates that it is not just the high-technology variety which is in demand. Products and services that are linked to risk avoidance are doing well. In the UK, bottled water has been the fastest growing sector in the drinks market. Perfectly safe tap water is increasingly regarded as not safe enough.

'Better safe than sorry' has become the fundamental principle of public life. And once a preoccupation with safety has been made routine and banal, no area of human endeavour can be immune from its influence. Activities that were hitherto seen as healthy and fun – such as enjoying the sun – are now declared to be major health risks. In the UK, some local councils are worried that children might get injured through conkering – the age-old custom of playing with chestnuts. Consequently, local councils have implemented the policy of 'tree management' – cutting down trees – to make horse-chestnut trees less accessible to children. Moreover, even activities that have been pursued precisely because they are risky are now recast from the perspective of safety consciousness. In this spirit, a publication on young people and risk takes comfort from the fact that new safety measures were introduced in mountain-climbing:

> Nobody is going to prevent young men and women from taking risks. Even so, it is obvious that the scale of such risks can be influenced for the better. During recent years rock-climbers have greatly reduced their risks thanks to the introduction of better ropes, boots, helmets and other equipment.[15]

The fact that young people who choose to climb mountains might not want to be denied the *frisson* of risk does not enter into the calculations of the safety-conscious professional, concerned to protect us from ourselves.

The evaluation of everything from the perspective of safety is a defining characteristic of contemporary society. When safety is worshipped and risks are seen as intrinsically bad, society is making a clear statement about the values that ought to guide life. Once mountain-climbing is linked to risk aversion, it is surely only a matter of time before a campaign is launched to ban it altogether. At the very least, those who suffer from climbing-related accidents will be told that 'they have brought it upon themselves'. For, to ignore safety advice is to transgress the new moral consensus.

3. Changing narrative of harm

Through the media, we are all continually reminded of the risks we face from environmental hazards. When the survival of the human species is said to be at stake, then life itself becomes one big safety issue. The tendency to treat human survival as an everyday problem is paralleled by a constant inflation of the harms that face us.

Most serious commentators accept that in real terms people live longer than before, and that they are more healthy and better off than in previous times. But many argue that the social, economic and scientific advances which made these improvements possible have only created new and bigger problems. Influential writers and thinkers now argue that new technological hazards have given risk a boundless character. They suggest that it is no longer possible to calculate the dangers involved in scientific developments. Because of the fast pace of events today, and the global forces that are now at work, it is argued, human actions have more far-reaching and incalculable consequences than ever before. Consequently, it is not just a question of not knowing. The outcome is not knowable.

Disasters and catastrophes have happened throughout history. But the reaction to these events has varied according to the mood that prevailed in society at the time. The definition of what constitutes a hazard changes over time. According to a study of the American media's reporting of risk, in 1960, most stories about nuclear energy 'emphasized benefits rather than costs; by 1984, the proportions had reversed'. The study also pointed to a dramatic shift in the way that stories about abortion were framed; in 1960, they emphasized the risks of illegal abortions to the women, while in 1984 the focus was the risks of legal abortions for the fetus.[16] The selective way in which the media and other institutions pick and choose what constitutes a risk underlines the social dynamic behind the formation of risk consciousness.

The different public reaction to the destruction of the first Apollo space craft in January 1967, and of the space shuttle Challenger, 19 years later, is instructive in this respect. When Apollo caught fire and three astronauts were killed, America was shocked and horrified. However, despite widespread anguish and concern about the incident, the future of the prestigious moon project was not put to serious question. In contrast, the response to the destruction of Challenger turned into a full-scale panic that led to a loss of nerve. For many this tragedy was proof that technology was out of control. The US space agency NASA was itself so badly traumatized that it took almost three years to launch another space shuttle.

Two comparable tragedies, two very different reactions. Why? Because public perception and response to any event are subject to influences that are specific to the time and place. Such responses are likely to be shaped not so much by the disaster itself, as by the public attitudes that prevail in society. A perspective which situates events more in their historical and social context would suggest that today's increased concern with safety and risk has little to do with the advance of technology and science. After all, it is not just the outcome of technological and scientific developments which provoke anxiety and fear. Our fear of crime, our obsessive concern with the safety of children or anxieties towards intimacy have little to do with society's response to technological advance.

A Historical Detour

A comparison to the way Britain responded to floods in the 1950s with those of recent times highlights the points under discussion. On the night of 12 October 2000, the south-east of England was severely flooded. The flood and storm accounted directly and indirectly for 12 deaths and many more injuries. Almost half a century earlier, on 15 August 1952, one of the worst flash floods ever to have occurred in Britain swept through the Devon village of Lynmouth. As a result, 35 people died as a torrent of 90 million tons of water, and thousands of tons of rock poured off a saturated Exmoor and into the village destroying homes, bridges, shops and hotels. This catastrophe was followed by the Big Flood of 1953, 'the worst natural disaster to befall Britain during the twentieth century'.[17] 307 people were drowned along with thousands of cattle, pigs, sheep and poultry. 40 perished on Canvey Island, Essex, alone.

There is a striking difference in the way that people were expected to deal with the calamity they encountered. In the 1950s, people were encouraged to interpret disaster as a test or challenge to be overcome. In contrast in 2000, the flood was represented as a uniquely threatening event that was likely to overwhelm the coping capacity of individuals. In 1953, a report from *The Times* on the Queen's visit to the afflicted areas clearly transmitted officially sanctioned expectations that people would respond to the flood with 'courage and fortitude'. It was reported that the Queen was 'impressed by the stoic and heroic manner of the people who had obviously been through a bad and trying time, suffering heavy losses'.[18] The familiar sounding rhetoric of the Queen was amplified and transmitted through metaphors and powerful symbols that at once affirmed the sense of loss, while communicating the belief that Britain's sturdy folk would prevail over the hardships it faced. In contrast, newspapers in 2000 transmitted the conviction that flood victims would suffer serious psychological damage. According to one account in the *Guardian*, 'up to 20% of natural disaster victims may suffer from post-traumatic stress disorder'. It added that many feel 'depressed and isolated, losing their sense of place and attachment, or developing obsessive anxieties as a result of the ordeal'.[19]

These two contrasting representation of events were paralleled by a fundamentally different orientation in the moral orientation towards harm. In 1953 the floods were not politicized. Criticism of officials, public agencies and professional groups was rarely expressed. A handful of politicians criticised the BBC for its inaccurate weather forecast. The response to the flood of 2000 was totally different. From the outset, the project of blaming was vigorously promoted by claims makers. At various times, greedy property developers, the Environmental Agency, public planning and politicians were blamed for the disaster. Not surprisingly arguments about who to blame encouraged suspicion and mistrust in the aftermath of the floods of 2000.

The different evaluation and responses to the floods are in part linked to the significance and meaning attached to the role of informal networks of the community. If the floods of the 1950s were about a disaster inflicted on communities, those of 2000 are about individual and private distress. It is striking how in comparison to the disasters of the 1950s, the role of the community, its altruism and resilience, is rarely endowed with significance in 2000. A review of the press indicates that reports of resilient behaviour are virtually absent from the discussion. One of the few reports of community altruism focused on a group of 22 people who were stranded in a pub in Yalding for three days. The owner of the pub was noted as saying 'we were petrified, but it has been like the Dunkirk spirit'. According to this account, everyone pitched in and provided help to one another.[20]

It was the populist tabloid the *Sun* that attempted to resurrect the traditional narrative of the 'British Bulldog Spirit' to represent the response to the flood. One of its writers noted that 'as the nation comes to terms with the worst deluge in living memory, a small band of people leave us feeling proud to be British'.[21] But it was a 'small band' of emergency workers, and not the community that constituted the focus of the *Sun*'s celebration of British courage. In contrast, a study of the 1953 floods, observed that thousands of volunteers took part in the rescue and salvaging operations. 'Many thousands of civilians, belonging to civil defence or voluntary organizations, played their part, and large drafts of officers and men were sent by the army and the R.A.F.' noted a report at the time.[22]

In contrast to the representation of the flood in 2000, during the 1950s, reports continually valorized the response of the community. Individual stories of human suffering were rare. In *The Times* there is only one story of an individual coping with adversity.[23] At all levels of society, the informal community networks that emerged in the course of the disaster were seen as the heroes of the hour. For many flood victims, it was the response of neighbours and other community members that gave them the strength to cope with their perilous circumstances. Christopher Manser from Canvey Island, who lost three of his siblings, recalls 'the warmth generated by the spontaneous reaction of local people to the need for clothes'. He notes that 'women had taken their husband's jackets and trousers straight from the wardrobe without emptying pockets' and gave it to victims of the flood. 'I found money, cigarettes, diaries and so on', he added.[24] For scores of individuals a sense of community meant something positive. John Peddler, who was 17 when he rescued his father as the Lynmouth flood engulfed the post office, stated that 'we are a very close community, and we remember the kindness of ordinary people who sent us things at the time'. He added, 'that is how we coped'.[25]

Ideas about how people are likely to cope in an emergency or a disaster are shaped by prior experience, but also by a cultural narrative that creates a set of expectations and sensitizes people to some problems more than others. It provides a frame through which people understand and make sense of their experience. Twenty-first century Western culture frequently transmits the view that we live in a uniquely dangerous era where humanity faces hazards and potential disaster. 'The modern era is often cast as an age of catastrophe, of global conflicts, genocides and "ethnic cleansings", disasters of industrial and agrarian change and of technological hubris, and — increasingly — environmental cataclysms', note two British historians.[26]

The experience of disasters – major and minor – is a social phenomenon which is mediated through the public's cultural imagination and attitudes towards loss. Our culture of fear both amplifies the dangers we face and undermines our capacity to engage with the experience of adversity. As a result when we face adversity we do so as vulnerable individuals who are unlikely to cope on their own. This is one of the most distinct features of the way we fear.

Notes

1. Garland, D. (2001) *The Culture of Control: Crime and Social Order in Contemporary Society* (Oxford University Press: Oxford).

2. Independent Expert Group on Mobile Phones (IEGMP) (2000) *Mobile Phones and Health* (IEGMP: Chilton, Didcot).

3. 'Men could be dying from fear, warns cancer expert', *Daily Telegraph* 26 May 2004.

4. Cited in Filler, D. M. (2003) 'Terrorism, Panic and Pedophilia', *Virginia Journal of Social Policy & the Law*, Spring 2003, p. 345.

5. Hale, D. (2002) 'Insuring a Nightmare', *Worldlink*; 19 March 2002.

6. Stearns, P. N. and Haggerty, T. (1991) 'The Role of Fear: Transitions in American Emotional Standards for Children, 1850–1950', *American Historical Review*, 96, pp. 85 and 88.

7. Parkin, D. (1986) 'Toward an Apprehension of Fear' in Scruton, D. L. (1986) (ed.). *Sociophobics: The Anthropology of Fear* (Westview Press: Boulder), pp.158–9.

8. Parkin (1986) p.159.

9. Garland, D. (2003) 'The Rise of Risk' in Ericson, R.V. and Doyle, A. (2003) (ed.) *Risk and Morality* (University of Toronto Press: Toronto), p. 52.

10. Ewald, F. (2002) 'The Return of Descartes's Malicious Demon: An Outline of a Philosophy of Precaution', in Baker, T. and Simon, J. (eds) (2002) *Embracing Risk: The Changing Culture of Insurance and Responsibility* (University of Chicago Press: Chicago), pp.273–301.

11. Dynes, R. (2000) 'The Dialogue Between Voltaire and Rousseau on the Lisbon Earthquake: The Emergence of Social Science View', in *International Journal of Mass Emergencies and Disasters*, vol.18.

12. Bourke, J. (2005) *Fear; A Cultural History* (London: Virago), p. 293.

13. See Furedi, F. (2005) *The Politics of Fear; Beyond Left and Right* (London: Continuum).

14. 'BMJ bans "accidents"', in *British Medical Journal*; 2 June 2001, p. 1320.

15. Plant & Plant (1992), pp.142–3

16. Singer and Endreny (1993), p.160.

17. Baxter, P. J. (2005) 'The east coast Big Flood, 31 January–1 February 1953: a summary of the human disaster', in *Philosophical Transactions: Mathematical, Physical and Engineering Sciences*, vol. 363, no. 1831, p. 1293.

18. 'The Queen Sees The Floods', *The Times*; 20 February 1953.

19. 'In deep trouble', *Guardian*: 6 December 2000.

20. 'Anguish as flood victims return to find their homes looted', *Daily Mail*; 16 October 2000.

21. Yates, C. 'They're floody heroes', *Sun*; 18 October 2000.

22. *The Times*; 3 February 1953.

23. *The Times*; 6 February 1953.

24. Cited in Pollard, M. (1978) *North Sea Surge: The Story of the East Coast Floods of 1953* (Terence Dalton Limited: Lavenham), Suffolk, p. 89.

25. Cited in *The Sunday Times*; 31 August 1997.

26. Gray, P. and Oliver, K., 'The Memory of Catastrophe', *History Today*, February 2001, p.1.

CHAPTER 2

The Explosion of Risks

That society is gripped by an ever-expanding preoccupation with risk is widely recognized. The aim of this chapter is to survey some of the patterns that recur in the discussion of risk. The chapter seeks not so much to explain but to identify what this concern about risks represents. The identification of the problem is a necessary prelude to the explanation of what lies behind the explosion of risks, which is the subject of the next chapter.

In any discussion of risk, it is useful to make a distinction between the likelihood of accidents, injury, disease or death and the perception that people have of the dangers they face. Often people's perception of what constitutes danger has little to do with the real likelihood that they will suffer a misfortune from that source. For example, in January 2001, Europe was gripped by a panic about the so-called Balkan War Syndrome. A significant section of the European public appeared to believe the claim that there was a link between depleted-uranium munitions dropped during the bombing of Yugoslavia and a variety of illnesses suffered by NATO troops who served in the area. Although even the most aggressive promoters of this scare acknowledged that the risk from depleted uranium was purely theoretical, sections of the public regarded it as a real danger. For many soldiers, this newly invented syndrome explained their post-war personal problems and illness. That was proof enough. Such panics are counterproductive and even distract from the dangers that confront us. After the Paddington rail crash in Britain, thousands of commuters to London abandoned the trains and took to driving to work. Yet the possibility of suffering an injury in a car accident was far greater than the risks associated with rail travel.

It is well known that what we dread and what tends to kill and maim are not always the same. In the USA, surveys of Americans continually place nuclear power at the top of the list of risks in life. Although it is not possible to prove that a single American has died from radiation from the civil nuclear industry, the fear of this technology continues to influence public opinion. There is a similar divergence between public fear and the actual incidence of danger in the sphere of human relations. The divergence between perceptions and incidence of crime parallels the reactions to environmental hazards. Reports based on the experience of the USA indicate that people are often wildly inaccurate in how they evaluate the situation that confronts them. Surveys have found substantial discrepancies between the rate at which a group is victimized and its concern about crime. 'Young black males, for example, report the largest number of victimizations and the smallest number of fears whereas older females (both black and white) report the highest level of fear and the lowest number of victimizations', according to a study of the media's reporting of risk.[1] The relationship between the perception and the real threat of crime is far from evident. On university campuses on both sides of the Atlantic, there is a widely held perception that life has become more and more violent. In fact, this reaction is contradicted by the reality of life on campus. Research shows that in the USA, since 1985, rates of both violent crime and property crime have been falling. Moreover, students are considerably safer on campus than in the cities and communities surrounding them.[2]

The divergence between subjective perception and the actuality of danger constitutes one of the main subjects of discussion among specialists in the field of risk. Traditionally, the field of risk studies was mainly oriented towards technical tasks. Models were developed to minimize or eliminate the adverse consequences of technological innovation. In recent decades, this approach has given way to a broader one. This shift in focus was a response to the growing divergence between expert and public opinion about what was safe and what was risky. The emergence of a profound sense of risk, which was often at variance with expert opinion, required a major reorientation of the field. As a result, the field of risk studies has become more absorbed in the social dimension of risk. Such studies suggest that it is not particularly helpful to characterize risk perceptions as right or wrong. Nor are these perceptions the simple reactions of the individual mind. The explosion of anxieties about risk takes place within the imagination of society as a whole. The constitution of this imagination is subject to a variety of influences, which form an integral part of the prevailing social and cultural climate, and express a mood, a set of attitudes, which cannot be characterized in terms of rational or irrational any more than the individual expression of happiness or sorrow. That is why officials and experts who try to influence public perception through better risk communication are often ineffective. The many panics or overreactions to a particular incident are by no means mainly the outcome of poor communication. They often provide interesting insights about how society makes sense of itself. Such reactions can only be understood in relation to the wider social processes that will be considered below.

There is little that is precise about the use of the term risk. It is a term that is deployed in a variety of contexts and used in relation to different themes. It is common to discuss the risk of crime, the risk posed by the nuclear power industry or reproductive technology, the risk of skin cancer, the risk of Gulf Syndrome, political risks, or the risk of using the Internet. Often, the term is used to focus on the outcome of specific activities: the risk of catching AIDS, the risk of a football injury or the risk to health through consuming fatty foods (which are converted to cholesterol in the body).

Defining risk

The term risk refers to the probability of damage, injury, illness, death or other misfortune associated with a hazard. Hazards are generally defined to mean a threat to people and what they value. Hazards are not merely such obvious threats as poison, bacteria, toxic waste or hurricanes. At various times peanuts, tampons, automobiles and contraceptive pills – to name a few – have been represented as hazards.

When reports refer to the risk of jogging or drinking or travelling, it is the probability of that particular activity leading to a hazard that is referred to.

No definition, including the one above, can exhaust the meaning and usage of the risk concept. Moreover, since the usage of the term is changing all the time, it is important that it is considered in relation to specific societies and contexts. Ideas and values about society and its future that prevail at any one time influence the way in which risk is perceived.

All risk concepts are based on the distinction between reality and possibility. The concept would not make any sense if the 'future is either predetermined or independent of present human activities'.[3] The relationship between the present and the future depends on how society feels about itself today. Fears about the future are linked to anxieties about problems today. And, if the future is feared, then reaction to risk is more likely to emphasize the probability of adverse outcomes. As a result, the very meaning of risk is shaped by how society regards its ability to manage change and deal with the future. For example, until recently, people frequently talked of good as well as bad risks. 'To risque the certainty of little for the chance of much' was how Samuel Johnson used the term in the eighteenth century. At various times, risk-taking was represented as an admirable enterprise. In recent decades, this neutral quality of risk has given way to one which is by definition a problem. The weighing up of positive and negative outcomes, which was traditionally involved in thinking of risks, has been replaced by an outlook where only danger enters into the equation. So today, when we speak of risk, what we have in mind is the danger of an adverse outcome. We describe less and less the decision we are likely to take as a 'good risk'. Not surprisingly, as risks become more and more equated with danger, there is a tendency to adopt strategies that are self-consciously about risk avoidance. Indeed the positive connotations traditionally associated with 'risk-taking' have given way to condemnation. Consequently, in many situations, 'to take risks' is to court social disapproval.

Another contemporary feature of the deliberation on the subject is that there is a tendency to highlight the intrinsic riskiness of virtually every type of human activity. So for example an advert for the July 1996, British consumer guide *Which?* declared:

SAFE JOURNEY

JUST HOW BIG IS THE RISK WHEN YOU TRAVEL BY PLANE, FERRY OR COACH? WE INVESTIGATE

Investigations such as this are carried out in relation to activities in the home, in school or in the workplace. Not surprisingly, their effect is to elevate safety into a cardinal virtue of contemporary society. It is worth noting that the promotion of such values endows virtually every experience with new meaning. A journey that is self-consciously about safety is very different to one that is about exploration and discovery. A safe journey attempts to avoid the unexpected – since the unexpected is more than likely to be dangerous.

Contemporary discussion is best expressed through the conceptualization of being 'at risk'. This new and original way of framing the term is so pervasive that it is easy to overlook the fact that it is only recently that risk has been thought of in this way. To be at risk is an ambiguous concept. It is used to denote certain types of people who are particularly vulnerable to a hazard. Children who are at risk are usually associated with a particular lifestyle. It also represents a statement about human beings. Their range of options and their future are circumscribed by the variety of risk factors that affect them. To be at risk also refers to certain situations, encounters and experiences. Sex, family life, living near power stations or walking out at night are experiences which are said to place people at risk.

The emergence of the 'at risk' concept ruptures the traditional relationship between individual action and the probability of some hazard. To be at risk is no longer only about what you do – it is also about who you are. It becomes a fixed attribute of the individual, like the size of a person's feet or hands. Consequently, experts in different professions draw up profiles of who is at risk. Thus, social workers look at the background of parents and believe that this information can be a useful indicator of whether or not their children are at risk. Surveys of risk factors isolate forms of behaviour which are symptomatic of those who are most likely to be at risk. Smoking, obesity and stress are only some of the more publicized risk factors in the field of health promotion.

Being at risk also implies the *autonomy* of the dangers that people face. Those who are at risk face hazards that are independent of them. This implies that danger is not merely the outcome of any individual act but is something that exists autonomously, quite separate from the actor. Thus the probability element, where choices about loss and gain informed the decision to take a risk, has given way to an emphasis on avoiding danger. Once risk is seen to exist in its own right and is therefore only minimally subject to human intervention, the most sensible course of action is to avoid it altogether. The diminution of the human agency that is implicit in the 'at risk' concept has dramatically changed the calculation of risk. As will be made increasingly clear throughout this book, the contemporary meaning of risk has little in common with its usage in the past. Openness to the positive as well as negative possibilities of an activity has been overwhelmed by the certainty of adverse outcomes.

If risk is autonomous, it suggests that it exists independently of any act or individual. Like the Greek gods, risk factors exist in a world of their own. The role of society is to warn its members about this complex of hazards with which they are compelled to live. To be at risk is a condition of life. That is why the traditional conceptualization of risk in relation to a specific hazard or technology is far too limiting. The system of risk factors is represented as prior and independent of any individual act, so the experience of being at risk transcends any particular experience. Attitudes towards personal security express this consciousness no less than reactions to problems of the environment. Consequently, the consciousness of risk influences human behaviour in its totality. The autonomization of risk factors reverses the human-centred relation between individual and experience. In this new scenario, the autonomous individual disappears and returns as one who is subjected to the authority of autonomous risk factors.

One of the central arguments of this book is that the perception of being at risk expresses a pervasive mood in society; one that influences action in general. It appears as a free-floating consciousness that attaches itself to (and detaches itself from) a variety of concerns and experiences. The pre-existing disposition to perceive not just major technological innovations but also mundane experiences as potentially threatening means that there is a heightened state of readiness to react to whatever danger is brought to the attention of the public. An understanding of the workings of this free-floating anxiety requires an examination of the different dimensions of risk consciousness.

The inflation of danger

Society today seems preoccupied with the dangers that people face. The past decade has seen a veritable explosion of new dangers. Life is portrayed as increasingly violent. Children are depicted as more and more out of control. Crime is on the increase. The food we eat, the water we drink, and the materials we use for everything from buildings to cellular phones, have come under scrutiny. However, reactions to such routine dangers pale into insignificance in relation to the big threats, which are said to put humanity's survival into question.

During the past decade, supposed threats to human survival have been declared so frequently that the expectation of an apocalypse has become rather banal. Our imagination continually works towards the worst possible interpretation of events. Expectations of some far-reaching catastrophe are regularly rehearsed in relation to a variety of risks. Thus fears about an explosive epidemic of a lethal infectious disease reinforce anxieties about the dangers of nuclear war, global warming and other environmental disasters. AIDS has retained its status of the modern equivalent of the plague, only to be joined by new threats to health such as Ebola, Mad Cow Disease, Severe Acute Respiratory Syndrome (SARS) and the Avian Flu – and the re-emergence of old dangers, notably cholera, tuberculosis and diphtheria, often in drug-resistant forms.

The inflation of danger is now systematically pursued and widely believed. The tendency to revel in the worst-case scenario is well summed up in the title of John Leslie's book, *The End of The World: The Science and Ethics of Human Extinction*. Its opening pages reel off a series of dangers, which Leslie believes could wipe out the human species. The list includes seven risks, such as nuclear war and the destruction of the ozone layer, which he states are 'already well recognised'. He also adds sixteen risks, such as a stellar explosion and disasters associated with computers, which he claims are often 'unrecognised'.[4] Leslie's grim prognosis may be a bit eccentric, but it does echo the consensus that humanity is in grave danger from a range of natural, social and technological factors. In fact, publications on the environment regularly use the discourse of crisis. For example, a review of the state of the environment in 2005 in the *Guardian* is typically titled 'Climate of Fear'. It notes that 2005 'was one of the four hottest years recorded since 1861'. It states that in this 'monumental year for the environment', 'the greatest number of hurricanes and tropical storms were recorded'.[5] From such reports it is difficult to avoid concluding that planet earth is in a state of terminal decline.

Anxieties about the environment appear positively restrained when placed alongside the new genre of medical doomsday scenarios. Recently published bestsellers like Arno Karlen's *Plague's Progress: A Social History of Man and Disease*, and Laurie Garrett's *The Coming Plague: Newly Emerging Diseases in a World out of Balance*, have had a major impact on both sides of the Atlantic. They give coherence to a new strain of panic about plagues and epidemics, which is spreading like wildfire through the worlds of science and popular culture. Never has the word epidemic been used in association with so many different phenomena. Thus Karlen can project a 'massive global die-off', which might result from a 'revived bubonic/pneumonic plague, a virulent new flu virus, a new airborne haemorrhage fever, or germs that lurk undiscovered in other species'.[6] In fact, one of the main objections to proceeding with primate-to-human organ transplant is the apparent risk of transferring unkown viruses from animals to humans. Thus while there are questions about which disease will threaten human survival, the existence of such a threat as such is not under discussion. In this scenario, plagues are waiting to be discovered by our free-floating anticipation of danger.

Since the AIDS panic first swept the Western world, there has been a series of dramatic encounters with infectious disease. Some have been associated with contaminated foods (eggs with *Salmonella*, soft cheeses with *Listeria*) and others have emerged from exotic foreign locations (such as the Ebola outbreak in Zaire). Others still are old-fashioned diseases like tuberculosis and diphtheria. A recent large-scale public health scare in the UK erupted in March 1996 in response to the fear that beef infected with BSE has led to cases of CJD in humans. In recent years, exotic viruses have been the main focus of concern.

The most common feature of these disease scares is the systematic exaggeration of the scale of the threat. In the 1990s, newspaper reports claimed that as many as 100,000 people would perish from an incurable brain disease due to BSE in the UK. By 2005, there were around 150 deaths due to this disease. But instead of informing the world that the previous catastrophic predictions did not materialize, the media tends to treat BSE as a prelude to more dangers to come. Nor was the public reassured about the good news concerning SARS. At the height of the 2003 panic about this 'killer pneumonia', SARS was represented as a terrifying disease that threatened the whole world. There were calls for mass screenings at airports and for closing down national borders. Fortunately SARS led to only a couple of hundred deaths. Nevertheless, alarmist accounts about the risks of this disease continued to be circulated warning the public that SARS was the prelude to wave of new viral pandemics.

Scares about infectious plagues are complemented by the continuous discovery of new health problems. Along with epidemic, 'syndrome' was one of the most overused concepts of the 1990s. An increasing range of experiences invites an association with a syndrome. We have everything from the Gulf syndrome to chronic lateness syndrome. In many accounts the impression is created that people living in the industrialized world are getting more unhealthy. Some writers point to the large number of people who die from cancer as proof that we live in an essentially unhealthy environment. According to Shrader-Frechette 'cancer already takes more American lives, each year, than were lost during all of World War II, the Korean War, and the Vietnam War combined; it is responsible for eight times as many annual deaths as automobiles'.[7] When the incidence of cancer is presented in such striking terms, it is difficult to avoid the conclusion that an epidemic of cancer is sweeping the USA. The reality is actually quite different. Figures show that the age-adjusted mortality rate for all cancers combined, except lung cancer, has been declining since 1950 for all individual groups except those 85 and above. Thus cancer rates are not soaring. Indeed the fact that so many people still die from cancer is due to an improvement in the general levels of health, which have allowed people to live longer than before. Cancer is a disease whose rate increases with age. In the past, many would not have survived to the age where their life would be threatened by cancer.[8]

Many observers acknowledge that there is something perverse about a society that is continually obsessed with health and is continually in the throes of some medical or environmental panic. However, many writers who can see a problem in relation to health are often not aware that virtually every area of society is dominated by the explosion of risks. The association of problems with plagues is by no means restricted to the sphere of health. Child abuse is often portrayed as a modern plague.

For example, the American Association for Protecting Children has argued that there was a 225 per cent increase in the reporting of all forms of maltreatment of children between 1976 and 1987. Others contend that child abuse has acquired epidemic proportions. According to one writer on the subject:

> Sexual abuse is a significant problem in America, as well as in other countries. With figures cited that as many as one in five children, both male and female, risks being sexually abused before their 18th birthday, some consider sexual abuse to be of epidemic proportions.[9]

Similar claims have been made about an explosion of domestic violence, bullying in schools and a variety of other kinds of harassment.

Perceptions about the inexorable rise of crime parallel the panic-like reactions in the sphere of health and the environment. Most studies reveal widespread public concern about personal security. The fear of violent crime influences human relations at all levels of society. As with health scares, society's free-floating consciousness of risk attaches itself to one type of crime on Monday, a different one on Wednesday and yet another on Sunday. During the last few years, in the UK, public attention has at one time or another focused on road rage, criminal children, stalking and random violence in public places.

It is also unfortunate that high levels of anxiety about crime can only make the world more insecure. In the USA publicity about road rage has helped fuel paranoia amongst insecure drivers, which in turn has contributed to more deaths. During the late 1980s, 1200 road-rage-related deaths were reported. Consequently, people became so afraid that they began to drive with a gun on the passenger seat. The predictable outcome of this reaction was that more lives were lost.

Anxieties regarding the threat of crime against children often take on panic-like proportions. In the USA, where FBI statistics indicate that fewer than 100 children a year are kidnapped by strangers, the public concern with child abduction is pervasive. For example, a study of schoolchildren in Ohio reported that nearly half of them thought that they would be kidnapped. Such reactions are not surprising. Public information campaigns on milk cartons, posters and videos have helped reinforce the impression that kidnapping is a widespread threat. The same inflated sense of danger prevails in the UK. Many parents simply do not believe that, over the years, the number of children murdered by strangers has remained fairly static. On average it has been five per year. A few highly publicized child murders have helped shape the impression that such tragedies 'could happen to every child'.

One of the most worrying symptoms of the reaction to crimes involving children is the cavalier manner in which facts are treated. Consider for example, a recent contribution by child-rearing expert, Penelope Leach: 'Whatever the real scale and scope of the horrors perpetrated on or by children, there are not hundreds, not thousands, but millions more who are being failed by Western society and are failing it'.[10] A statement which begins with the rather unspecific 'whatever the real scale' ends with the confident assertion about millions of victims. In a similar vein, Rosalind Miles warns her readers: 'the prevalence of today's news stories about criminal children, abused children, children out of hand, however much they smack of newspaper hype and moral panic, point to a genuine, growing and justified concern'.[11] From this perspective, 'hype' and 'moral panics' are presented as instruments for exposing genuine concern. That the concern is genuine is beyond doubt. But what this concern is based on is not clarified by the attitude of 'don't worry about the figures, the problem has to be enormous'!

In recent years the highly sensational manner in which issues to do with children are treated has been widely acknowledged. Many have pointed out the tragic consequences of scare campaigns, like the 'Stranger Danger' initiative organized by the Home Office in Leeds in 1988. The campaign, which saturated the whole town with the warning to children that they should mistrust people they did not know, helped contribute to the climate of near hysteria concerning this subject. It is not surprising that in the UK, more than in most places in Europe, children have little freedom to walk the streets on their own. In some places, parents who do not escort their children to school are regarded as placing their young ones at risk. The consequence of this culture of 'Stranger Danger' is well summed up in a recent study of children's independent mobility.

We have created a world for our children in which safety is promoted through fear. The message of campaigns such as 'One false move and you're dead' is one of deference to the source of the danger. That such a world can be advertised without apparent embarrassment by those responsible for the safety of children, and without provoking public outrage, is a measure of how far the unacceptable has become accepted.[12]

Unhappily, the use of fear has become a widely accepted device for the promotion of a variety of good causes.

The promotion of fear and the propagandist manipulation of information is often justified on the grounds that it is a small price to pay to get a good message across to the public. For example, the health promotion campaign about the dangers of skin cancer focus on exposure as the cancer-inducing factor. However, it has been suggested that the crucial determinant has to do with the genetic make-up of the individual concerned, and that most people can continue to enjoy the sun without worrying about the risk of skin cancer. Many health promoters are aware of these suggestions, but argue that if the information they provide was qualified, then its impact on the public would be seriously undermined. In other words, rather than provide people with the information to make an informed choice, everyone is warned that they are at risk. The refusal to make a distinction between people who are clearly at risk and those who are not has also been the hallmark of successive AIDS awareness campaigns. It is only recently, after almost a decade of campaigning, that the media have begun to acknowledge that AIDS is not a significant threat to heterosexuals. Most supporters of this campaign are unapologetic about the promotion of dishonest propaganda. Writing in the *Guardian*, Mark Lawson declared: 'the

Government has lied, and I am glad'. Lawson concedes that the government had promoted 'exaggerations and inaccuracies', but so what since this was a case of a 'good lie'.[13] It appears that a widespread panic that has significantly influenced sexual behaviour and personal relationships is in itself such a worthy cause that telling the truth can be negotiable.

Advocacy groups self-consciously use scare tactics to promote their cause. In June 2006, Greenpeace responded to President Bush's attempt to promote his nuclear energy policy during his visit to Pennsylvania by releasing an alarmist statement about the 'threat' posed by the local reactors. A memo accidentally released by Greenpeace illustrated this organization's embrace of the propaganda of fear. It stated;

> 'In the twenty years since the Chernobyl tragedy, the world's worst nuclear accident, there have been nearly [FILL IN ALARMIST AND ARMAGEDDONIST FACTOIDS]'.[14]

Later the author of this memo claimed that he was making a joke in this 'mistakenly' released document. However, jokes like this appear with frequent regularity in the press releases of his organization.

There appears to be no restraint on publicity and information warning of an expanding variety of dangers. One would have thought it unlikely that everything is becoming all at once more dangerous. The laws of probability would suggest that at least something should be going in a different direction. But the words 'and it's getting worse' are used with ever-increasing frequency in relation to an astounding range of experiences. Moreover, the tendency is to expand the range of activities which are now considered risky, so everything from a major threat to human survival to the mundane everyday affair of walking to school is subject to risk consciousness. At times it seems that there is no escape. Health promoters advise people to take exercise to avoid certain risks, but then exercising has its own risks. As one author wrote: 'Risk taking and pushing the body to extremes are part of many sporting activities. The numbers of risks have increased considerably as an increasing number of adults take regular exercise'.[15] So it seems that it is possible to choose between exercising or becoming a couch-potato. But it is not possible to avoid risks – in one case the risk associated with sport, and in the other the risk of poor health.

The constant amplification of danger in virtually every sphere of social life must be symptomatic of some underlying problem. As the American critic Susan Sontag remarked, the 'striking readiness of so many to envisage the most far-reaching catastrophes' must point to some failure within society.[16]

The fear of side-effects

Fears and anxieties about danger are surprisingly selective. The outbreak of the Ebola virus in Zaire during 1995 attracted a high level of international publicity. The media devoted considerable resources towards reporting this story and the Western public was soon made aware of yet another danger. But the purveyors of this risk neglected to mention that Ebola was a relatively minor health problem, even in Africa. In Zaire, more people died of sleeping sickness than of the Ebola virus during the outbreak of the epidemic. To place the reporting of this virus in a comparative perspective, it is worth considering how the media dealt with other tragedies during this period. The epidemic coincided with a three-day storm which led to an outbreak of diarrhoea in Bangladesh. Although the casualties – 400 dead and more than 50,000 infected – were far higher than in Zaire, the Western media were distinctly uninterested in the story. The sense of risk was attached to Ebola, not to diarrhoea, the far greater killer of people throughout most of the world.

There are many explanations of why people dread some dangers more than others. It has been suggested that experts differ from the public when it comes to risk perception. Experts tend to regard the risks posed by hazards such as nuclear waste or power plant operations as being less significant than do the public. It is suggested that the reverse is the case when it comes to so-called lifestyle risks, such as smoking or alcohol. Others have pointed to the quality of the risk as being the decisive pointer to the reaction. It has been suggested that people are more prepared to accept 'voluntary' risks such as mountain-climbing than ones, like chemical pollution, over which they have no control. Recently, it has been argued that it is unnatural hazards which cause most anxiety. Concepts like that of 'manufactured risk' have been used to characterize the unnatural dangers that cause the most consternation.

The distinction drawn between natural and unnatural represents an important theme in the discussion of risk. As with all couplets, the natural–unnatural one raises important questions. Why are some risks called natural and some unnatural? In reality, the line that separates one from the other is far from clear. It is true that, today, 'natural' is often portrayed as wholesome and intrinsically good, but just what constitutes the natural is not straightforward. For example, some people object to taking medicine containing hormones, like the contraceptive pill, because they do not want to introduce any unnatural agents into their bodies. When these objections are countered by the information that the body contains many hormones, there is often a hint of surprise in the reaction.

Often, benign natural substances are contrasted with unnatural, synthetic toxins. As in the case of hormones, life is more complicated. Many of the most beautiful wild flowers and plants are full of carcinogens. Many plants survive because the toxins they produce deter the animals that would otherwise devour them. Because of our system of values, a plant's natural pesticide is usually described as 'natural resistance', whereas something that comes out of a bottle is said to be poisonous. Yet both pesticides – natural and synthetic – may have carcinogenic or teratogenic properties.

The rigid contrast drawn between natural and unnatural and the benign image that Western societies have of nature is very much bound up with contemporary culture and values. In the past, benign interpretations of nature coexisted with ones that were far more negative. At times, the overwhelming mood was to see nature as threatening, even destructive. Even today, in many agrarian societies, natural forces are far more feared than loved. Today, people in Western societies have little to fear directly from such dangers. The damage caused by floods, earthquakes and hurricanes has been minimized through technological innovation. Consequently, danger appears to be mainly manufactured by human beings. Traffic accidents, chemical pollution and violent crime rather than floods or lightning cause death and injury. As a result, perceptions of danger are increasingly focused on technology: human-created or manufactured risk.

The close association that is made between technology and our heightened sense of danger describes but does not explain very much about the explosion of risks. A more useful way of understanding the discussion is to ask the question: what lies behind the celebration of the natural and the disparagement of the unnatural? The ascendancy of this sentiment is of relatively recent origin. Human history can be interpreted as a protracted process of transforming, altering and rearranging nature. There can be nothing more unnatural than domesticating animals, injecting ourselves with vaccinations or reclaiming land from the sea. Many of these formerly unnatural acts – such as the keeping of pets – are seen as entirely natural. At the same time, deeds that were once described as great achievements are today dismissed as destructive. This mood is very much linked to the end-of-the-twentieth-century culture, which regards human creation as at best a mixed blessing and at worst wholly dangerous. From this perspective, human beings are seen to spoil, pollute or destroy nature. The very attempt to control or transform nature is depicted as the source of hazard. That may be why we dread Ebola, one of a number of new viruses that are considered to have become a threat to humanity as a result of people's interference in natural ecosystems, especially rainforests. Our inflated sense of danger is at least indirectly linked to the sentiment which regards human innovation with suspicion. Many of the panics discussed previously reveal a tendency to denigrate innovation and to dismiss the human potential. It is the destructive side of the human experience which captures the imagination. The metaphor 'population explosion' symbolizes the consciousness which believes that the less people that inhabit the world, the better. As the American commentator Malcolm Gladwell has observed, contemporary culture concerning the danger of new plagues exhibits a 'self-loathing' of humanity – one that goes far beyond the old Cold War images of the enemy as alien, beyond even biblical notions of pestilence as punishment for wickedness.[17] The scale of such profoundly anti-humanist sentiments is vividly illustrated in a passage from Richard Preston's bestselling thriller, *The Hot Zone*. Preston's story of the arrival of the Ebola virus in the USA portrays humanity itself as the plague! 'The earth is attempting to rid itself of an infection by the human parasite. Perhaps Aids is the first step in a natural process of clearance.'[18]

Preston's welcoming of new epidemics as a sort of natural purge of human parasites may be an eccentric one, but his equation of humanity with such negative qualities is not. It is a pattern that recurs throughout cultural and political debate. Indeed, the same sentiment has influenced discussions of violence, crime and abuse. The debased human being, an abuser in the making, 'a natural-born killer', is a character type that has caught the imagination of popular culture and the media.

Perceptions of risk are strongly shaped by the prevailing absence of trust in humanity. The decline of trust has been widely acclaimed as the cause of society's sensitivity to risk. As an explanation, the decline of trust is not particularly helpful. Such explanations beg the question of why trust has declined. Trust is not so much a cause as a symptom of our consciousness of risk. As a result of the decline of trust, there is a tendency to view people's actions as at least potentially dangerous. As one major study of risk argued, 'both institutions and individuals have a strong interest in under-assessing and underestimating risk'.[19] The belief that risks are continually 'underestimated', 'ignored' or 'covered up' strengthens the conviction that in many situations there are hidden or invisible risks lurking under the surface. One of the consequences of this development is a strong undercurrent of fear about the side-effects of any technological innovation or social experience. This suspicion of side-effects is one of the central motifs of risk consciousness.

'What are its side-effects?' is a question that is asked in relation to an ever-expanding list of subjects. The question is not asked merely in relation to drugs or complex technological processes. Virtually any innovation is likely to be assessed in this manner. The fear of side-effects influences whole communities, who sometimes believe that their well-being is affected by the side-effect of some industrial process. Complaints by communities that some unknown or invisible toxic substance is responsible for illness are readily given credence by the media. In the USA the suggestion of an epidemiological association between a factor in the environment and illness provides the basis for litigation.

Today, the belief that the risk of side-effects outweighs the benefits of many innovations is deeply embedded in contemporary Western culture. One of the consequences of this attitude is that both relationships and products are regarded as inherently risky. Sooner or later virtually anything can be perceived as a tangible risk. The result of this process is a mind-set that continually expects the worst in every situation. An example is the completion of the Channel Tunnel. Instead of celebrating the realization of this centuries-old dream of linking France to Britain, the tendency of the media was to look for problems and side-effects. Soon the British public was made aware of a variety of new risks connected with the Channel Tunnel. At first the discussion focused on the likelihood of a major accident which could claim many lives. Then the focus shifted to the risk that international terrorists would blow up the tunnel, causing major damage. The public was even warned about the danger that rabies could be introduced into Britain from the Continent through the Channel Tunnel. As a result of all these warnings, the positive contribution of this development to improving the quality of life became obscured. The Channel Tunnel was seen not so much as an example of human ingenuity, rather as the transmitter of new hazards. And when in November 1996 a fire on a lorry led to the closure of a section of the tunnel, it seemed to confirm the wisdom of the sceptics.

The conviction that innovations are inherently risky often leads to speculation about side-effects. Such discussions are usually directed towards a deliberation about how best to pre-empt any adverse outcomes. This compulsion to pre-empt danger sometimes leads to the tendency to imagine and to hypothesize about problems that may occur in the future. An examination of such speculation indicates that it invariably takes the form of projecting contemporary social problems onto the plane of technology. Anxieties about rabies and terrorism are not the creation of the Channel Tunnel. Rather, this tunnel gave shape and form to pre-existing concerns.

Reproductive technology provides another example. Instead of celebrating the important contribution that new developments in this sphere have made towards tackling the problem of infertility or the potential it has for giving women greater control over their fertility, the tendency has been to warn people of its consequences. The media revel in publishing sensational accounts about how this technology is misused by elderly women and lesbians. Reports continually warn of the ethical problems, whilst conservative writers condemn assisted conception as unnatural. What lies behind these warnings? An examination of the debate indicates that it is the difficulty of negotiating changing relations within the family, between men and women and parents and children, that informs the concerns. Even if this technology did not exist, anxieties would be expressed about lifestyles which did not conform to the traditional norm.

The obsession with the side-effects of reproductive technology has led some to investigate the possibility that children born through assisted conception may be subject to some special risk. These investigations were not a response to any empirical evidence of such a problem. They were motivated by the belief that reproductive technology must pose some adverse outcomes to those born in this way. A study on parent–children relationships, which compared 24–30-month-old single-born children conceived by *in vitro* fertilization (IVF) with those born through natural conception, could not find any significant differences in the parent–children relationship. This has not stopped researchers from imagining that those children born through IVF must be at some special risk.[20]

A recent monograph on the risks that reproductive technology represents to the safety of children is paradigmatic of the current search for side-effects. Without producing any factual evidence, the author, Ruth Landau, seems utterly convinced that this technology constitutes a risk to the safety of children. She does this by abstractly speculating about possible dangers. The first risk she enumerates is to do with the fact that children born with the assistance of medical technology are planned. Because they are planned, parents are less likely to be satisfied with children who do not meet their high expectations. Since parents have such high expectations, she asks, 'should it come as a surprise that abuse, neglect or abandonment may follow'? It is interesting that Landau does not entertain the possibility that parents who plan and devote considerable resources towards overcoming the barriers to reproduction may well create an environment that is uniquely good for the welfare of children. The sense of being wanted, an important factor in stable child development, is simply not discussed by Landau. Instead, parents who plan conception (which in reality includes not just those who use medical technology but a significant proportion of parents in Western societies) are represented not only as having the worst possible motives, but also as being abusers in the making.

The second argument that Landau uses for supporting her interpretation of risks concerns the time-honoured conservative fears regarding the erosion of traditional bonds between the biological parent and child. She argues that artificial insemination, IVF and surrogate parenthood blur the line between parent and child. This lack of clarity on the parents' part may introduce a 'possible breach of parental responsibility'. This could 'complicate the bond between parent and child, and eventually also weaken the incest taboo'. Why people who devote considerable time and resources to having children should be more irresponsible than others is not explained. At a time when large numbers of children are not brought up by both their biological parents, the validity of concern for the absence of a traditional bond for those born through assisted conception is not at all self-evident.

Landau herself is far from certain about what the risks are for the offspring of assisted conception. However, she fervently believes that there must be some risks. This belief is rooted in the fashionable doctrine that innovation is dangerous. She is not obliged to identify any dangers; all she needs to state is that the 'medical and the social costs' of reproductive technology are 'still unknown'. 'Thus the exponentially increasing medical advances in general and the new technologies in particular, create new and unprecedented forms of risk to children's personal safety and their well being in the family'.[21] This vision of 'new and unprecedented forms of risk' is based on the assumption that any interference with nature will exact a heavy price. The belief that the side-effects outweigh the advantages is the corollary of this vision.

Whether or not such a vision is substantiated by evidence is irrelevant. It is enough to dread, in a society which routinely feels ill at ease with its own creation. More specifically, what inspires Landau's reaction logically and chronologically precedes the development of IVF technology. Uncertainties about parenting reappear yet again in the new form of a technological risk.

It was not so long ago that the Internet was treated as a powerful instrument for improving the quality of our lives. However, as with reproductive technology, before too long society's obsession with side-effects attached itself to cyberspace. Increasingly, the deliberations about the sociology of cyberspace have begun to mirror the contemporary disquiet about adverse outcomes. As a result, the theme of new risks and dangers on the Internet has become an important focus of discussion. Danger lurks in cyberspace. 'Cyberporn' has become a big issue. According to many accounts, cyberspace has become a risky territory populated by paedophiles, cyberstalkers and other perpetrators of on-line sex crimes. One leading American weekly argues that cyberspace 'seems a harsh and unforgiving place ... where it's all too easy for villains to snatch your digital valuables – by ripping off your work or stealing your credit-card information'.[22] This characterization of the Internet appeared to be confirmed when the FBI arrested Jake Baker, a 20-year-old student, for alleged 'cyber-rape', after he posted a torture and murder fantasy which referred to one of his classmates by name. The charges were later dropped.

Most new technologies, the Internet included, are liable to be portrayed as inherently risky. There is a tendency to take seriously virtually any discovery of a new risk. When, two years ago, Dr Ivan Goldberg, a New York psychopharmacist, first identified Internet addiction syndrome (IAD), it was treated as something of a joke. However, it has since been 'confirmed' by other experts that Internet users are at risk from addiction to on-line communication. According to one account IAD 'has been blamed for broken relationships, job losses, financial ruin and even a suicide'.[23]

What we already fear can now thrive in the new space provided by the Internet. The worries expressed regarding the Internet suggest it is not merely the physical material aspects of technology which are in question. Some question the benefits of technological innovation on the grounds that it provides new opportunities for those who threaten people's well-being and safety. A recent Labour Party document pronounced that

New forms of violent and sexual threat have developed through technological change. Telephones have always been used for abusive and threatening phone calls, by men both known and unknown to women. Computers now offer an additional route, especially in work settings.[24]

From this vantage point of risk sensitivity, every innovation merely increases the potential danger. This is why most innovations soon come under the critical scrutiny of those who see in every development the potential for more danger.

If an innovation like the Internet can provoke such anxiety about its dangerous side-effects, it is not surprising that more stigmatized technologies — such as biotechnology and genetics — are so often embroiled in controversy and public hostility. Such technologies have provoked some intensely speculative responses. Critics have focused on the dangers of 'hypothetical risks'. Thus opponents of genetic engineering have argued that organisms which are harmless in themselves could be manipulated in such a way as to produce dangerous human or animal pathogens, which could spread all over the world and kill millions of people. Such a scenario is not based on any examples in the here and now — it is based on the invention of a possible nightmare. The premise of a hypothetical risk is that anything can happen. That what used to pass for science fiction is now considered to be of direct relevance is a statement about society's anxieties.

However, regardless of the scale of public anxiety, it is important to understand that it is not a direct response to a particular technological process. For example, panics about the Internet are predicated on an already heightened sense of anxiety within society, particularly in relation to the safety of children. The Internet provides a framework through which concern with what children see and hear and who they talk to can be made tangible. This anxiety concerning the safety of children could have just as well attached itself to the danger of videos or computer games. Experience suggests that it is only a matter of time before an innovation is inspected to ascertain whether it puts children at risk or provides opportunities for sex crimes or international terrorism.

Hidden, invisible and always getting worse

Statements about side-effects and dangers are often unsubstantiated. There is a presumption that what is visible or quantifiable is only the tip of the iceberg. Such conclusions often make sense, since many people expect that those in authority are unlikely to tell the truth. That people so readily expect cover-ups and hidden agendas is in part an understandable reaction to past experience. However, it has also contributed to a climate in which the most extreme claims about virtually any issue can be taken seriously – at least until they are disproved. The task of contesting such claims is sometimes relatively straightforward. But what happens when attention is drawn to risks that are said to be invisible or hidden or whose adverse consequences will not be known for another generation?

The explosion of risk which characterizes Western societies is accompanied by a consciousness which imagines destructive side-effects as boundless. Not only is society's sense of risk a free-floating one, ready and able to attach itself to any experience; it is also not limited by what is visible or what exists in the here and now. Consequently, even if a particular product or technology creates no apparent problems today, that is not the end of the matter. There is a tendency to presume that the adverse outcomes will only be known by future generations. This outlook strongly influences strands of environmental thinking. Indeed many of the policies of environmentalists are justified on the grounds of protecting future generations from the risks that we thoughtlessly set in motion today. However, as we shall see, this sentiment also influences social policy and academic research on human relations.

Risks, especially the varieties that are intensely disliked, are also often said to be invisible. Like the plague, they are out there, ready to strike. Such invisible risks range from HIV to toxic pollutants. In contemporary society, pollution is important not just as a byproduct of industry but as a metaphor for making sense of a variety of experiences. The existence of this invisible process is confirmed by the regularity with which people's illnesses are now attributed to some kind of pollutant. But pollution today, as in the past, is inextricably linked to imagination, social values and culture. For some societies, the act of defiling a temple is experienced in physical and material terms. This perception is no less real than the belief that an outbreak of some illness in a community could not be a coincidence but must be a physical reaction to an act of pollution.[25]

Even a periodical like *Nature*, which is devoted to science, is ready to accept the idea of invisible risk and interpret it negatively. A 'reminder of the insidious threat posed by environmental pollutants' was its comment on the publication of a study, in February 1966, which argued that the sperm count of British men was falling.[26] The link between pollutants and falling sperm counts required no elaboration – it was established *a priori*. Yet there is little proof of the connection between environmental pollution and falling sperm counts. Indeed, the very meaning of the 'facts' is open to question. It has still not been established whether sperm counts are falling, and we are even less certain whether such a fall has any significance. Along with the popular media, *Nature* simply assumed that this 'insidious threat' represented a significant risk to society. But what is the danger that is alluded to in the UK, where the rate of reproduction is primarily influenced by attitudes to contraception rather than men's sperm counts?

The tendency to dread hidden dangers invites speculation of science-fictional proportions. Such a perspective often informs both academic and non-academic deliberations about the future of the world. 'How do you calculate risk in an era when nightmares are becoming headlines?' asks the *New York Times*.[27] A study published in *Foreign Affairs* predicts that 'if an influenza struck today, borders would close, the global economy would shut down, international vaccine supplies and health-care systems would be overwhelmed, and panic would reign'.[28] Like our reaction to global terrorism, these are boundless fears – threats without boundaries, from which there is no hiding place.

It is the inflated consciousness of danger which expresses itself in risks which are, by definition, without boundaries, either in time or in space. According to an American study of community traumas, people have a particular dread of 'toxic emergencies', because, states the author, 'they never end'. 'Invisible contaminants remain a part of the surroundings, absorbed into the grain of the landscape, the tissues of the body, and, worst of all, the genetic material of the survivors. An all clear is never sounded.'[29]

The sentiment that whole communities have been contaminated for life by some invisible or unknown substance and that the dreadful consequences will not be known until the indefinite future now has the character of an established truth. As a result, unexplained outbreaks of illnesses or of birth defects, within a particular area, often lead to speculation that some unknown factor in the environment is the cause.

The preoccupation with unexplained and invisible risks has stimulated a retrospective re-examination of processes that were, until recently, never thought of as anything but safe. Potential health risks from exposure to power-frequency electromagnetic fields (EMF) have become an issue of significant public concern in the USA and, to a lesser extent, in the UK. It has been suggested by some critics that people living near power transmission cables or electricity substations might be in danger from certain forms of cancer. The focus on cancer causation has led other technologies and processes to be regarded with suspicion. As a result, more and more products are investigated for evidence of human carcinogenicity. Since the world is full of pollutants and since every living thing and every industry 'pollutes', it is not difficult to arrive at an inflated perception of the risk of cancer. 'Even sunlight is carcinogenic and it is likely that oxygen will be found to be carcinogenic as well' write two critics of the contemporary obsession with cancer risks.[30]

The current official disapproval of sunbathing indicates that it is not merely technologies that are liable to be reinterpreted as dangerous. The idea that the sun is dangerous must have come as a surprise to generations who have believed that the sun was actually good for their health. In the UK, a vigorous campaign launched in 1995 by the Health Education Authority (HEA) helped to equate sunbathing with skin cancer. 'In an ideal world we would stay out of the sun all the time' was how the July 1995 issue of *Top Sante* magazine summed up the new wisdom.

The readiness with which the media and the public accepted the HEA's new message was a testimony to the unbounded character of risk consciousness. No one in the media asked how something regarded as beneficial to human health by so many experts, for so long, could become suddenly such a danger to the public. It was only in specialist medical publications that the alleged melanoma epidemic was placed under scrutiny. Indeed, some dermatologists have argued that the advocates of sun-avoidance in fact may be creating a problem for people. According to Professor Jonathan Rees, 'most melanomas occur on skin that is only intermittently exposed; individuals with higher continuous sun exposure have lower rates than those exposed intermittently'. Rees and others have also questioned the use of sunscreens on the grounds that they may 'actually increase rather than decrease the melanoma risk'.[31]

Since scientific opinion is still unclear about the relationship between melanoma and sun exposure, it is surprising that such a solid and unquestioning consensus was established in the media, so quickly. A practice which had been long seen not only as healthy but as a source of pleasure suddenly became a danger to all. The speed with which the new interpretation of sunbathing was assimilated into the psyche of British society was also remarkable. Its clearest symptom was the widespread concern with children playing outdoors. Indeed, the vulnerability of children to exposure to the sun became the main selling point of public health promoters. Their message was that if children will not cover up in the sun, they should be kept indoors. The many new safeguards that have been put in place in nurseries and infant schools to protect children from the sun indicate how everyday behaviour can be modified by a health promotion campaign based on relatively skimpy evidence. Questions about what we give up in order to be safe are rarely explored. Instead, patronizing health promotion campaigns seek to reassure that there is nothing wrong with a lily white coloured face. They also aim to scare women off sunbathing on the grounds that those with a tan age faster than those without one.

The redefinition of hitherto uncontroversial technologies and processes as dangers is assisted by society's disposition to focus on their problematic and destructive side. The anticipation of risks, at least hidden risks, precedes the identification of any specific object of fear. It is not just technologies which are deemed to be dangerous that are approached in this way. Human relationships are also increasingly interpreted as the site of new or hitherto unrecognized risks. The American term 'toxic families' indicates that our boundless imagination of dangers transcends the technical and influences the domain of social relations. Indeed, the many scares about the risks involved in human relationships have the same structure and dynamic as those which prevail in discussions of the environment or technology.

Susan Forward, author of *Toxic Parents*, regards the effects of bad parenting as akin to 'invisible weeds that invaded your life in ways you never dreamed of'. Parents who exude invisible poisonous substances to pollute their vulnerable offspring are the perfect personification of what we dread. As Forward explained,

> *As I searched for a phrase to describe the common ground that these harmful parents share, the word that kept running through my mind was toxic. Like a chemical toxin, the emotional damage inflicted by these parents spreads throughout a child's being, and as the child grows, so does the pain. What better word than toxic to describe parents who inflict ongoing trauma, abuse, and denigration on their children.*[32]

The ease with which Forward shifts from technical to human toxins is indicative of the imagination of unbounded risks. The premise of this imagination is the belief that people pollute – not just the environment but also each other. The reinterpretation of human relations as toxic suggests that it is driven by a moralizing impulse. This conceptualization of pollution is influenced by the traditional meaning of the term.

Pollution as a morally defined act traditionally involves the act of defilement and desecration. In the past, to pollute was understood to mean to render ceremonially or morally impure, to profane, to stain, to sully or to corrupt. These concepts of moral defilement are like acts of physical pollution, invisible. They leave it to the imagination to think the worst.

Academic and non-academic discussions of social problems use an approach and a vocabulary which parallel the discussion of environmental, health and technological hazards. It is customary to claim that a problem is underestimated or underreported and that, in fact, its incidence is far greater than we suspect. The use of the metaphor of *invisibility* appeals to our imagination to look beyond the obvious boundaries of perception. Indeed, the very fact that a problem is not visible invites us to speculate about its intensity. Those involved in public communication routinely invite people to speculate about some unacknowledged phenomenon. The following press comment from the RAC is illustrative in this respect: 'Road rage is not supposed, officially, to exist but we think it is a very serious problem'.[33] The construction of the argument is based on the assumption that the reader is already disposed to believe that important information is withheld by official authority from the public domain. Indeed, the very strength of the argument is that road rage is 'not supposed, officially, to exist'. Lack of official recognition merely strengthens the plausibility of the argument.

Warnings of risks in the sphere of human relationships invariably claim that a particular condition is either hidden or consciously made invisible. Consequently, the diagnosis of a disorder or of a social problem often takes the form of a discovery of a condition that has existed for some considerable time. Typically, an article on attention deficit disorder (ADD) is titled 'The Hidden Handicap'. The discovery of this hidden condition among children invariably leads to its siting among adults. 'Now it is one of the fastest growing diagnostic categories for adults', wrote *Time* magazine.[34] Everyone seems to adopt the metaphor. Fredrick Lynch's advocacy of the white American male is titled *Invisible Victims: White Males and the Crisis of Affirmative Action* (1989).

Appeals designed to raise awareness about the recently discovered condition, social phobia, emphasize its undetected prevalence. After noting that 'social phobia is a disabling disorder that has only recently become a focus of investigation', a study into the problem remarked that 'epidemiological studies have shown social phobia to be far more common than previously thought'. Other studies have used terms like 'neglected', 'trivialized' and 'stigmatized' to draw attention to what they consider to be a major anxiety disorder.[35] Claims of past neglect are meant to indicate the gravity of the problem. The view that such past 'neglect' may have been based on a sound diagnosis is not entertained. Similar claims about the underestimated importance of post-traumatic stress disorder (PTSD) and dyslexia also use the argument of professional and official ignorance and neglect. One of the growth areas for the discovery of hitherto hidden diseases is amongst children. Whereas in the past clinicians believed that children were not susceptible to major depression, some specialists now argue the opposite view. According to one account, it not only exists among children, but it also constitutes an 'insidious and major public health problem'.[36]

The assumption of unacknowledged and hidden risks informs the approach of many contributors to the debate on crime statistics and on family violence. The amplification of the danger of crime transcends the traditional ideological divide. The right often has an inflated perception of the risk of violent crime, whereas more liberal writers are disposed to a heightened sensitivity to the dangers lurking within the private space of family life. It is paradoxical that writers often criticize others for promoting a sense of panic in relation to one type of crime, whilst they themselves amplify the risks of others. For example, a handbook on victimization recognizes the relatively low rates of crime compared to the public panic they generate before issuing the warning that 'there appears to be a vast murky area of hitherto unacknowledged acts of violence such as child abuse, domestic violence, racial assault, sexual harassment and obscene telephone calls which are only now beginning to filter through into public consciousness'.[37] But why should so many new abuses, crimes and conditions filter through into the public consciousness at the same time? If the author had reflected on this question, the 'vast murky area' would have been seen in a different perspective.

The debate on child abuse has seen a clash of opinion about the dimensions of the problem. Many specialists adopt the tip of the iceberg approach. They claim that the incidence of abuse is far greater than society is prepared to accept. Consequently, many of those involved in the sphere of child protection are convinced that what is invisible is more relevant than the so-called facts. Therefore, their vocation becomes the detection of a pre-existing risk. An excerpt from a leaflet directed at those involved in this vocation in Hackney, an inner-London borough, is illustrative of the current mind-set:

The detection of child sexual abuse is low in Hackney, yet as those who work in primary care know, disclosure by parents of past childhood abuse is common. Can we improve our ability to recognise sexual abuse and what support is available if we do?[38]

The possibility that the low rate of detection corresponds to the actual incidence of child abuse is simply not entertained. The assumption that families in Hackney inhabit an invisible world of sexual and physical violence has the character of a self-evident truth. As with the Spanish Inquisition, more effective and vigorous detection is required to uncover widely practised but hidden acts.

Once our unbounded consciousness of risk is disposed to expect hidden or invisible dangers, new discoveries will inevitably follow. No part of the human experience is immune from the risk of violence. 'Elder abuse and neglect is the latest discovery in the field of familial violence' trumpets an introduction to the problem. The authors of the study were confident that the importance of elder abuse will be quickly acknowledged and that it will become for the 1990s what 'child abuse and spouse abuse' were in the preceding two decades.[39] It seems that there are many abuse experts who are prepared to publicize this newly identified phenomenon and turn it into a new cause. 'Granny-bashing is common and unreported' was the title of a survey in the British *Medical Monitor* in April 1996.

However, there are many other new contenders for the abused label. In recent years *peer abuse* has been identified as a major menace facing the children of Western societies. According to one influential study, 'peer abuse is an underestimated and neglected social problem'. Anne-Marie Ambert, the author of this study, has suggested that because of its greater frequency, peer abuse may be a bigger problem than parental abuse.[40] Similar words are used and claims made on behalf of the problem of bullying. Terms like 'unrecognized' or 'underestimated' are used to draw attention to the alleged scale of the dangers. At a conference on male rape at De Montfort University in Leicester in July 1996, speakers emphasized how this act was 'far more common than previously thought' and that up to 3 per cent of men may have suffered this abuse.[41] The same argument is repeated time and again for a variety of hitherto undisclosed abuses.

Contributions on the hidden risks of human relationships are surprisingly uncritical about their subject matter. Society's sensitivity to hidden risks and hitherto unacknowledged abuses requires to be questioned as much as its past attempts to cover up these conditions. Can it be a coincidence that numerous psychological disorders, sex crimes and a variety of abuses are now regularly excavated? Most serious studies of these problems concede that there is little evidence of an increase of any particular abuse. Rather, there has been an increased sensitivity to and interest in these issues.

The growth of interest in the so-called dark side of the family and in hidden medical and psychological disorders expresses the sense of self-loathing discussed previously. The perception of human beings as polluters transcends the line that separates the physical from the spiritual. As a result, whether rearing a family or building a power station, the destructive side of people is what is emphasized. From this perspective, imagining the worst – both about human motives and about human creations – makes perfect sense. It is what we anticipate and expect. In the past, lack of confidence in human passions and motives inspired a conservative outlook which demanded a lowering of expectations and restraint. Today, ideology is not decisive in the formation of risk consciousness. The entire political spectrum – left to right, conservative to liberal – shares a common consciousness of risk. Whilst there may be debate about what constitutes the gravest risk, there is an acceptance of the consensus that we live in an increasingly dangerous world. Why we feel this way is the subject of the next chapter.

Notes

1. See Singer, E. and Endreny, P. (1993) *Reporting on Risk: How the Mass Media Portray Accidents, Diseases, Disaster and Other Hazards* (New York: Russell Sage Foundation), p. 62.

2. See Volkwein, J. F., Szelest, B.P. and Lizotte, A. J. (1995), 'The Relationship of Campus Crime to Campus and Student Characteristics', *Research in Higher Education,* vol. 36, no. 6.

3. See Renn, O. (1992), 'Concepts of Risk: A Classification', in Krimsky, S. and Golding, D. (eds) (1992) *Social Theories of Risk* (Westport, CT: Praeger), p. 56.

4. Leslie, J. (1996) *The End of the World: The Science and Ethics of Human Extinction* (New York: Routledge), pp. 4–10.

5. 'Climate of Fear', *Guardian*; 21 December 2005.

6. Karlen, A. (1995) *Plague's Progress: A Social History of Man and Disease* (New York: Random House), p. 276.

7. Shrader-Frechette, K. (1991) *Risk and Rationality: Philosophical Foundations for Populist Reforms* (Berkeley: University of California Press), p. 24.

8. For an interesting discussion of this issue, see Ames, B. and Swirsky Gold, L. S. (1989) 'Misconceptions Regarding

Environmental Pollution and Cancer Causation', in Moore, M. (ed.) *Health Risks and the Press* (Washington, DC: Media Institute).

9. Freeman-Longo, R. E. (1996) 'Feel Good Legislation: Prevention or Calamity', *Child Abuse and Neglect,* vol. 20, no. 2, p. 95.

10. Leach, P. (1993) *Children First: What Society Must Do – and Is Not Doing – for Children Today* (London: Penguin), p. xiii.

11. Miles, R. (1994) *The Children We Deserve: Love and Hate in the Making of the Family* (London: Harper Collins), p. 46.

12. Hillman, M., Adams, J. and Whiteleg, J. (1990) *One False Move . . . A Study of Children's Independent Mobility* (London: PSI Publishing), p. 111.

13. Lawson, M. (1996) 'Icebergs and Rocks of the "Good" Lie', *Guardian,* 24 June.

14. Cited in the *Washington Post;* 2 June 2006.

15. Quick, A. (1991) *Unequal Risks: Accidents and Social Policy* (London: Socialist Health Association), p. 81.

16. Sontag, S. (1990) *Illness and its Metaphors* (London: Penguin), p. 28.

17. See Gladwell, M. (1995) 'The Plague Year: The Unscientific Origin of Our Obsession with Viruses', *New Republic,* 17 and 24 July.

18. Preston, R. (1994) *The Hot Zone* (London: Corgi), p. 367.

19. Leiss, W. and Chociolko, C. (1994) *Risk and Responsibility* (Montreal: McGill-Queen's University Press), p. 259.

20. See Colpin, H., Demyttenaere, K. and Vandemeulebroecke, L. (1995) 'New Reproductive Technology and the

Family – The Parent–Child Relationship Following In-Vitro Fertilization', *Journal of Child Psychology and Psychiatry and Allied Disciplines,* vol. 36, no. 8.

21. Landau, R. (1995) 'The Impact of New Medical Technologies in Human Reproduction on Children's Personal Safety and Well-being in the Family', *Marriage and Family Review,* vol. 21, no. 1–2, p. 133.

22. See *Business Week;* 27 February 1995. For an excellent treatment of computer panics see Calcutt, A. (1995) 'Computer Porn Panic – Fear and Control in Cyberspace', *Futures,* vol. 27. Also see Faucette, J. F. (1995) 'The Freedom of Speech at Risk in Cyberspace', *Duke Law Journal,* vol. 44, no. 6.

23. See Hammond, R. (1996) 'Internet Users Risk Addiction to Computers', *The Sunday Times,* 9 June.

24. Labour Party (1995) *Peace at Home* (London: Labour Party), p. 4.

25. On this subject, see the interesting work of Mary Douglas (1992).

26. *Nature;* 7 March 1996, p. 48.

27. 'Risk managers face Challenge of Bracing for the Unimaginable', *New York Times;* 20 October 2001.

28. Michael Osterholm 'preparing for the Next Pandemic', *Foreign Affairs,* July/August 2005.

29. Erikson, K. (1994) *A New Species of Trouble: Explorations in Disaster, Trauma and Community* (New York: W.W. Norton & Company), p. 148.

30. See Ames, B. and Swirsky Gold, L. S. (1989) 'Misconceptions Regarding Enviromental Pollution and Cancer Causation', in Moore (ed.) *Health Risks and the Press,* p. 21.

31. Rees, J.L. (1996) 'The Melanoma Epidemic: Reality and Artefact', *British Medical Journal*, vol. 312, p. 137.

32. Forward, S. (1990) *Toxic Parents: Overcoming the Legacy of Parental Abuse* (London: Bantam Press), pp. 5–6.

33. Cited in the *Guardian*; 11 January 1996.

34. *Time*, 18 July 1994. See 'The Hidden Handicap', *Guardian*, 30 January 1996.

35. See Rapaport, M., Paniccia, G. and Judd, L. (1995) 'A Review of Social Phobia', *Psychopharmacology Bulletin*, vol. 31, no. 1, p. 125 and Hirschfeld, R. (1995) 'The Impact of Health-care Reform on Social Phobia', *Journal of Clinical Psychiatry*, vol. 56, no. 5.

36. Lamarine, R. (1994) *Journal of School Health*, vol. 65, no. 9, p. 390.

37. Kirsta, A. (1988) *Victims: Surviving the Aftermath of Violent Crime* (London: Century), p. 6.

38. Leaflet by City and Hackney Community Health Services Trust; 24 May 1995.

39. See Bennett, G. and Kingston, P. (1993) *Elder Abuse: Concept, Theories and Intervention* (London: Chapman and Hall), p. 1.

40. Ambert, A. M. (1994) 'A Qualitative Study of Peer Abuse and Its Effects', *Journal of Marriage and the Family*, vol. 56, February, p. 119.

41. See report in the *Guardian*; 3 July 1996.

CHAPTER 3

Why Do We Panic?

Panic: A sudden and excessive feeling of alarm or fear, usually affecting a body of persons, and leading to extravagant or injudicious efforts to secure safety.

(The Shorter Oxford English Dictionary, 3rd edn, 1965)

That 'sudden and excessive feeling of alarm or fear' that we usually associate with panics is clearly reflected in surveys and opinion polls. Polls conducted in the UK and the USA suggest that people are anxious about the future and are afraid of a variety of dangers. Despite this evidence, there is hardly any serious discussion of society's disposition to panic. From time to time, observers engage in a discussion of a specific event or panic, such as the periodic outbreak of anxiety about crime. Most of these contributions are reactions to a specific event. There is virtually no attempt to compare the different types of panics to see whether they are part of any wider pattern. Instead, analyses of specific panics treat their causes as separate and unconnected events. Thus fears about radiation, crime or child abuse are not discussed as part of a wider social pattern. Consequently, the central question which this chapter attempts to address, 'why do we panic?', is rarely engaged.

Many observers actually question whether the many outbreaks of fear that were discussed previously are anything like a panic. The view that the many risk-averse responses that people display constitute at least an overreaction, if not a panic, is in general not intellectually accepted. Sections of the media actually interpret such reactions as the only sensible way of negotiating a life that we do not fully comprehend. Influential contributions on the subject argue that risk-averse reactions represent a sensible, indeed the only responsible, appreciation of the situation. 'It makes no sense to talk about risks versus perceived risks, as if experts had some magic window on reality', argued one major study. This equation of perceived risks with reality treats people's reactions as unproblematic. The popular perception of hazards becomes by definition the issue. 'We must deal with all hazards as they are perceived' is the study's conclusion.[1] Leading writers are full of praise for public manifestations of anxiety. 'Be Very Afraid' is the title of an article in a major British daily. According to its author, strong manifestations of anxiety are 'but a cry for a new accountability'.[2] Individual and collective expressions of anxiety are therefore more likely to be praised than to be interpreted as irrational panics.

The sentiment that one person's panic is another one's rational reaction runs through the literature on the subject. A double standard also permeates the writing on the topic. Authors are clearly selective about which responses are treated as panics and which are not. Consequently, some intense anxieties and fears are interpreted as panic-like, while others are not. Otherwise critical social scientists can recognize some manifestations of panics but not others. This double standard often corresponds to the writers' social, cultural and political outlook. Liberal and feminist writers are sensitive to right-wing panics regarding crime and family values. At the same time they are oblivious to the many panics generated about the dark side of the family, such as child abuse. In contrast, many conservative and right-wing intellectuals are vociferous in their condemnation of panics about impending environmental catastrophes and various forms of family abuse, whilst they ignore the hysteria generated by law and order campaigns.

The following are a few illustrations of this double standard at work. The authors of an important work on child victims in the UK drew attention to recent law and order panics about street crime, muggings, race riots and the sanctity of the family. They connect these reactions to instances of public backlash against social workers such as that which occurred over the highly publicized child abuse scandal in Cleveland, in the mid-1980s. In this small city in northeastern England, 121 children were taken into local authority care over a three-month period in early 1987 following the diagnosis of child sexual abuse made by a small team of paediatricians and social workers. A public inquiry into these cases reported 12 months later, by which time 98 of the children had been returned to their families. Those involved in the child protection industry interpret the targeting of Cleveland social workers by sections of the media as an exemplar of the classical moral panic, but it never occurs to the authors that the invention of an epidemic of child abuse in Cleveland, by doctors and social workers, was in scale a far more significant event. It helped unleash widespread anxieties and fears which affected millions of people. It seems that many social scientists and social workers distance themselves from the concerns of wronged parents in Cleveland and other places. They feel aloof from the effects that accusations of child abuse and satanic abuse panics have on the life of parents and are extraordinarily indifferent to their plight. This sentiment is no doubt sustained by the conviction that professionals were entitled to raise the alarm about their suspicions of child abuse. From this perspective, instances of overreaction and zealous policing do not constitute a panic. On the contrary, society's preoccupation with the safety of children is a responsible response to the threat posed by millions of abusing parents.

The view that moral panics are targeted against caring professionals and not against wronged parents is systematically pursued in a collection of essays, *Scare in the Community: Britain in a Moral Panic*. This text, published by *Community Care*, a periodical written for social and community workers, attempts to defend its readers from the vilification of the right-wing media. Predictably, the contributors to this text tend to equate moral panics with attacks on social workers. The editor, Geoffrey Pearson, rightly notes that frequently 'child protection workers have been subjected to ferocious rituals of public shame' which 'suggests that they are situated within a larger moral drama which is barely understood'. Unfortunately, this sensitivity to the difficulties faced by social workers is not matched by any sensitivity to the humiliation of parents caused by the actions of child protection workers. There is a clear selectivity about which types of social obsessions are worthy of the term moral panic.[3]

Right-wing and conservative contributions on panics constitute the mirror image of the liberal ones. They are some of the most interesting exposés of the contemporary obsessions with sex crime, harassment and abuse. However, since such contributions are motivated by their writers' concerns about the erosion of so-called family values, they tend to be one-sided and selective. The American publication *Public Interest* illustrates this approach. Whilst articles have pointed to the inflation of panics about the environment and abuse, they themselves are vociferous in their condemnation of single mothers and welfare recipients. Such attitudes mirror the approach of the zealous child protection workers in the Cleveland scandal. 'Can a single welfare mother who has been beating her children, or failing to feed and bathe them, be turned into a responsible parent?' is the rhetorical question posed by Heather MacDonald in the Spring 1994 issue of *Public Interest*. Unlike liberal child protection workers, who identify abusive men as the problem, MacDonald targets 'illegitimacy and social dysfunction'. However, her solution, taking children away from their mothers, is identical to the approach adopted by child protection professionals.[4]

The selectivity with which panics are discussed by writers from across the entire political spectrum also demonstrates a conviction that the manufacturing of fear is not necessarily a bad thing. Some writers actually contend that moral panics help to increase social awareness. Thus one contributor, who deplores panic when it is addressed against social workers, believes that not all moral panics are bad. He wrote:

> *We tend to think of 'moral panics' as unfortunate and disreputable episodes. Yet in so far as they represent eruptions of social anxiety, albeit distorting and ideologically driven, they may be an index of important shifts in public awareness.*[5]

He added that each 'wave of child abuse panic' in the UK helped to breach 'social illusion' and helped raise awareness of the problem. This view of panic as an instrument of enlightenment is by no means an eccentric one.

A contribution on a previous UK government's attitude to lone parents positively welcomes certain types of panic. 'One consequence of the moral panic may be judged to be the higher political exposure fatherhood attained, and the beginnings of a more informed debate about the roles of fathers and the nature of modern fatherhood', was the conclusion drawn by the authors. What we have here is a moral panic with a happy ending, since the target shifted from single mothers to errant fathers. From this perspective, the outcome of the panic is greater clarity about the dynamic of family life in the UK.[6] Conservative authors prefer different panics. Many of them are pleased with the public reaction to AIDS because the 'notion of sexual responsibility has shaken off its puritanical image'.[7] Here, public anxiety about AIDS is seen as an important sentiment for popularizing a more restrictive and puritanical sexual ethos.

Such uncritical, even positive, representations of the manufacturing of fear by so many observers helps to explain why the sociology of contemporary panics is so underdeveloped. If scaring people is seen as a legitimate way of educating the public, then what is the problem?

Such attitudes are further reinforced by many leading social scientists and journalists who are convinced that the scale of the threat facing people is so great that it is not possible to exaggerate the dangers. Contrary to common sense, many experts believe that abuse is routine or that the environment is heading towards extinction. Consequently, the reactions to a variety of hazards are seen as proportional to the dimension of the problem. Individuals and groups who are involved in 'raising awareness' about the many hazards – environmental or personal – are celebrated as the enlightened vanguard of an otherwise complacent political culture.[8]

That panics can be associated with raising awareness is, perhaps, an indication of a loss of faith in reasoned arguments. As Chapter 1 suggested, the outcome of the inflation of the consciousness of risk is not clarity but insecurity. Such events do not always lead to a full-blown panic – but they do create unnecessary anxieties and fears. A few examples follow.

Toxic shock syndrome (TSS) is a classic example of how a trivial matter was turned into a major scare campaign which affected the lives of millions of women. In the USA, a media campaign created a situation where a virtually unknown disease led to a multimillion dollar recall of Rely tampons. Public awareness of TSS led to significant changes in women's tampon-buying habits. To this day, TSS is often discussed as a serious health risk to women.

TSS is a nasty reaction to a toxin produced by a normally harmless bacterium, *Staphylococcus aureus*, which lives on nearly a third of the population and in the vaginas of about one in ten women. Very rarely this toxin causes its carrier to become very ill with a sudden high fever, vomiting, low blood pressure, sore throat and a sunburn-like rash. If it is caught early, it can be wiped out with a course of antibiotics; left to its own devices, it kills, but only very rarely.

TSS was linked to tampons after a number of cases in the USA occurred in women using high-absorbency tampons – and it remains the case that tampon users seem to be particularly prone. Nobody has established exactly what the link is. The link between TSS and tampons does not suggest a relation of causation. Even organizations such as the Women's Environmental Network, which employs a dedicated toxic shock information officer, have to admit that about half of the reported cases of TSS have nothing to do with menstruation at all. Infections after surgery are a common cause, as are burns and gardening injuries. Also, women who are stricken with TSS during their periods are not always tampon users. In the USA two reported cases of TSS were in women who, worried about tampons, had switched to natural sponges.

Not only is the relationship between TSS and tampons far from clear; this highly publicized disease is very, very rare. There are about twenty confirmed and probable cases of TSS in the UK each year, so assuming even a 50 per cent link to tampons, only ten women are affected out of about 14 million tampon-using menstruating women. Put another way, the chances of getting TSS from using a tampon this year is 1 in 1,400,000. Not only is this a very rare disease – it is also a curable illness. Deaths do not even figure at one a year.

Public awareness of TSS is proportional to its insignificance. It is one of those fashionable complaints about which awareness is mandatory. Despite its insignificance, when someone says that this is a 'very important issue' everybody nods sagely and advises women to cut down their use of tampons. In Britain, public sector unions have circulated information to their members and personnel departments about the risks of TSS. Even the manufacturers take the concern at face value and print warnings on their leaflets. Tambrands, which makes Tampax, produces a helpful, earnest special leaflet which gives similar figures to those above and then runs into advice on what a woman should do if she thinks she has TSS.

According to one account, the reason why an insignificant cause, like that of TSS, got so much media attention is that a 'rare hazard is more newsworthy than a common one'.[9] Whatever the merits of this argument as far as media strategy is concerned, it does not explain why a rare and curable illness is treated as a major public health issue. The promotion of concern over TSS can only be understood in the context of a moral climate where few dare to question claims of dangers and risks.

Technical explanations

The media play an important role in shaping society's perception of risk. Studies have shown that the media's emphasis on certain crimes or diseases leads the public to acquire a heightened sense of danger in relation to them. Singer and Endreny note how the reporting of a single terrorist incident involving US citizens in Greece led to a major decline in the numbers prepared to travel to Europe. Despite the fact that more Americans drowned in their bathtubs than were killed by terrorists, travelling to Europe seemed like a dangerous enterprise.[10]

The influence of the media can be seen through comparing its reporting of risks associated with oral contraceptive pills in the UK in October 1995 and June 1996. In October 1995 the Committee on Safety of Medicines (CSM) issued an advisory notice claiming that certain brands of combined oral contraceptives were associated with a slightly higher risk of venous thromboembolism. The communiqué advised doctors to switch women from the higher-risk pills to other formulations. Pill users were advised to consult their doctors for advice. The action, prompted by the CSM's consideration of three (then unpublished) papers, took the medical profession, the family planning establishment and journalists – not to mention women – by surprise. Shock-horror 'Pill Kills!' headlines were the inevitable response of a prime-time press conference – the means by which official concern was made public. Health officials justified what they refer to as an 'alert' by claiming that although the increased risk of venous thromboembolism was small (women on the more dangerous pills faced a risk of 30 per 100,000 compared with 15 per 100,000), it nevertheless existed and the public had a right to know the facts. It was subsequently reported that some 12 per cent of women stopped using the pill, and abortion rates soared.

In the light of this interpretation, it is interesting to note that research suggesting that all brands of combined oral contraceptives are associated with an increased relative risk of breast cancer, leaked to *The Sunday Times* prior to publication in the *Lancet* in June 1996, was handled entirely differently – by health officials and by journalists. The reported association between oral contraceptives and breast cancer was small, but nevertheless greater than that between oral contraceptives and venous thrombo-embolism. Furthermore, far more women die from breast cancer – whether they are 'on the pill' or not – than die from circulatory diseases. But there was little public reaction to the June announcement, despite the fact that this research was a collaborative peer-reviewed study co-ordinated by the Imperial Cancer Research Fund (ICRF) which involved almost all the world's experts.

The different reactions were due, at least in part, to the role of the media. In October the risks had been played up and elevated into scare headlines. In the following June, the risks were played down. The media, following careful briefing by the ICRF and family planning organizations, self-consciously chose to treat the story in a neutral manner and, despite the reporting of the risks, no panic ensued.

The media play an important role in the shaping of perceptions of risks. Since most people gain their information through the media rather than through direct experience, their perception is moulded by the way information is communicated. According to one account, the following are important in the shaping of perceptions of risk:

> the extent of media coverage; the volume of information provided; the ways in which the risk is framed; the interpretations of messages concerning the risk; and the symbols, metaphors, and discourse enlisted in depicting and characterising the risk.[11]

However, it is important to remember that the media amplify or attenuate but do not cause society's sense of risk.

There exists a disposition towards the expectation of adverse outcomes, which is then engaged by the mass media. The result of this engagement is media which are continually warning of some danger. But the media's preoccupation with risk is a symptom of the problem and not its cause. It is unlikely that an otherwise placid and content public is influenced into a permanent state of panic through media manipulation.

The media are not the only technological agents held to be responsible for the contemporary inflation of the sense of risk. In many accounts, the development of sophisticated screening techniques and of measurement is presented as the reason why we perceive risk on an altogether different scale than previously. According to one proponent of this interpretation,

> The power of technology to extend our perceptions of the natural world has challenged even our strongest principles. 'Thou shalt not kill' is still a sound idea, but because we can see into wombs, fertilise human eggs in a test tube, and pump air and blood into people after their brain had died, we are now arguing over the very definition of life and killing . . . we are using sophisticated biological investigation and computer calculations to measure risk. We are going to have to decide how much risk is too much, and even how many deaths we will tolerate.[12]

But why should greater technological sophistication lead to a heightened concern with risk? One could plausibly argue the opposite view and conclude that more refined screening methods should minimize the sense of risks and enhance society's sense of control. And, of course, new instruments of calculation have little relevance for explaining the growing sense of risk in the domain of human relationships and family life.

For many writers, society's preoccupation with risk is the product of the theoretical gains made through scientific, medical and actuarial research. In other words, the development of knowledge has helped create an increased sensitivity towards hitherto unseen hazards. An important study of the subject argues as follows:

> To some extent what has happened recently is that we have become more aware of the riskiness present in our environment, simply because we are able . . . to 'put a number on' the efforts arising from our encounters with hazards.[13]

According to this approach, the insights gained through scientific research help people to become more aware of the risks that they face.

The association between scientific advance and the parallel growth in risk awareness is, in fact, far from self-evident. The assumption of an automatic growth in risk awareness alongside the development of knowledge ignores the social influences that shape human consciousness. In principle, the advance of knowledge does not necessarily lead to anxiety about hazards. In some situations it can lead to a high degree of confidence. Indeed, many critics of scientific reason have criticized nineteenth-century industrial culture for its 'arrogance' and its 'overconfident' conviction in its ability to control events. Technological and scientific advance was no less significant a century ago than today, but instead of promoting a heightened sense of risk, it helped consolidate a mood of confidence in the power of science and society to shape human destiny. Even tragic manifestations of the destructive side of certain technologies did not necessarily lead to a culture of risk consciousness. Although hostile to nuclear weapons, postwar Japan has retained a strong belief in technological development, despite the horrific experience of Hiroshima and Nagasaki.

Nor is there any direct causal relationship between the advance of science and knowledge and the growth of risk consciousness. The equation of risk consciousness with increased awareness is widely acclaimed today, but the awareness of risk should not be confused with real danger. To do so would be to flatter our disposition to panic and overreact with the claim of new insight and awareness. What are we to make of a claim by a leading British Sunday newspaper that 'the world really is becoming a more dangerous place' because of an increase in potential climatic disasters?[14] Is this anticipation of disaster warranted by contemporary experience?

It is striking that, despite the many problems that face humanity, we live in a world that is far safer than at any time in history. The very fact that Western society has become concerned about its ageing population reflects the dramatic progress that has been made in recent years in humanity's struggle against disease. Since 1950 there has been a 17 per cent increase in life-expectancy worldwide: this increase has been most spectacular in the poorer countries of Asia where it has reached 20 per cent.[15] Advances in food production have been phenomenal and demonstrate humanity's capacity to feed itself. Advances in medicine have been equally impressive. Although many people are convinced that we are being choked and poisoned by pollution, there is much evidence of improvement. In 1952, the London fog was responsible for killing 12,000 people. As late as 1962, *The Times* could carry a story with the title 'Fog Menace to the Lungs – 55 Deaths in London'.[16] The death of 136 people in London due to smog in December 1962 did not lead to a major public outcry. Today, such an event would be perceived as comparable with the disasters in Bhopal or Chernobyl. The difference in reaction has little to do with awareness of actual risks. Paradoxically, in the 1960s, people who were actually at greater risk of pollution than are Londoners today felt far more secure.

Another variant of technical explanations of risk consciousness is to link it to the dangerous consequences of accelerated technological development. The argument is based on the commonsense assumption that the more we develop technology, the greater is the power to cause danger. This point has been argued by a leading German sociologist, Niklas Luhman. He propounds the view that, more than any other single factor, 'the immense expansion of technological possibilities has contributed to drawing attention to the risks involved'.[17] Luhman's argument shifts the focus towards a perspective where scientific development itself creates the dangers that help to consolidate a consciousness of risk.

As with all technical explanations of risk, that of Luhman does not address why society is also disposed towards fearing dangers in spheres that lie outside the domain of technology. Unfortunately, this emphasis on the consequences of technological developments recurs in many of the influential explanations of the subject.

Risk as the product of knowledge

Influential authors on the subject of society and risk often combine Luhman's aversion to technology with the conviction that it has led to new hazards. The identification of science and technology with dangerous outcomes is common. This hostility towards scientific advance has led to growing scepticism about the claims made on behalf of knowledge. Indeed, many of the leading authorities on the sociology of risk associate its development with the advance of knowledge.

Leading European sociologists, such as the German academic Ulrich Beck and the Cambridge academic Anthony Giddens, argue the case for the close association between the sense of risk and the increase of knowledge. 'Many of the uncertainties which face us today have been created by the very growth of human knowledge', wrote Giddens,[18] and Beck noted that the 'sources of danger are no longer ignorance but *knowledge*'.[19] In this scenario, knowledge through its application creates both new hazards and an awareness of their risk.

The association of knowledge with risk is based on a model of society which is continually under threat from technological development. Beck, who provides the most eloquent version of the knowledge-as-risk thesis, regards modernization as the producer of unparalleled dangers. Indeed, he characterizes 'risk society' as a stage in modernity 'in which the hazards produced in the growth of industrial society become predominant'. Such a society faces major threats to its survival from the unintended consequences of technological development. The scale of the dangers that are consequent on modernization changes the very character of risk. This is because the forces of destruction unleashed by modernization increasingly outweigh the benefits. Beck contrasts old and new risks in the following way:

> *Anyone who set out to discover new countries and continents – like Columbus – certainly accepted 'risks'. But these were personal risks, not global dangers like those that arise for all of humanity from nuclear fission or the storage of radioactive waste. In the earlier period, the word 'risk' had a note of bravery and adventure, not the threat of self-destruction of all life on Earth.*[20]

This intimate link between the taking of risk and the act of destruction endow the act with intrinsic irresponsibility. Moreover, since the act of risk-taking ceases to be a private individual matter, as others are put at risk, society is entitled to take measures to protect itself from this danger. What is at issue is not a specific hazard but the act of risk-taking.

The image of science as a producer of dangers of Frankenstein proportions informs the contemporary academic debate on the nature of risk. It is a vision which has traditionally been connected with conservative interpretations of science. According to this version, science and knowledge invariably overstep the limits posed by nature, leading to chaos and catastrophes. It is not surprising that contemporary conservatives have been quick to join in the condemnation of belief in science and technology. No opportunity is missed – AIDS, greenhouse effect, BSE – to remind the world that humanity has gone too far. John Gray, a leading British conservative thinker, has observed that the current crisis of confidence in the powers of technology provided a vindication for a 'genuinely conservative policy'. According to Gray, the explosion of risks – from BSE to the threats posed by genetic engineering – reflected nature's revenge on human arrogance.[21]

Paradoxically, arguments which associate knowledge with risks are implicitly questioning the ability to know. It is said that human knowledge is overwhelmed by the unpredictable chain of events which are set in motion by global capitalism. The impossibility of knowing or calculating the consequences of technology and human action is widely insisted upon. This view is motivated by the belief that technological development in a globalized environment has become so complex as to destroy the foundation for prediction. As a result, Luhman claims that 'no one is in a position to claim knowledge of the future nor the capacity to change it'.[22] For Luhman, knowledge is restricted to providing insights about what has already happened, and rather limited insights at that.

The negative sentiments about knowledge, technology and science reflect the belief that they are the causes of risk. These so-called manufactured risks created by humanity are sharply counterposed to the 'natural' risks of the past. Such a model of the world is, in fact, extremely one-sided. The assumption that risk is the outcome of technical advance does to some extent correspond to contemporary experience in the Western world. Few Americans or Europeans perish from famines or from such natural dangers as floods or lightning, because of the high levels of safety assured by scientific and technological advance. However, such levels of security only prevail in a small part of the world. That is why far more people die of a poor diet than from toxic residues in food. Even in the Western world, traditional dangers outweigh the risks posed by the high-technology sector. According to one study, the number of fatal accidents per capita of those employed in occupations with a long pre-industrial tradition is 'incomparably higher' than fatality figures in high-technology industry. Thus the chance of a chemical worker in Switzerland dying in the course of work is over eighteen times less than for a lumberjack.[23]

The accent on the unnatural and technological foundation for our concern with risk continually underestimates the social influences of such perceptions. In this worldview, the mechanism of risk is driven automatically by a process unleashed by modernization. Consequently, the distribution of hazards has a logic which spares no one. That is why many sociologists of risk seem convinced that the distribution of hazards is blind to social inequalities. Whether it is Chernobyl, AIDS or the greenhouse effect, no one is immune to the risks. Writing in this vein, the authors of a collection of essays on the subject state that in 'risk society the distribution of hazards seems blind to inequalities, they flow easily across national and class boundaries'.[24] According to this logic, a poor peasant eking out a living in the Nile delta and the middle-class engineer living a comfortable life in Munich are equally at risk from a range of hazards.

The random distribution of risk by a society that is fundamentally out of control is the intellectual foundation of the commonplace platitude, popularized in the 1980s, that 'we are all at risk'. It is not just sociologists but advocates of a multitude of causes who profess their faith in this belief. As it happens, we are *not* all at risk and certainly not to the same degree. Studies show that even apparently random accidents are not randomly distributed. For example, research into accidents affecting British children has shown that those between the ages of 0 and 14 years from a working-class background are twice as likely to die from an accident than those whose parents are middle-class. They are also five times more likely to die through being hit by a car. The relationship between social inequality and health is also well documented. The danger of being poor in the USA is highlighted by the fact that living in poverty reduces life-expectancy by about nine years, and, predictably in the USA, unemployment beat steeplejacking as the riskiest occupation. According to one account 'so heightened is your risk of suicide, liver cirrhosis from drinking alcoholic beverages, and other stress-related diseases while not working, that being unemployed rates as the equivalent of smoking ten packs of cigarettes per day'.[25]

It should be clear that risks do not transcend society. Rather, on balance, hazards affect people in relation to their power and influence. The very fact that so many important observers regard risk in such a non-social and technical manner is itself worthy of note. The corollary of the view that risk is the product of human action, of knowledge and of science, is the contention that it is not subject to control and regulation. Like the genie let out of the lamp, risk is no longer subject to human control. The representation of risk as a transcendental technical problem, caused by human endeavour, demonstrates a clear attitude about the human character. It suggests that we have the power to destroy but not to do very much about the dangers which hover over our everyday life.

Why do we panic?

The technical approach that dominates explanations of risk consciousness stresses the process of technological advance in creating the hazards we face. It pays very little attention to the influence of changing social relations and their role in influencing perceptions. Such explanations are based on the assumption that the long-term consequences of human action are not only incalculable today, but are also beyond control in the future. This objectification of danger renders the human response of panic and fear self-evident. It concludes that we are right to worry about the unintended consequences of our actions.

In many cases, even those who are critical of the tendency to fetishize technology and nature are reluctant to situate risk in its social and historical specificity. For example, the editors of an interesting collection of essays on this subject criticize those who objectify nature but warn that 'the occasional sociological tendency to criticise such scientific reification by advancing the alternative view that all such problems are "mere" social constructions and hence (it is implied) not real is equally misleading'.[26] Of course, the issue at stake is not whether perceptions of risk are real or not, but what the basis is for such responses. It is not particularly fruitful to counterpose the real to the unreal. A 'real' hazard like industrial waste can be seen as acceptable in one situation but interpreted as a deadly threat in another. The question worth investigating is how society goes about selecting its 'problems'. The focus on the process of problematization would raise the most significant question of all: why is there, today, such an increase in the range of experiences that are problematized?

In fact, there is no direct relationship between the process of problematization and the experience to which it refers. The activities that we label 'bullying' or 'sexual harassment' have a long history – but it is only in the specific circumstances of the recent period that they are defined as problems. Thus the very definition of something as a risk is bound up with changing relations and perceptions within society. That is why the development of risk consciousness has both a historical and a social context. For example there is a contemporary equation between sex and risk. The positive views about recreational sex in the 1960s have given way to the conviction that sex is by definition a risk. Why this elementary form of human activity should be interpreted through the prism of risk will not be clarified by an investigation into the physical act. To gain insights into this process, a more fruitful approach is to examine changing relationships within the family, and between men and women, and other forms of human interactions.

The tendency to elevate the technical and natural foundation of risk consciousness contributes towards a fatalistic interpretation of danger. The weight which observers attach to technical factors in the explanation of risk consciousness is itself significant. It indicates an approach which in an intellectual form expresses the sentiment that we are all at risk. Or, at least, it assumes that this sentiment is a self-evident reaction to clearly defined dangers. Consequently, it is the risks rather than the way in which they are interpreted and perceived which require investigation. In this way, analysis reinforces the stress on technical factors whilst underestimating the importance of social influence.

To treat risk from a technical point of view is to underestimate the crucial social processes that it expresses. The negative representation of risk and its relentless inflation do not take place in a vacuum. Many writers have tried to link these reactions to the prevalence of social anxiety and the widespread mistrust by the public of traditional sources of authority. The many outbursts of panic about matters of health, food and the environment are, no doubt, symptoms of some underlying malaise. Clearly, such reactions manifest a clear distrust of authority. The emphasis on the erosion of relations of trust has helped to throw light on aspects of the problem. However, as we shall see, the explosion of panics also reveals a lot more about the workings of contemporary society. The following themes may help to provide insights into the influence of the consciousness of risk.

Change is often experienced as risk

Perceptions of risk are influenced by the previous experience of change. The failure of numerous social experiments – from the Soviet Union to the European-type welfare state – has strengthened conservative suspicions about the consequences of change.[27] Today, terms like planning, social engineering and reform often have a negative connotation. Even the attempt to formulate a state interventionist strategy is dismissed as utopian. Whereas, in the past, state intervention was seen as a possible solution to a problem, today such policies are presented as the cause of many of society's difficulties. And, more broadly, change is seen not so much as a solution but as a cause of problems. Such reactions pertain not only to political experimentation. Initiatives in the field of science and technology are regarded with scepticism. Such scepticism is matched by the certainty that something will go wrong. The fear of side-effects, discussed in Chapter 1, is the clearest manifestation of this association between change and danger.

Scepticism towards change indicates that belief in finding solutions to the problems facing humanity lacks plausibility. The discrediting of solutions has gone furthest in the sphere of politics but it has spread to all fields of social engagement. As solutions appear to lose their relevance for our lives, problems assume an overwhelming form. The absence of obvious solutions endows problems with extra weight and importance. The inflation of problems which is a characteristic feature of today's risk calculus follows logically from the decline of support for the perspective of social change. The failure of the human endeavour to discover solutions to serious problems in the past is recast as a warning to those who would seek change in the future. The main legacy of the acknowledgement that society lacks solutions is the consolidation of a culture of uncertainty.

Concern about the future

Suspicion about change inexorably influences the way in which people regard the future. The underlying expectations are that the situation is likely to get worse. Most opinion polls confirm that the public regards the future with fear. For the first time since the end of the Second World War, parents expect that life for their children will be worse than it was for them. Such perceptions of the future reflect contemporary anxieties – indeed, they project into the future the collective insecurities of society today.

The future is seen as a terrain which bears little relationship to the geography of the present. Since the process of change appears unresponsive to human management, its future direction becomes more and more incomprehensible. Society's estrangement from the process of change is expressed in a future that is so strange as to be unrecognizable. This is most clearly represented in the media, where the future is treated in a way that highlights its dehumanized difference to the present. Science fiction today projects future society as either a wasteland or a high-technology purgatory. A similar message is enunciated by some theorists of risk. According to the editors of an influential text on the subject, 'the future looks less like the past than ever before and has in some way become very threatening'.[28]

There have been times before when the future was perceived in such negative and anxious terms. What is distinctive about the way in which the relationship between the present and the future is constructed is that the future that we dread is the direct result of our action today. This is clearly expressed in the belief that the potential for human destruction is so great that its dreadful results will not become evident until many generations to come. In this way our fear of danger today is compounded by the knowledge that the full extent of the risks facing humanity will only be clear in the indefinite future. This helps to strengthen the perception of risk as unbounded. The riskiness of our action will not be known until many decades hence. Consequently, our actions put at risk not only people today, but also those of generations to come. It is this model of the future which informs the mainstream of ecological thinking. Terms like intergenerational equity and sustainability suggest that our actions should be restrained by considerations of future development.

It is important to note that when the future is deemed to be very threatening, it is present-day society that is condemned. For if our actions are likely to have such an impact on the future, then it is we who are responsible for what happens in the period ahead. As Luhman wrote, 'more and more of the future apparently comes to depend on decisions taken in the present'.[29] Since our actions are likely to increase the dangers faced by people in the future, the most enlightened strategy is to minimize the risks faced by future generations. That requires that we do as little as possible of anything that is likely to have future consequences.

Impossibility of knowing

Increasingly, risk is intellectually defined in relation to our inability to know. What is at issue is not just not knowing but the impossibility of knowing. This attitude – strikingly expressed in the idiom of unknown unknowns – informs policy towards the war on terrorism and climate change. The inability to predict outcomes is often linked to the fast and far-reaching consequences of modern technology. Many observers argue that since the consequences of technological innovations are realized so swiftly, there is simply no time to know or to understand their likely effect. The lack of time is also posited in relation to the long-term effect of actions taken today. Many supporters of the so-called precautionary principle argue the need for caution on the grounds that by the time the outcome of a particular innovation is understood, processes which will cause damage to generations to come will have been unleashed.

According to Luhman, the absence of time required to obtain the necessary information weakens hope in rationality.[30] It is simply not possible to know much about future trends of development.

The association of knowledge with danger, discussed previously, is based on a profoundly anti-humanist intellectual outlook. In this model, knowledge and science are both limited in their grasp of truths. But because they set in motion innovations that have unintended effects, they also create problems. Such an outlook is, of course, strongly shaped by the negative experience with the record of political change in the twentieth century. The failure of political experimentation in the Soviet Union and China is interpreted as direct proof that ambitious political programmes do not work; and, retrospectively, such negative experiences confirm that we simply do not know how to know.

Not knowing the outcome of our actions strengthens uncertainty and the negative expectations of events. Not knowing and the sentiment that it is not possible to know weakens the human capacity to take chances. The expectation of negative outcomes is not hospitable to social experiments, and when suspicion of outcomes is so deeply entrenched throughout society, the quality of reactions to new events becomes at least unstable and anxious. Such responses are but a step away from overreactions and panics.

A diminished humanity

The negative interpretation of society's ability to manage social experimentation and of the claims of knowledge and science are linked to a vision of society where human beings play a rather minor, undistinguished role. The very use of the risk discourse signifies a world view in which technical factors outweigh social ones. It is worth noting that risk analysis developed in relation to the technological domain. The growth of risk thinking demonstrates the spread of technical calculations into the social domain. The concern with probabilities and predictions inherently points towards outcomes which are to a considerable extent independent of human action. Currently fashionable models portray a semi-conscious humanity that is desperately attempting to take control of the forces – mainly destructive – that it has created. In this model, technologically driven processes have the upper hand and people are reduced to minimizing damage and harm. Such a model represents a powerful statement about the limits of human control.

The representation of humanity as too powerless to repair past damage and too ignorant to shape the future is in wide circulation. The limited role assigned to human subjectivity is most clearly expressed through risk consciousness. Risks are increasingly posited as autonomous forces that are, to a large extent, beyond human manipulation. Risks have little to do with any individual or with his or her experience. Risks emerge from a variety of factors which render an individual's action more or less risky. The risks are the active agents and people – at risk – are the passive agents in society.

The growth of risk consciousness is proportional to the diminished role assigned to human subjectivity. During the past decade the role of the human species and the human-centred worldview (humanism) has been subject to a systematic attack from a variety of directions. Political experimentation has been denounced for leading to totalitarianism. Those who uphold the benefits of science and technology for society are often condemned for an irresponsible lack of concern for the planetary ecosystem. Similarly, the affirmation of the superiority of human reason over animal instinct is often attacked as 'speciesism'.

The diminished role assigned to human subjectivity also implies a redefinition of our humanity. During the past decades the elevation of the passive as opposed to the active side of humanity has been paralleled by concern with people's destructive and abusive potential. The risky individual is also the one at risk. The association of human relationships with risk – the subject of Chapters 4 and 5 – helps to consolidate a life of permanent alertness. Such attitudes breed suspicion and the disposition to panic.

Reconciling limits

The spread of risk consciousness has influenced the way in which people make sense of their circumstances. The diminished role assigned to subjectivity is often discussed in terms of a heightened sense of limits. For Beck, risk society poses the 'question of the self-limitation' of modernization.[31] Others have called for restraint in other forms – consumption, technological development, etc. Sentiments supporting restraint are presented positively as expressions of responsibility and care. Recycling is represented as a moral virtue.

Heroes are definitely out of fashion. The virtues of the 1990s are those of caring and suffering. At the level of the individual, these virtues celebrate the respect of limits. Not taking risks is positively advocated. Since people's powerlessness relative to risks is widely affirmed, limited ambition has become increasingly acceptable. Outcomes beyond human control relieve the stigma of failure. The growth of therapeutic strategies, such as counselling, is based on helping people to live with experiences that have put them at risk. The emphasis of such strategies on 'self-esteem' help to make indistinct the line that divides success from failure. Knowing your limits, accepting yourself, is held to be more important than actual outcomes. The separation of responsibility and accountability from action – at least in an inchoate form – is the most destructive accomplishment of the creation of the diminished subject.

Accountability acquires different qualities in a situation where people live a life of being permanently at risk. The limited scope for human action that this situation affords means that most outcomes are outside any one individual's control. Since the situation is so unpredictable, individuals can demonstrate their responsibility only by playing it safe and not putting anyone else at risk.

The disposition to panic

The themes discussed above express a mood where problems are inflated and where possible solutions are invariably discounted. Such sentiments influence the discussion of the economy as much as they inform child-rearing or education. Not only is there the absence of the elusive feelgood factor, but every hint of a difficulty has a tendency to become exaggerated. Most people find it difficult to remain confident about the workings of Western society.

The loss of confidence of capitalist society cannot be directly attributed to economics. However, economic problems do not inexorably lead to a loss of confidence in society. Indeed what is particularly interesting today is that even the beneficiaries of the capitalist system express doubt and anxiety about the future. Indeed, affluence itself is increasingly indicted for making people feel unhappy. Along with technology, affluence is portrayed as a disease of the market.

It is ironic that the captains of industry and most sections of the ruling elites, who so recently emerged triumphant from the Cold War, should feel so insecure about the future, yet it increasingly appears that leading executives have become scared to manage. As many pass the responsibility for the most elementary decisions to specialist advisors and consultants, a veritable industry of management training and consultancy has come into existence. This phenomenon has spread to other sections of society. The loss of nerve of authorities in both the private and public sectors has led to a proliferation of rituals which help them to avoid problems and postpone confrontations. Thus many institutions now rely on 'facilitators' or 'consultants', 'mentors' or 'counsellors' to supervise everyday human relations in a variety of spheres.

The trends outlined above do not simply constitute a response to uncertainty. The response is to uncertainty in the specific conditions of today, when the role of human potential is called into question. Risk consciousness pertains not only to uncertainty but also to the inability of the human species to do very much about the problems it faces. The fear of risks and the discrediting of experimentation is society's way of acknowledging its inability to tackle the problems which confront it. This works both at the level of wide social processes and at the level of individual interactions.

The clearest expression of society's loss of nerve has been the institutionalization of intermediaries who are invited to contain the tensions and conflict that inevitably arise from the struggle to survive. This tendency is underwritten by the sentiment that people are both unable and unfit to manage their problems. This conviction is highlighted in the recurrent comparison that was drawn between the 'greedy' 1980s and the 'caring' 1990s. Such comparisons articulate a criticism of individual pursuit of self-interest and an implicit demand for regulation. Although this standpoint often seems like an enlightened attack on private greed, it can also be seen as an invitation to curb the human potential.

The main reason why today's insecurity has created an intense consciousness of risk has to do with the changing relationship between society and the individual. Many observers have commented on the relentless process of individuation that has occurred in recent decades in Western societies. Changing economic conditions have created an insecure labour market, while the transformation of service provision has increasingly shifted responsibility from the state to the individual. The individuation of work and the provision of services have made survival much more of a private matter. As a recent BBC poll showed, most people think that Britain is a worse place to live now than 20 years ago. Many are worried about crime, terrorism and personal security. An intensely individuated concern with survival prevails.

But of course the changes in the labour market alone cannot account for the process of individuation. Economic change has been paralleled by the transformation of institutions and relationships throughout society. The decline of participation in political parties and trade unions points to the erosion of traditional forms of solidarity among people. This has been most clear with the demise of traditional working-class organizations. Many mainstream commentators have interpreted this trend through what they call the decline of community. Even a fundamental institution such as the family has not been immune to this process. The changes in family ties and relations have had a deep impact on people's lives. Today, one out of three children is born outside of wedlock. Among those who marry, the rate of divorce is very high. In these circumstances the security of family life is an ideal that is rarely realized.

The mutually reinforcing combination of economic dislocation and the weakening of social institutions has accentuated the tendency for society to fragment. This problem of social cohesion has implications for the daily routine of individuals. Many of the old routines and traditions of life can no longer be taken for granted. Even the role of the family as a system of support is questioned. Under these circumstances, expectations and modes of behaviour inherited from the recent past cannot be effective guides to future action. Relationships between people 30 years ago may not tell us very much about how to negotiate problems today.

The process of individuation is by no means a novel phenomenon. The break-up of communities and old forms of solidarities, the decline of organized religion, geographical mobility and urbanization are all important elements in the development of capitalism. However, today's individuation is not merely more of the same. In the past, the erosion of institutions took place in conditions where new forms of solidarities were created. Thus the growth of the private sphere in the nineteenth century coincided with the emergence of co-operatives, trade unions, mass movements and other collective arrangements. Today, the absence of such arrangements is a widely recognized problem. It has led to the flourishing of initiatives which attempt to provide a substitute for wider social networks. Self-help groups, helplines and counselling are initiatives designed to compensate for the absence of more organic links between individuals.

The relative weakness of institutions which link the individual to other people in society contributes to an intensification of isolation. The process of individuation enhances the feeling of vulnerability. Many people are literally on their own. Such social isolation enhances the sense of insecurity. Many of society's characteristic obsessions – with health, safety and security – are the products of this experience of social isolation.

The sense of fragmentation is reinforced by a lack of consensus about what society's values should be. Many traditional norms are now strongly contested. When British newspapers reported that one out of three children were born out of wedlock, some used the traditional term 'illegitimate' while others took strong exception to this pejorative appellation. One *Guardian* columnist accused *The Times* of superstition and prejudice.[33] Such disputes over fundamental questions of what is right and wrong have always existed. The difference is that today issues to do with morality and basic norms are contested far more often and more intensely. This lack of consensus on elementary norms of behaviour fuels uncertainty about life. The lack of agreement about basic matters like the relationship between children and the family helps to generate confusion about every aspect of human conduct.

When social roles are continually subject to modification and when what is right and what is wrong is far from settled, people are entitled to feel unsure about the future. All of these processes strengthen the process of individuation. What emerges is a decidedly cautious individual.

Diminished sense of control

Probably the most important consequence of the changes described above is a diminished sense of individual control. Since so many aspects of everyday life can no longer be taken for granted, many activities that were once routine have become troublesome. This leads us to one of the main theses of this book: that when attitudes and ways of behaving can no longer be taken for granted, experiences which were hitherto relatively straightforward now become seen as risky. This is the key to understanding the obsession with risk and safety in society today.

For example, consider the uncertainty which now prevails over the so-called crisis in parenting. This insecurity is in part due to the changing character of the family; but it is also due to the shift in relationships between parent and child and between men and women, coupled with a lack of clarity about what is acceptable behaviour today. Parenting and the conduct of family life, long taken for granted as something you just got on with, have now become far from self-evident. Nothing seems straightforward. It is as if parenting has become a minefield. The diminished sense of control which results from these developments exacerbates insecurity and the sense of being at risk. Not surprisingly, the family comes to be seen as a dangerous site where many of the participants are held to be continually at risk. The family home is no longer portrayed as a refuge, but as a jungle where children are at risk of abuse and where women are at risk of domestic violence.

In the same way, changing practices at work mean that relationships between colleagues can no longer be taken for granted. The new pre-occupation with harassment and bullying indicates that work is now seen as a place where one is at risk. Changing relations between men and women certainly mean that little can be assumed. A look or gesture may now be interpreted either as a routine sign of affection or as a mild form of harassment. Debates about the definition of rape and of abuse show how an explosion of risks follows from a situation where nothing can be taken for granted.

Confusion about appropriate forms of behaviour has always existed, but today such confusions are expressed through a highly charged moral climate of risks. One of the arguments elaborated in Chapter 7 is that moral sentiments are often expressed through the vocabulary of risks. Those who put others at risk are condemned and blamed for the misfortune that they caused. However, this condemnation does not take place through an overtly moral discourse. Instead, risky individuals are attacked on the grounds of health and safety. Instead of the old morality, which targeted the promiscuous single mother, the new etiquette attacks a pregnant woman for smoking or drinking alcohol and thereby placing her future child at risk.

But the new morality of risk does not necessarily resolve the problem of the contestation of values, as the decline of old conventions creates a situation in which individuals feel that they have less control over their lives. This in turn inevitably helps to consolidate a sense of insecurity. We feel exposed and unsafe. It is this experience, rather than any fear of technology running out of control, which makes us so preoccupied with personal safety today. As a result, being at risk itself comes to be portrayed and accepted as a way of life.

The notion that being at risk is the same as being alive is clearest in the case of children. In discussion of childhood today, one threat seems to give way to the next. Children are assumed to be at risk not only from abusing adults, but from bullies and abusers among their peers. During the past decade, the issue of safety has also dominated discus-sions on the position of women, who are presumed to be at risk – permanently – from male violence. Even men are now said to face new risks. The recent literature on masculinity has argued that those who have a strong 'masculine orientation' are risking their health, since the rigidity of male gender roles prevents men from asking for the help they need.[34] The diminished sense of control turns even the most basic of human activities into issues of safety. We are continually warned of the risks posed by sex and by the food we eat. Is it surprising that such preoccupations increase our suspicions of strangers, and make us vulnerable to panics about crime, road rage and other dangers to our personal safety?

The insecurity inherent in an existence where little can be taken for granted is evident. However, such insecurity does not automatically transform itself into a consciousness of risk. That transformation has been mediated through the experience of disenchantment with humanity. The coincidence of the process of individuation with a mood of social pessimism helps to produce a sense of cynicism regarding the merit of social engagement. This lack of belief in the problem-solving ability of human beings helps to heighten the sense of vulnerabilty. It is this convergence of insecurity with the sense that we have run out of answers that makes society feel that it is entitled to panic.

Notes

1. Shrader-Frechette, K. (1990) *Risk and Rationality: Philosophical Foundations for Populist Reforms* (Berkeley: University of California Press), pp. 82–4.

2. Vidal, J. (1996) 'Be Very Afraid', *Guardian*; 29 May.

3. See 'Introduction' by G. Pearson (1995), in *Scare in the Community: Britain in a Moral Panic* (London: Community Care*, Reed Business Publishing), p. 4.

4. MacDonald, H. (1994) 'The Ideology of "Family Preservation"', *Public Interest*, Spring, pp. 45 and 60.

5. See 'Child Abuse' by A. Cooper in *Community Care* (1995), p. 35.

6. See 'Lone Parents' by C. Roberts and L. Burghes in *Community Care* (1995), pp. 23–8.

7. See Sykes, C. (1992) *A Nation of Victims: The Decay of the American Character* (New York: St Martin's Press), p. 246.

8. See, for example, Luhman, N. (1993) *Risk: A Sociological Theory* (New York: Walter de Gruyter); and Beck, U., Giddens, A. and Lash, S. (eds) (1994) *Reflexive Modernisation: Politics, Tradition and Aesthetics in the Modern Social Order* (Cambridge: Polity Press).

9. Singer, E. and Endreny, P. (1993) *Reporting on Risk: How the Mass Media Portray Accidents, Diseases, Disasters and Other Hazards* (New York: Russell Sage Foundation), p. 83.

10. Singer and Endreny, *Reporting on Risk*, pp. 1–2.

11. See Kasperson, R. and Kasperson, J. (1996) 'The Social Amplification and Attenuation of Risk', *Annals of the American Academy of Politics and Social Science*, no. 545, p. 97.

12. Kaufman, W. (1994) *No Turning Back: Dismantling the Fantasies of Environmental Thinking* (New York: Basic Books), p. 172.

13. Leiss, W. and Chociolko, C. (1994) *Risk and Responsibility* (Montreal: McGill-Queen's University Press), p. 7.

14. See 'Storms, Drought, Floods on Rise as Climate Spins Out of Control', *Independent on Sunday*; 30 June 1996.

15. Simon, J. (1995) *The State of Humanity* (Oxford: Blackwell), p. 46.

16. *The Times*; 6 December 1962.

17. Luhman, *Risk*, p. 83.

18. Giddens, A. 'Risk, Trust, Reflexivity', in Beck *et al.*, *Reflexive Modernisation*, p. 185.

19. Beck, U. (1992) *Risk Society* (London: Sage), p. 183.

20. See Beck, U. (1996) 'Risk Society and the Provident State', in Lash, S., Szerszynski, B. and Wynne, B. (eds) *Risk, Environment and Modernity: Towards a New Ecology* (London: Sage), pp. 28–9; and Beck, *Risk Society*, p. 26.

21. 'Nature Bites Back', *Guardian*; 26 March 1996.

22. Luhman, *Risk*, p. 48.

23. Lubbe, H. (1993) 'Security: Risk Perception in the Civilization Process', in Bayerische Ruck (ed.) *Risk Is a Construct: Perceptions and Risk Perception* (Munich: Knesebeck), p. 25.

24. See Lash *et al.*, *Risk, Environment and Modernity*, p. 2.

25. Ross, J. (1995) 'Risk: Where Do Real Dangers Lie?' in *Smithsonian*, November, p. 46. For a useful study of accidents involving children, see Roberts, H., Smith, S. and Bryce, C. (1995) *Children at Risk? Safety as a Social Value* (Buckingham: Open University Press), p. 6.

26. Lash *et al.*, *Risk, Environment and Modernity*, p. 2.

27. This point is elaborated further in Furedi, F. (1992) *Mythical Past, Elusive Future* (London: Pluto Press).

28. Beck, U., Giddens, A. and Lash, S. (eds) (1994) *Reflexive Modernisation: Politics, Tradition and Aesthetics in the Modern Social Order* (Cambridge: Polity Press), p. vii.

29. Luhman, *Risk*, p. 147.

30. Luhman, *Risk*, p. 44.

31. Beck, U., 'Risk Society and the Provident State', in Lash *et al.*, *Risk, Environment and Modernity*, p. 29.

32. See the BBC News; 4 September 2006.

33. *Guardian*; 3 June 1996.

34. See Kaplan, M. and Marks, G. (1995) 'Appraisal of Health Risks: The Role of Masculinity, Femininity, and Sex', *Sociology of Health and Illness*, vol. 17, no. 2, p. 207.

CHAPTER 4

The Culture of Abuse

The literature on risk consciousness is primarily concerned with the relationship between the perception and reality of hazards. Its orientation is towards physical risks such as the environment and health. The analysis of the risks rooted in human relations is at best a subsidiary theme in this literature. One of the key arguments of this chapter and indeed of this book is that the inflation of concern about physical pollution is merely one side of the contemporary outlook. Anxiety about physical pollution is intertwined with existential and moral fears. Consequently our era is characterized not only by intense levels of anxiety about environmental pollution but also by a unique obsession with abuse, or the defilement of the individual.

The explosion of risks discussed previously runs in parallel with the amplification of abuse. Since the 1980s, the representation of people has been transformed by the normalization of the experience of abuse. Claims that abuse is rife, that most people are affected and damaged by it are now widely believed. Such claims thrive in a moral climate where visions of a rising tide of violence help to generate a consensus that everyone is potentially a victim or an abuser. The abused, the individual damaged by another human being, is the subject of this chapter.

The normalization of abuse

If any enlightened American or British social commentator living around 1900 had been informed that by the end of the century their society would revert to witch hunts, they would have responded with incredulity. Since the eighteenth century, intellectuals have been in the forefront of fighting superstition. Despite widespread prejudice on a number of fronts, Western societies regarded themselves as enlightened communities that had nothing in common with the superstitious past. Yet today something has changed. Not since the Dark Ages has there been so much concern about organized forces of evil. Small panics about satanic abuse have erupted on both sides of the Atlantic, and serious intellectuals have criticized those who deny its existence. This belief in the flourishing of satanism is all the more disturbing as serious investigations into the subject have failed to find any evidence for ritual abuse.

There is a morbid expectation that just about every home contains a potential abuser. The belief that predatory molesters routinely prey upon their victims has imprinted itself on everyday imagination. People regard others with the kind of suspicion that would have been rare just a few decades ago. Parents wonder whether the day-care-centre workers looking after their children can be trusted. In schools, children with bruises are apt to arouse the suspicion of teachers about what their parents have been doing. For their part, parents wonder whether the cuddling of their children by their teachers is entirely innocent. Such mistrust also extends to relatives and neighbours. Nor have relations between fathers and mothers been left untouched by a climate where abuse is seen as a routine hazard of the human condition. Children as young as 5 and 6, who have been 'sensitized' to be 'aware', are growing up with the value of mistrust deeply embedded in their imaginations. For some experts, this education of mistrust has not gone far enough. One monograph decries the fact that children have only been sensitized to mistrust adults: 'children are currently socialised to recognise, resist, and report child abuse perpetrated by adults, but there is no parallel effort made with regard to peer abuse'.[1] The implications of a process of socialization which rests on the premise of fear and mistrust is rarely explored by its advocates.

The intense suspicion of human motives bred by the routinization of the experience of abuse has encouraged people to alert the authorities to acts of possible perversion. Words and deeds are often given the worse possible interpretation, especially when a child is involved. Consider a couple of examples. In November 1995, detectives accosted Toni Marie Angeli, a Harvard photography student, at a local photo laboratory after technicians alerted police to the potentially pornographic photographs that she had taken of her 4-year-old son. The photographs showed a naked boy grinning as his father held him up in the air. A picture that in the past would have been seen as an image of love and affection now evoked the interpretation of depravity at work. Toni Marie Angeli's class assignment was titled 'The Innocence of a Child's Nudity'. The police, who handcuffed and manhandled her, had a more up-to-date cultural interpretation of the legitimacy of such an assignment.[2]

In the UK, the Julia Somerville case illustrates how the expectation of abuse serves to create an atmosphere that is both prudish and misanthropic. In November 1995, Julia Somerville, a well-known British news broadcaster, and her boyfriend, Jeremy Dixon, were arrested after a tip-off from a photo-lab assistant. The assistant working for the chain shop, Boots the Chemist, had reported one of the films that Dixon had taken in to be developed to his superiors because it contained 28 pictures of Somerville's daughter in the bath.

Neither Boots nor the police claimed that the pictures in question were any different from the millions that parents take of their nude children on the beach, in the garden or in the bath. Even Sheldon Atkinson, who alerted the world about the pictures, conceded that the child 'was smiling and didn't seem miserable or worried'. Apparently, what alerted the shop assistant was the fact that Dixon had asked for a duplicate set of photos. Moreover, if it had just been one or two snaps, he said, that would have been all right, but 28 was 'too many'. In the event, no case could be found against the two suspects and they were not charged with any crime.

The incident revealed a number of interesting features about the moral climate in the UK. The celebrity status of Somerville ensured that the case would gain widespread publicity and thereby draw attention to practices that otherwise go unnoticed. The controversy revealed that people working in photo-labs are expected to work as unpaid spies on the look-out for family pornography and paedophilia. For example, a mother was arrested for taking photographs of her 3-year-old daughter lying naked by the fireplace, with the intention of giving them to the little girl's grandmother as a Christmas present. The incident also revealed just how obsessed so-called experts have become with discovering abuse.

Although many people felt uneasy about the treatment of Somerville and Dixon, few felt able to challenge the right of Boots and the police to investigate the pictures and arrest the couple. Public criticism was largely confined to the media's role and the manner in which the story was leaked to the papers. Very few were prepared to ask the question, 'what kind of a society has Britain become where a few pictures of naked children taken by their parents could arouse such concern'? There was a time when images of nude children represented beauty and innocence. The classic definition of a cherub, 'a beautiful and innocent child', has inspired artists through the ages. Such visions, of course, were products of the human imagination as it tried to rediscover its lost virtues in the idea of childhood. Today, society's imagination cannot stretch to the idea of human beauty. What was once a celebration of purity has become a temptation to perversion. The inability to imagine innocence coincides with a readiness to diagnose a depravity of the soul.

Typically, the British child protection industry portrayed the Somerville incident as a positive contribution to fighting abuse. Organizations like the National Society for the Prevention of Cruelty to Children (NSPCC) defended free-lance snooping by Boots on the grounds that one could never be too vigilant. Clive C. Walsh, director of the British Association of Social Workers, even wrote to the *Guardian* suggesting that, instead of complaining about her treatment, Somerville should be using the spotlight to aid the anti-child-abuse crusade by 'helping us all to be confident enough to welcome being asked to explain'. Walsh's implicit message, 'prove that you are not an abuser', crisply summed up the misanthropic mood of the times.

The theme of abuse has become one of the most distinct features of contemporary Western culture. The frequency with which the term is used and the growing number of experiences that are defined as abusive are symptomatic of the significance of this artefact of contemporary culture. Ironically, those who publicize the danger of abuse insist that this danger is not given enough publicity by educators and by the media. Their demand is for the transmission of more warnings about the danger of abusive behaviour. In fact, virtually every form of the media has already become obsessive about this subject. Popular soap operas in the UK revel in the theme. In the USA, talk shows have normalized the experience of abuse. Sexual abuse has become a fashionable theme for Hollywood films and novels. Concern over physical and sexual abuse now constitutes a mainstay of the entertainment industry. The Liverpool-based soap opera, *Brookside* (Channel 4), featured wife-battering and child sexual abuse in its Jordache storyline (wife Mandy killed husband Trevor after he molested their younger daughter). *Coronation Street* subsequently took up the wife-battering theme, while *Brookside* has moved on to brother-and-sister incest.

Crime shows (fictional and documentary) are similarly preoccupied. The American-made *Murder One* is an in-depth investigation of the gruesome sex murder of a 15-year-old girl. The central plot-line hinges on identifying which of two characters is more guilty of sexual abuse. Various subplots involving a whole host of characters are focused on sexual abuse and harassment. In the documentary field, Channel 4 transmitted a season of documentaries during the autumn of 1995, entitled 'Battered Britain', which portrayed British society as a nexus of abusive relationships.

In films such as *The Net* (starring Sandra Bullock) and *Strange Days* (directed by Kathryn Bigelow) Hollywood's rendition of cyberspace has correlated the Internet with sexual harassment and rape. Not to be outdone, the music industry, which once seemed dedicated to the notion that 'chaste is waste', is now given to bouts of soul-searching about the allegedly abusive effects of 'hard-core' music (note the pornographic connotation) such as rap, ragga, heavy metal and jungle. Child abuse has even featured in a pop music video by Madonna.

Not to be outdone by Hollywood, popular fiction has turned abuse into a bestselling theme. Dorothy Allison's highly acclaimed *Bastard out of Carolina*, Marilyn French's *Our Father* and Jane Smiley's Pulitzer Prize-winning *A Thousand Acres* are only a few of the well-known texts focusing on this subject. As Kate Roiphe wrote in *Harper's* magazine: 'by the early nineties incest had swept across the literary map of America – into Mona Simpson's California cities, Jane Smiley's flat Midwestern farmlands, Mary Gaitskill's middle class suburbs, Russell Bank's small upstate New York towns, and even E. Annie Proulx's icy Canadian islands'.

The representation of abuse as normal in the media has been backed up by the phenomenal growth in the literature on family violence. Histories of ideas in the future will no doubt look upon the past three decades as an era dominated by interest in the so-called dark side of the family. As one review of research in the 1980s remarked:

> *The expansion of research on the topic of domestic violence in the last decade has been substantial, perhaps greater than in any other substantive area in the social sciences. In addition to work on child and wife abuse, a substantial body of research developed on the topics of violence toward parents, especially elderly parents, courtship violence, and sexual abuse.*[3]

This major reorientation of social science research indicates that the expectation of what constitutes normality has undergone a dramatic transformation. The postwar image of the wholesome nuclear family has been replaced by a vision of unbounded depravity.

The normalization of abuse has been underwritten by the conviction that human relations are inherently risky. The eternalization of risk has been recast at the level of the individual as one of permanent abuse.

Children, women, the elderly and even men are defined as being permanently at risk of abuse. Thus being at risk has been assimilated into the very conditions of childhood and womanhood. The statistics on abuse make truly phenomenal reading. They suggest that male violence against women is so deeply structured that virtually every women is subject to it. Alarmist accounts warn that one in four or one in three or one in two women will be raped. An example of such panic-driven research was the CanPan survey in Canada which argued that 98 per cent of women in that country are sexually violated.[4] Comparable claims of epidemics are made in relation to child abuse, elder abuse and bullying.

The amplification of abuses by family violence research is realized through a conceptualization of abuse which is entirely arbitrary. The act of abuse lacks any structure or fixity because it is defined through the eyes of those who believe that they have been abused. One of the most absurd consequences of this perspective is the belief that truth is always on the side of those who claim abuse. Consequently, insistence on evidence and the close interrogation of the claim is often dismissed as irrelevant or as insensitive to the condition of the victim. This approach to evidence is well illustrated by Lucy Berliner, an American feminist social worker, in her comments on child abuse:

> *A legal decision should never be confused with the truth. If we believe what children say we will be right 95–99 per cent of the time. If we want signs and symptoms as proof we will be right 70–80 per cent of the time. If we require medical evidence we will be right 20 per cent of the time and if we have to wait for a witness we will be right 1 per cent of the time.*[5]

From this perspective, the demand for proof simply detracts from the transcendental truth of abuse. Even the manifest examples of false accusation are seen to contain some intrinsic truths. Thus according to one account, false accusations in child sexual abuse are rare but 'when they occur it is nearly always a cry for help'. The authors add that it is 'clear that the children who make false allegations require help and support and as such these allegations should not be ignored'.[6] Such sympathy is rarely extended to the accused, and since allegations, even when they are false, 'should not be ignored', those at the receiving end cannot be absolved of suspicion.

By placing the emphasis on the importance of believing the accuser, experts in the field of family violence have freed themselves from being accountable to the facts. Proponents of satanic abuse disarm sceptics by contending that probably the worst thing that can happen to the victim of sadistic sexual abuse is not to be believed. Patrick Casement argues this thesis in the following way:

> *It may be that some accounts which are reputed to be of 'satanic' abuse are delusional, and the narrators may indeed be psychotic in some cases. But we must still face the awful fact that if some of these accounts are true, if we do not have the courage to see the truth that may be there . . . we may tacitly be allowing these practices to continue under the cover of secrecy, supported also by the almost universal refusal to believe that they could exist.*[7]

By stigmatizing the refusal to believe, the accuser is accorded monopoly over some transcendental truth. In this way, thinking the worst about people is interpreted as an act of courage rather than what it really is – an expression of misanthropy.

The *a priori* belief in the prevalence of abuse has led to a standard of evidence which is characteristically flexible. Indeed, even the very definition of what constitutes an abuse depends on the interpretation of the defiled victim. Manuals on abuse, harassment and bullying insist that the act is 'defined largely by the impact of the behaviour on the recipient not its intention'.[8] This means that the act is defined by the recipient's feeling of stress and humiliation and not by the intent. Many disciplinary codes in British universities contain the expression 'harassment should be defined by the victim'.[9] Because of this arbitrary representation of abuse, there can be a multitude of coexisting definitions of the problem. The literature on elder abuse offers a vivid illustration of this pick-and-mix approach. A well-known training manual on the subject concedes that 'even researchers who have been working for many years on the subject cannot agree on a straightforward definition'. But that does not matter since the intention of the manual is to help the reader 'to develop his or her definition'.[10]

That just about anything that happens to old people can be categorized as abuse is confirmed by the policy documents that are intended to inform the work of social workers. The British Social Services Inspectorate Practice Guidelines note that 'Abuse may be described as physical, sexual, psychological or financial. It may be intentional or unintentional or the result of neglect. It causes harm to [an] older person, either temporarily or over a period of time'.[11]

In other words, elder abuse can be anything. The unpleasant

experiences to which old people are subject are represented in the discourse of abuse. Acts of petty theft and cheating acquire gravity by being labelled as financial abuse.

The subjective interpretation of abuse does not only provide the foundation for the exaggeration of family and other forms of inter-personal violence. It also leads to the continuous expansion of the range of human experiences which can be labelled as abusive. Many practices that in the past might have been considered to be bad habits – eating, drinking – are characterized as abuse. More importantly, forms of behaviour that were accepted as routine in the past are now redefined as abuses. Once one type of experience is defined as abusive, it is only a matter of time before the same claim is made for another.

The trivialization of the abusive relationship is evident in the case of elder abuse. When neglect and unintended insult become equated with physical violence and incorporated into an all-purpose generic concept of abuse, the life of an old person becomes a perpetual nightmare.

> *Elder abuse can be described as the mistreatment of an older person which results in suffering and distress . . . it can be a single incident, or part of a repeated pattern as a result of a conscious act, or neglect by the abuser. Both men and women are abused and carers can be abused by those for whom they care. Abuse can take place in someone's home, in the home of the carer, where day or respite care is being provided and in any form of institutional care, whether in a residential or nursing home or a hospital.*[12]

The coherence of a concept that embraces a single incident and a repeated pattern or which fails to distinguish neglect from conscious intent is dubious. As in the stories which adults tell to warn their children from straying too far, the big bad wolf is everywhere.

Bullying has emerged as one of the most thriving of abuse relationships. Whereas in the past bullying was interpreted as one of the unpleasant aspects of growing up, today it is seen as a pathology that deeply scars its victim. The growth of the bullying industry has been truly phenomenal, as has the definition of what constitutes bullying. As with elder abuse, definitions of bullying vary. However, the emphasis is on repeated 'negative action' towards another person. As in the case of other abuses, experts on the subject justify the importance of their issue on the basis of alarming statistics. It seems that one in four or one in five schoolchildren are bullied. A closer inspection of the evidence indicates that as usual the meaning attached to the act of bullying is very flexible. Most of the experiences which they define as bullying are what used to be called name-calling. Some experts make a distinction between direct bullying and indirect bullying, i.e. between open attacks and social isolation. The failure to involve someone in one's circle of friends is but one variation on the bullying theme. Experts have redefined elementary forms of peer-to-peer interactions, such as rejection and exclusion, in the discourse of bullying. Social exclusion, now presented as emotional bullying, is also interpreted as the most painful type of bullying.[13] In this way, the common difficulties that children have in developing social skills and self-confidence are seen as the outcome of yet another abusive relationship.

The inflation and trivialization of bullying has turned virtually every peer-to-peer relationship which is stressful into an experience of abuse. The ease with which the stressful experiences of children have come to constitute a widely accepted pathology has led others to claim the status of being bullied. It is not just children who face bullies in schools. A recent study by the psychology department of the University of Surrey has concluded that many 'poorly-trained' school heads were bullying their teachers. The report found that 'victims were most frequently shouted at, put down in front of colleagues and pupils, and had their confidence undermined'. Another report, which claimed that the bullying of teachers was widespread, added that this experience 'reduces adults to the state of frightened children'.[14] It appears that teachers are not the only adults who face an epidemic of bullying. A survey by the British trade union MSF disclosed that 30 per cent of the respondents 'thought that bullying was a significant problem in their workplace'. Upon closer examination, it becomes clear that what the MSF categorizes as bullying in the workplace is what used to be called office politics. Personality clashes, mismanaged relations and petty jealousies are the stuff out of which workplace bullying is born. By endowing the everyday tension of the experience of work with the quality of bullying, human relations become diseased. 'The mental torture now recognised as workplace bullying', claims one reporter, 'is emerging as one of the key employment issues of the day, with the lives of tens of thousands of employees being ruined by corporate tyrants and shop floor "Hitlers"'.[15]

The culture of abuse has its intellectual foundation in the field of family violence research. During the past fifteen years the research provided by this field has offered a relentless escalation of the numbers of victims. The rise in the numbers of victims has been matched by the expansion of the definition of violence and abuse. The redefinition of the meaning of violence has been most innovative in the area of male violence against women. In numerous accounts, violence against women has been portrayed as the normal state of affairs. It has been claimed by American researchers that one out of four women are raped. This allegation, made by Mary Koss in a well-known article in *Ms* magazine, has helped to authenticate the reality of a rape epidemic. As usual, it does not take long for American intellectual fashion to be aped in the UK. 'Half of all girls experience some form of unwanted sexual experience, from flashing to rape before they are 18', is the expert opinion of the British Labour Party on the subject.[16]

Arguments about male violence and rape are based on a fundamental revision of the interpretation of interpersonal relations. Sexual violence is an emotive term; but it is a term that embraces a variety of actions – from an unwanted touch to an act of rape. Acts which are ambiguous and which at the most constitute a minor irritation and which involve no violence are now classified together with rape and battering. In this way, every unsolicited touch helps to increase the numbers of victims of sexual violence. A similar approach is used in the categorization of sexual harassment. The instrument used in a well-known survey of the subject at the University of Iowa defined eight categories of behaviour: sexist comments, undue attention, verbal sexual advances, body language, invitations, physical advances, explicit sexual propositions, and sexual bribery.

What underpins the methodological exaggeration of male violence is a model where any act by a man towards a woman can be interpreted through the prism of abuse. In the writings of some feminist writers, the boundary that separates normal male acts from violence is difficult to distinguish. This pertains to the most ambiguous of all interpersonal relations of all – that of sex. Thus Catharine MacKinnon, professor of law at Harvard University, is anxious to point out the similarity between 'the patterns, rhythms, roles and emotions, not to mention acts, which make up rape (and battery) on the one hand and intercourse on the other'. MacKinnon finds it difficult to distinguish 'pathology and normalcy' and 'violence and sex'.[17] From this perspective, sexual intercourse is rendered pathological and the male lover is at once a rapist.

Other contributors on the subject portray male violence as a 'unitary phenomenon'. Jalna Hanmer and Mary Maynard contend that it is wrong to portray male violence – rape or domestic violence – as a discrete act. They argue that such acts are closely linked to other manifestations of male behaviour. They also demand that all such acts – rape, domestic violence, flashing, obscene phone calls – should be understood as the projection of what they term 'male power'.[18] In this way, a variety of distinct acts become methodologically connected to rape. The synthesis of male acts into a unitary phenomenon of violence leads to a loss of proportion in the meaning to be attached to each individual act.

The expansion of the meaning of male violence is most coherently argued in the continuum of sexual violence thesis. According to this thesis, male violence can be understood as a continuum of acts of sexual coercion. With the ever-widening definition of abuse, the milder end of the continuum can begin with a look and the harder end culminate with ritual murder. This thesis helps to augment the number of violated victims, since everything from a dirty joke to physical assault is defined by its common quality of male violence. Normal male behaviour becomes but a precursor to rape.

The methodology deployed to substantiate the continuum of violence thesis helps to seriously misrepresent human relations. Although arguments about the continuum rely on empirical research, the conclusion of what constitutes violence and rape depends on the interpretation of the researchers. For example, Mary Koss's figure of one in four women being raped is based on her interpretation of events and not on the alleged victim's perception of the act. According to one of her critics, 73 per cent of those classified as rape victims by Koss did not think that they had been raped, and 42 per cent of them reported having consensual sex with the same men.[19] Once researchers feel comfortable with disregarding the views of their sample and assuming a monopoly over the definition of rape, then the numbers can become astronomical.

The ever-widening interpretation of rape and other forms of male violence provides the foundation for the woman-as-victim perception. One of the implications of the argument is that all women, most of whom have never experienced violence, should behave and feel as though they have. In this way all women become part of a 'collective victimhood'. As one proponent of the thesis argued:

> Using the concept of a continuum highlights the fact that all women experience sexual violence at some point in their lives. It enables the linking of the more common everyday abuses women experience with less common experiences labelled as crimes.[20]

Through this methodological fusion of qualitatively different experiences, sexual violence becomes the dominant motif in the relation between men and women, and male violence – a normal feature of masculinity – is reconstituted as the all-purpose cause of the defilement of women and children.

The characterization of male violence as normal and intrinsic to the daily experience of women has acquired great currency amongst the intelligentsia. Even leading sociologists adopt this quasi-religious interpretation of male violence as a recycled manifestation of the original sin. Such an approach is evident in the writings of Anthony Giddens, who is probably the most influential British sociologist today. Giddens not only accepts the continuum of male violence thesis, but extends it to incorporate the fundamental heterosexual experience. He argues:

> It seems clear that there is a continuum, not a sharp break, between male violence towards women and other forms of intimidation and harassment. Rape, battering and even the murder of women often contains the same core elements as non-violent heterosexual encounters, the subduing and conquest of the sexual object.[21]

By reducing human experience to 'core elements', the most unlikely links can be drawn. One such possible example is the continuum between eating and cannibalism – they, too, contain the same core elements.

The fervour with which male violence is imagined is demonstrated by the cavalier manner with which sociologists can ignore the social aspects. The isolation of male violence endows it with an almost transcendental character. According to Giddens, 'the impulse to humiliate women' is 'probably a generic aspect of male psychology'.[22] If indeed this is so, and if heterosexual encounters invariably contain the implication of violence, abusive relations are by definition the norm.

There seems to be little resistance to the representation of most forms of human relations as abusive. This outcome is not surprising in a society where the dominant consciousness is that everyone is at risk. Panics about abuse do at the level of the individual what risk consciousness does in relation to the environment and wider social processes. Through abuse, our very being is invaded – after the experience, according to expert opinion, we will never be the same. *Abuse is the form that our concern about pollution assumes at the level of individual relations.* The traditional meaning of the word abuse related to the act of misuse, improper use and perversion, but it also carried the connotation of violation, pollution and defilement. In the eighteenth century, the term self-abuse was defined as 'self-pollution'.[23] Today, the emphasis is not on the pollution of the self but on the defilement of others. Within our consciousness of risk, this type of pollution is as prevalent, probably even more prevalent, than the fear of wider environmental damage.

The key significance of the discourse of abuse is that it redefines relations of conflict and tension in terms of the metaphor of pollution. Like the effects of toxic waste, the effects of human pollution are long-term. This misanthropic tendency to define a growing range of experiences as potentially abusive represents an important condemnation of the human condition. Since human relations are all potentially toxic, they require careful management and control. Those who uphold this vision of human degradation regard private life in pathological terms. As Kaminer noted, they view families as 'incubators of disease', where 'they manufacture "toxic" shame, "toxic" anger, "toxic" self doubt, any number of "toxic" dependencies, and a "toxic" preoccupation with privacy'.[24] Like the old-fashioned religions which declared that we were all sinners, today's culture of abuse contends that as people we are damaged and are badly in need of help.

The cycle of abuse

The shift from portraying the snapshot of a naked child as a symbol of innocence to seeing it as an incitement to depravity corresponds to the misanthropic way in which human motives are represented. The culture of abuse expresses the loathing that society feels towards itself and its members. This culture provides a framework in which a variety of experiences can be reinterpreted as abusive. A characteristic expression of this was provided by the reports around the time of the 1996 Olympic Games in Atlanta which claimed that the rigours of competitive gymnastics amounted to child abuse. Such claims were backed up by a report in the *New England Journal of Medicine*. According to the authors of the report, pushy parents and coaches were seeking to experience vicariously the success of the child, and this 'achievement by proxy' could be seen as a 'sort of child abuse'.[25] Even in the Olympics there are no more heroes. The main protagonists in the drama are abusers and survivors. When adults can see in their childhood photographs the evidence of abuse, maturity becomes identified with survival.

Survival has become the axial principle of the culture of abuse, and human beings are increasingly perceived as survivors of traumatic experiences. Often, they are portrayed as damaged people. This in turn has encouraged a mood where acknowledgement of such damage is seen as being essential to one's public persona. According to one astute commentator:

Never has there been a time in history when people have represented themselves as so damaged – riven with anger, aggression, frustrated ambition, unfulfilled needs. Never has there been a time when people thought of themselves so strongly as victims or prisoners to our past.[26]

The use of the designation of 'survivor', with its connotation of wartime tribulation or even of the Holocaust, underlines how everyday life has been turned into a major test. The celebration of survival turns the ordinary existence of everyday life into an end in itself. Such lowering of horizons is justified on the grounds that the burden of our childhood trauma is so great that we can never be free of its effects. At no time since the emergence of modernity has the latitude for human action and control been so strongly denied as today. It appears that people are too weak to overcome the effects of their negative experiences and they therefore become 'scarred for life'. This expression is now recycled routinely to predict what will happen to a victim of abuse or crime.

The damaged person is often someone who has been abused. Experts on abuse all emphasize the long-term effects of the experience. It is a life sentence for the victim. This view is stressed in the literature on bullying. Bullying has left 'scars' on the minds of the victims. Little can be done to eradicate this spiritual mutilation. 'Very few children escape the experience of victimisation unaffected', concluded a study of child victims.[27] A similar conclusion was drawn by a study titled 'Peer Rejection Places Children at Immediate, Long Term Behavioral Risk'.[28] It argued that the long-term effects of peer rejection were delinquency, dropping out of school and psychopathology. Writing in the same vein, the authors of a study of adults with a history of child sexual abuse concluded that they are 'severely damaged people', who use the health services 'much more than other adults'. It appears that 'more of them have weight problems, misuse alcohol and drugs and have irritable bowel syndrome'.[29]

The long-term damage caused by abuse is given intellectual respectability by the 'cycle of abuse' theories. The intergenerational transmission of violence is one of the uncontested themes of the family violence literature. Those who uphold this thesis see abuse as an intergenerational disease. Abusers were themselves abused when they were children, and their victims will go on to manifest delinquent behaviour. Thus abuse does not end with the victim; it has a life of its own, which is then transmitted to future generations.

Despite a lack of hard evidence, the cycle of abuse thesis has acquired the status of an incontrovertible truth. Yet the evidence is open to serious interrogation. The view that violence breeds violence is based on retrospective studies. Such studies often depend on comparing aggressive and non-aggressive adolescents and men to see if those who are aggressive were more likely to have been abused when they were young. There are many problems with such studies. The status that one assigns to recollection is one area of contention. Another fundamental weakness of such studies is the relationship drawn between the experience of childhood abuse and the subsequent act of adult abuse. Is this a causal relationship? Was this experience of violence the cause of subsequent adult violent behaviour or are there other influences that shaped the response? To abstract one variable – abuse – and construct a direct lineage with future acts of abuse is to ignore a variety of social phenomena.

The elevation of the experience of violence to the level of a transcendental force is based on the commonsense assumption that people who have experienced brutality are likely to become more brutal themselves. In one account, speculation about elder abuse is based on this model of a brutalized lifestyle:

> there is a possibility that transgenerational violence occurs and that there are situations where children are abused who then go on to indulge in spouse abuse and abuse their own children and later become recipients of abuse themselves as elderly people.[30]

Although the authors qualify their remark by stating that it is only a 'possibility', the image of abuse as a self-reproducing phenomenon overwhelms perceptions of the problem.

Problems that in the past were seen simplistically as the result of the 'violent society' are today increasingly explained by the 'violent family'. The widespread credibility of the cycle of abuse thesis is a testimony to the decline of the sociological imagination. It is worth noting that in the debate about the so-called underclass, many social scientists rightly reject a cycle of poverty thesis as non-social. However, they seem quite happy to accept such a thesis in relation to abuse. The reasons for this shift away from social explanations are complex. One important factor has been the growing acceptance by leftist, feminist and liberal thinkers of the traditional conservative thesis that explanations of adult behaviour are rooted in family life. This trend is usefully illustrated by the Report of the Gulbenkian Foundation's Commission on Children and Violence. According to this report the creation of a non-violent society depends on positive parenting. This conclusion is based on the premise that violence is generated within the confines of family life before it spreads to other areas of social life. The solution to the problem lies in the domain of parenting because it 'minimises the chances of children experiencing violence and consequently, minimises the likelihood that they in turn will behave violently'.[31]

The Gulbenkian Foundation Report provides a coherent presentation of the cycle of abuse thesis. Although it accepts that the causes of violent action cannot be identified 'beyond doubt', it is absolutely certain that violence within the family is the main force at work. The report's main thesis is that violence begets violence. The authors of the report are prepared to consider influences other than family violence, such as poverty, family break-up, alcoholism and the media. However, the report considers the effects of all these factors on children to be 'indirect'. The only variable that is conceptualized as a 'direct' influence on children is parental violence. So it argues that

> very substantial research evidence highlights negative, violent and humiliating forms of discipline as significant in the development of violent attitudes and actions from a very early age. Effects of family structure and break-up are indirect, and they can be mediated through the quality of the parenting process.

In the same way, poverty, schooling and alcohol are said to be indirect. The report notes that 'low socio-economic status has been shown to be clearly related to delinquency and violence in many UK studies'. But it is careful to add that low economic status does not 'cause' violence. According to the report, poverty and low economic status increase 'the risk of violence through their inter-relation with other risk factors'. This careful nuanced approach disappears when it comes to parental violence. A simple relation of causality is difficult to sustain in any complex social relationship, yet for some reason family violence is treated as a phenomenon that is in a class of its own. Unlike any other social experience, family violence has the autonomous power to directly shape behaviour. Why violent discipline alone should be a direct and unmediated influence on behaviour is seen to be so obvious as to require no explanation.[32]

The fatalistic premise of the report is that once children have experienced violence, then all the damage has been done. It asserts that 'insofar as the best predictor of violence in adulthood is violent behaviour in childhood, we can assume that the most important causal contributions to adult violence have already been made by the time adolescence is reached'.[33] Adult violence is then hatched in childhood. The portrayal of violence as the independent variable, stripped of any social determination, transforms it into an incurable disease. The language of pathology best encapsulates a phenomenon which is immune to intervention once the damage has occurred. The report also uses this vocabulary when it observes that 'violence can escalate quickly, through a process of "contagion"'.[34]

The view that the experience of childhood violence is responsible for adult delinquency flatters society. The family bears the burden of responsibility for the creation of childhood thugs who will become the criminals of tomorrow. Violence is separated from broader relations of power. Taken out of context, the term violence can be used interchangeably to describe the act of an errant child, that of a rapist or of a group of soldiers fighting in the battlefield. Individual acts of desperation become equated to calculated projections of power, affecting the lives of thousands of people.

The importance attached to the character-forming role of childhood violence is based on a highly deterministic perspective of the human condition. It suggests that people's adult existence is predetermined by their childhood experience. The many experiences we have as adults pale into insignificance compared to an act of abuse we experienced as children. As in a Greek tragedy, through our life we merely realize our fate. People are encouraged to see themselves as victims of family life rather than as self-determining agents. The debilitating consequences of this culture are self-evident. The past acts as an all-purpose explanation of the problems of adulthood. Human beings are not only victims of their past – they are also destined to damage future generations.

The cycle of abuse thesis posits a world where abused children are already abusers in the making. This was the insight that informed the headline 'Cash to Catch Sex Menaces of the Future' in one local London newspaper. The *Hackney Gazette* reported that the local council had provided funding for a project 'to spot potential paedophiles and rapists before they became a menace to the public'. The aim of this young abusers project was 'to steer sex offenders and child molesters in their early teens away from abuse'.[35] What follows from the perspective that the family is a training ground for violence is a focus on managing the individual behaviour of the young.

Abuse, then, is a never-ending experience. It is an intergenerational disease passed on from parent to child. All this leads to an almost biblical conception of human beings. The sins of the parents are visited upon the children. What they did can never be undone. The experience of abuse leaves one scarred for life, and future generations may well pay the final price for these deeds.

The culture of abuse gives a new definition to powerlessness. Unlike traditional notions of crime, violence is no longer viewed as a one-off act. The effects of abuse linger on in the body and the psyche of the victim. Its effects are for life. Moreover, the effects are so significant as to influence virtually every aspect of the life of the survivor. Addictions, eating disorders and phobias are some of the manifestations of this life sentence. The acknowledgement of this trauma helps the survivor to cope. Many professionals in the abuse industry vociferously warn against victims trying to deal with their conditions themselves. Some therapists dismiss individual attempts to overcome addiction and other problems as futile expressions of a 'perfectionist complex'. 'Admit that you're sick and you're welcome to the recovering persons fold; dispute it and you're "in denial"', is how Kaminer described the attitude of many therapists.[36] Avoiding professional counselling serves as proof of the gravity of the problem facing the victim.

One of the most damaging consequences of the pathology of abuse is the way in which it undermines people's desire to control their lives. In the past, coping with experiences which today are labelled as abusive has been an integral part of life. Despite many terrible individual tragedies, most people have managed to overcome the pain that some of these experiences inflict. Indeed, the struggle to come to terms with the pain has been an important source of strength. According to the abuse industry, the attempt to manage such pain without expert intervention is itself a problem. For example, a study on child victimization in Edinburgh presented in negative terms the fact 'that children were forced back on their strategies for dealing with victimisation through offering each other mutual support'.[37] In other words, children in the course of growing up found their own solutions to the difficulties they faced. Instead of praising this extension of mutual support, the authors decried the absence of official intervention. Unfortunately, the pathology of abuse will probably have the effect of becoming a self-fulfilling prophecy. People who are forever told that they need help to deal with difficult experiences will find it hard to tackle problems on their own. The culture of abuse flatters personal weakness and lowers the aspirations of people.

Incompetent people

It seems that people's attempts to cope with and negotiate the problems they face are wholly inadequate. Terms like 'on their own' or 'coping alone' are used to highlight how inadequate individuals are in dealing with personal problems. The inadequacy of the individual is often contrasted with the special skills and resources which many encounters are presumed to demand. The variety of encounters and experiences which overwhelm the individual has increased enormously in recent decades. The representation of 'can't cope' encounters has followed the same pattern as that of abusive relations. Just as an increased range of experience has been labelled as abusive, so there has been an expansion of the situations in which an individual cannot be expected to be able to cope alone. Even some of the most elementary adult roles, such as parenting, have become subject to special consideration. People are trained in 'parenting skills', so that they can carry out functions which their poor ancestors had to perform without the help of trainers and counsellors.

The phenomenal growth of counselling has been one of the clearest manifestations of the 'can't cope' trend. In 1980 the British Association for Counselling (BAC) had just over 1800 individual members and 160 organizational members. By 1993, it had over 10,000 individuals and 500 organizational members. It is said that at present the BAC is recruiting over 300 counsellors per month.[38] According to a study of this subject, this growth 'has come about with the increasing acceptance that from time to time most people have problems that they may not have the necessary resources to cope with'.[39]

The view that people lack the 'necessary resources' to deal with experiences that used to be considered part of everyday life is now deeply entrenched. In schools, counsellors deal with a wide range of incidents which not so long ago were considered the private affairs of the family. They deal not just with school-related problems but with redundancy, divorce, alcoholism, eating disorders and death in the family. Counselling is now considered to be an obligatory service in most institutions. Trade unions, institutions like the police and professional bodies like the British Medical Association all provide counselling to their members. Camelot, the operator of the national lottery in the UK, offers counselling to all winners.

These days, whenever we want to underline the seriousness of a condition, we indicate that someone is receiving counselling. The expression 'they are still receiving counselling' is used in the media to indicate the gravity of the situation. In more serious cases, the viewer is informed that a particular group will need counselling for a long period of time. In one case of a tragic school accident which had been recounted to the author, parents were sent letters four years after the event, informing them of the availability of counselling services. Parents who were perfectly happy to carry on with life were made to feel that there was something odd about their reluctance to talk to the counsellors.

Increasingly, the message transmitted through counselling is that one is not expected to cope without professional intervention. The institutionalization of counselling is most developed in the sphere of education, particularly in higher education. Students at British universities are constantly offered the services of counsellors. Long lists of different counselling services are pinned to the walls of university toilets. A stranger arriving on a British campus could easily draw the conclusion that university life was fraught with so many complicated risks that no one could succeed without professional help. Counsellors, jealous of their skills, reinforce this impression and advise university teachers not to get drawn into student problems 'which require specific skills or training'.[40]

The inability to cope, which is the fundamental assumption of the counselling revolution, is explained through the language of disease and addiction. The pathology of abuse seems to offer the model through which human relations in general are explained. Through the language of disease, a variety of experiences become medicalized. The most dramatic effect of the medicalization of experience is the invention of a variety of new disorders and conditions. The transformation of behaviour into a disorder or a disease, which is one of the main accomplishments of the cycle of abuse theory, has acquired a practical reality through the birth of an ever-expanding range of psychological disorders.

These disorders – social phobia, post-traumatic stress disorder, attention deficit disorder, to name a few – all follow the same pattern as the experience of abuse. They are life-long conditions that shape behaviour. Like viruses, microbes or pollutants, when these diseases infect the person, little can be done to evade their effects. Their very existence helps to explain human behaviour. Thus when a person states 'I am stressed', we are meant to understand that some unaccountable force, external to the individual, is influencing his or her behaviour. No doubt such a statement is an invitation to a stress counsellor to perform the necessary ritual.

As in the case of abuses, conditions and disorders are continually being discovered. Virtually every form of behaviour has now become subsumed under a medical label. What used to be called bad habits are now called addictions. Indeed, every form of compulsive behaviour is now classified as an addiction. Alcoholism provides a model for other forms of obsessive activities – shopaholics, sexaholics and workaholics are all people who are addicted to their particular obsessions. Thus people who need to be loved and love others too often and too much are, in the USA, labelled as being addicted to sex. Throughout modernity, people have made foolish choices about their choices of partners, have sometimes stayed with them far too long and have spent too much of their time searching for lovers. Today, we use the discourse of disease and addiction to describe this all too common human experience. The American Association on Sexual Addiction Problems has estimated that between 10 and 15 per cent of all Americans – i.e. around 25 million – are addicted to sex![41]

The construction of sexual addiction as a distinct disorder indicates that the ambiguities of human relationships are simplified through the medicalization of behaviour. Monographs purporting to analyse this condition merely recast in medical terminology what people have known for a long time. In one such study, sexual addiction is diagnosed as the compulsive dependence on external actions as a means of regulating one's internal states. In other words, our difficulty in living with ourselves leads to attempts to gain external affirmation.[42] Terms like 'sexual compulsivity' or 'sexual dependency' merely render everyday behaviour pathological.

One way in which obsessive activity is transformed into a major addiction is to draw a comparison between its features and that of alcoholism. In this way we know that children obsessed with computer games have a serious problem because they get the same euphoria as do smokers and heavy drinkers.[43] We also know that people who get carried away with shopping and become addicted to it are suffering from a real disease, because shopping addiction 'can amount to a form of illness on a par with compulsive gambling and alcoholism'. According to Kay Sheppard, an American clinician and a self-confessed 'food addict in recovery', many food addicts come from alcoholic families. Sheppard also insists that food addiction is no less of a problem than alcoholism.[44] Historical familiarity with the destructive consequences of alcoholism is mobilized to claim a similar status for a variety of recently discovered addictions.

Also, addictions are increasingly represented as diseases. Food addiction, which in the past would have been characterized as overeating or obesity, is now medicalized as a physical disease. Kay Sheppard argues that 'it is a physical disease characterized by obsession with food, obsession with weight, and loss of control over the amount eaten'. These obsessions are presented as the outcome of a physiological or biochemical condition of the body, which creates 'cravings for complex carbohydrates'.[45] Advocates of sexual addiction also advocate a disease-focused treatment. An American expert prescribes a combination of therapy and pharmacotherapy, and a Malaysian contribution on the subject suggests among other things clomipramine (an antidepressant drug) as an effective cure for the disease.[46]

The medicalization of behaviour continually redefines the human condition. As more and more of our experiences are defined medically, the space open to human action contracts. At the same time, it leads to the systematic multiplication of the number of people who suffer from some condition or disorder. With the invention of the concept of *co-dependency*, virtually everyone can be depicted in this way. Co-dependence, which in the USA originally referred to the problems of women married to alcoholics, was redefined by addiction counsellors in the 1980s. 'Now it applies to any problem associated with any addiction, real or imagined, suffered by you or someone close to you', points out Wendy Kaminer. As a result, virtually every American can be defined as a co-dependent. It is worth noting that co-dependency is blamed on bad parenting or child abuse. In this roundabout way, the culture of abuse claims even more recruits. Every obsessive glance or act can be presumed to have its origin in an abusive experience.[47]

There has been a dramatic increase in the discovery of new anxiety disorders. Disorders such as social phobia or dependent personality disorder are held responsible for individual performance and behaviour. Uncertainty about issues, an inability to make decisions or the disappointments associated with setbacks in life are now routinely diagnosed as symptoms of some kind of anxiety disorder. Such a diagnosis helps make sense of the difficulty that people have in coping. The generic condition of 'can't cope' becomes naturalized. From this perspective, the attempt to assume a degree of control of one's life becomes a pathetic gesture, for we need help and not independence.

The medicalization of behaviour has helped create a climate in which people are continually looking for some organic or psychological explanation for their actions. Parents are relieved when they are told that their badly behaved offspring is suffering from attention deficit hyperactivity syndrome or a newly discovered anxiety disorder. In universities there is a veritable culture of medicalizing failure and poor performance. In this way the whole culture of abuse becomes complicit in legitimizing low expectations.

The culture of abuse encourages people to think of themselves as addicts or ill. Consequently, people's lives and actions are permanently subject to yet more influences which are beyond their control. This natural constraint on human self-determination has become an influential component of contemporary identity. Addictions and illnesses have become an integral and fixed part of people's identity. The insistence of counsellors that one can never cure addictions has given currency to terms like 'addict in recovery'. The damage that has been done to us can be contained but its influence cannot be transcended. We are seen as victims of what happened to us in the past, and we define ourselves by that which happened to us in the past rather than by what we have done to make this world our own.

The growth of the victim identity

Observers on both sides of the Atlantic have commented on the growth of the culture of victimhood. They have pointed to the frequency with which a wide variety of interests seem to be playing the victim card. American and British commentators have remarked on the growth of the 'culture of complaint' where competing victim groups demand special privileges and resources to compensate them for their suffering. A grotesque illustration of this process occurred in the aftermath of the Hillsborough football stadium disaster in Sheffield. Relatives of football fans who were injured or killed reacted with anger upon receipt of the news that a number of policemen in attendance had received substantial compensation before they had. Arguments broke out about which group was more traumatized by this tragedy – and, of course, who was most worthy of compensation.

It is in the USA that victimhood is most developed as an institution in its own right. The category of victimization is claimed by a variety of groups, from compulsive gamblers to addicts of junk food. Victims of 'toxic parents' compete with disabled sex addicts to recount their suffering in the media. Victimhood is one of the central categories of the culture of abuse. Celebrities vie with one another to confess in graphic detail the painful abuse they suffered as children. The highly acclaimed BBC interview with Princess Diana symbolized this era of the victim. She literally boasted of her suffering as she exposed her emotional scars to anyone who cared to look. Indeed, she advertised her ability to revel in pain as the main accomplishment to make her a suitable candidate for agony aunt to the nation.

The public exposure of inner pain has become a highly prized cultural artefact. It has inspired individuals and groups to stake a claim on behalf of their painful experience. The inability to cope and a variety of difficulties and complaints are blamed on some traumatic incident that occurred in childhood, and the number of experiences which are today redefined as traumatic is on the increase. In early 1996, the *British Medical Journal* published a letter signed by 20 men who had set up a victim support group for men who were circumcised in childhood. Their letter opens with the declaration that 'We are all adult men who believe that we have been harmed by circumcision carried out in childhood by doctors in Britain'.[48] They did not actually indicate how they had been harmed, but it is easy enough to get the gist of their complaint from the line put out by similar men's groups in the USA. They argue that they feel mutilated and psychologically damaged by circumcision, and they believe that sex for them is less satisfying than it should be, as a permanently exposed glans becomes less sensitive.

The attempt to transform infant circumcision into an abuse is yet another worrying manifestation of society's expanding demand for new victims. One wonders how Jewish and Muslim people have managed to survive all these centuries. But instead of dismissing this as an undeserving claim for victim status, the main reaction is to treat it as received wisdom.

In Britain, men's magazines and newspapers have treated the plight of circumcised adult men as a serious question. For example, *Maxim* carried sympathetic articles featuring the findings of American psychologist Jim Bigelow, author of *Joy of Uncircumcising! Restore your Birthright and Maximise Your Sexual Pleasure*. The *Guardian* reported accounts of circumcised men who complained that their ability to enjoy sex had been impaired and who felt a 'sense of mutilation and of loss'. Channel 4 commissioned a documentary to show what can and does (rarely) go wrong during the procedure. The cumulative effect of this whole campaign was to create the impression that circumcision was a form of child abuse. Yet another abuse was born.

Normally there would be little merit in recounting the the various attempts to transform circumcision into a form of child abuse. There are always groups of individuals who attempt to shift the blame for their circumstances onto the backs of their parents. However, what is most striking about this campaign is the lack of critical thinking on the part of journalists and the media. It was as if they were too embarrassed to interrogate the claims of the circumcised men. The assertion of mutilation was sufficient to enforce silence. There was a reluctance to ask the obvious question: why is it only now that we discover that one of the earliest operations recorded in history apparently has such devastating psychological effects? Or why have otherwise highly articulate Jewish and Muslim men kept quiet about their poor sex life all these centuries? It is obvious that a media that allows such a story to gain currency will also be complicit in transmitting reports of satanic abuse and similar claims for victimhood.

As with all the conditions discussed in this chapter, that of victimhood lasts into the indefinite future. The scars it leaves behind carry on to future generations. Advocates of victimhood integrate the themes central to the culture of abuse and imply that once a person has become a victim, he or she will always be a victim. Recently it has become fashionable to claim the status of second- and third-generation survivor. Merely being related to someone who was victimized decades before is sufficiently traumatic to have a major impact on one's life. Psychology provides its intellectual apparatus to legitimize the indefinite status of the victim experience. Conditions like post-traumatic stress disorder (PTSD) suggest that trauma is a perpetual phenomenon.

Victimhood has also been expanded through the concept of the indirect victim. For example, people who witness a crime or who are simply aware that something untoward has happened to someone they know are potential indirect victims. Advocates of child victims insist on the importance of this indirect experience:

> *Where an offence is committed against a member of the child's household or against another family member, the child is unlikely to be recognised as a victim in his or her own right. However, their experience may be such that they ought to be recognised as victims.*[49]

With the concept of the indirect victim, the numbers become tremendously augmented. Anyone who has witnessed something unpleasant or who has heard of such an experience becomes a suitable candidate for the status of indirect victim.

In all the discussion that surrounds victimhood, it is easy to overlook the fact that this way of conceptualizing human experience is a very recent one. Until recently the word victim was used in association with someone who was sacrificed to a deity or some supernatural force. It was also used to describe someone who was subjected to torture or put to death. In the nineteenth century, the concept expanded to include those who were badly treated. However, it was only in the 1960s that victimhood came to acquire the character of a permanent identity!

It is only in recent decades that people have been described as victims and that they have been given such a corporate identity. It is worth noting that victims were invented by criminologists and others involved in social policy during the 1960s. Their retrospective accounts criticized policy-makers for not recognizing this 'invisible' group. Others write of the long overdue recognition of victimhood. Criminologists add that because crime is underreported there are far more victims than we suspect. However, such criticisms miss the point. The victim is a social construction. People who have had bad or traumatic experiences do not think of themselves as victims unless society defines them in that way. The concept of an 'invisible' victim is nonsense, for it implies the existence of people with prior victim identities who were somehow ignored. In reality, such a constituency did not exist. It is interesting to note that most of the early initiatives that were implemented to help victims came from above. The author of a major text on the discovery of victims in the UK notes that the Criminal Injuries Compensation Scheme 1964 was 'not the result of any mass campaign waged by victims themselves'. This scheme was the product of lobbying by professional reformers.[50]

The widely held view proposed by criminologists that there existed a lonely and isolated group of individuals waiting to be discovered turns reality on its head. It retrospectively endows individuals with specific experiences with the character of victim. This procedure is most clearly exemplified in the retrospective construction of the child victim. One of the points emphasized by advocates of the child victim is that their recognition faced special obstacles from the adult world. Morgan and Zedner remark that children had to 'earn' the status of victim because 'many types of crime committed against children are not regarded by adults as sufficiently serious to merit any formal response'. They add: 'Routine acts of minor violence such as bullying, chastisement, or assault appear resistant to being defined as criminal when committed against children. To this extent, children are liable to be denied recognition as victims'.[51] With a sleight of hand 'routine acts of minor violence' between children have been defined as criminal. It is precisely this inflation of the meaning of crime or of abuse that is the precondition for the subsequent emergence of yet another group of victims.

It does not occur to Morgan and Zedner that, before the construction of the child victim, children were not striving to gain the status, for the very simple reason that they may not have identified themselves as victims. Yet their own statistics suggest that definitions of victimhood may be externally generated. They indicate that, in Oxford, the single largest category of known offences against children was bicycle theft – 57 per cent of all recorded offences. Today, children in Oxford who have their bicycles stolen are all considered to be victims. What is interesting about this development is not that so many bicycles are stolen. Many of us, when we were children, had our bicycles stolen. But did we react by silently identifying ourselves as victims? Did the experience traumatize us? Were we scarred for life? Did we need counselling? The interesting aspect of this Oxford story is the cavalier way in which relatively insignificant childhood experiences are integrated into the promotion of victimhood.

The term victim is now used so liberally in situations where children are concerned as to deprive it of any content. The Gulbenkian Foundation Report literally treats victimization as the defining quality of childhood. It does this by widening the meaning of violence so that the most trivial encounter becomes a mild variant of homicide. In this continuum of violence, 'sibling assaults' are discussed in the same breath as murder. The authors cite an American study, which noted the existence of a 'pandemic' of sibling assault in the USA. Apparently, 800 per 1000 children are 'victims of sibling assaults'.[52] There was a time when tugging each other's hair and lashing out at one another was seen merely as what children did. By reinterpreting these acts as sibling assaults, a huge pool of potential recruits to the victim cause has been created. The consequence of this development is that children will begin to think of themselves as victims. A society that expects its offspring to be in need of so much counselling will get all the victims that it needs.

Social scientists who specialize in victim studies rarely reflect critically on their subject matter and inquire why their specialty has so suddenly shot into prominence. They all note that recently there has been a long overdue recognition of all the invisible victims. But the issue that is rarely engaged is why has bullying become such a key problem of concern? Why has an experience that children lived with for centuries become so problematized during the past twenty years? And, more broadly, why has the victim become such a key symbol of our era?

Victim studies have become prominent in the past two decades. However, the reason for this development is not that hitherto invisible people have become more visible. The invention of the victim took place under special circumstances. The precondition for the emergence of the victim identity was the consolidation of the consciousness of risk. In the UK and the USA, the growing fear of crime and the growing perception of risks have contributed to the sentiment that everyone is a potential victim. However, crime and the fear of crime are only the most striking manifestations of the kind of insecurity that strengthens the belief that everyone is at risk.

In the past, people who suffered from a particular violent incident did not identify themselves as victims. This was not because they did not suffer, or because they did not carry their scars with them for the rest of their life, but because the experience was not seen as identity-defining. People regarded them as unfortunate incidents but not ones that polluted them. Even when people felt badly hurt and deeply aggrieved, their own self-identity was not defined by the experience. In contrast, today there is a belief that victimhood affects us for life – it becomes a crucial element of our identity. Since so much of our behaviour is the outcome of forces outside our control, our experience as victims acquires a new significance. The experience of being the objects rather than the subjects of life enhances the sense that something is being done to us. This has led to a situation where we continually feel the sense of loss. It is this sense rather than the sense of control that characterizes the mood of our time. Society encourages those who suffer from a crime or tragedy to invest their loss with special meaning. Parents of children who are killed insist that their 'offspring should not die in vain'. They set up campaigns and charities to publicize the cause of their children's death and thereby to warn others of a specific danger. In the UK there are almost 300 charities with the name victim in their title, many of them set up by relatives of victims.

Most critical accounts of victim culture emphasize the motif of financial or other forms of individual gain. There is no doubt that many people cynically cultivate their victimhood to strengthen their claim on resources. But the wholesale institutionalization of the victim cannot be explained as the outcome of cynicism and dishonest manipulation. Indeed, what is interesting is that even those who are accused of responsibility for victimizing others respond in the same terms. Thus men who have been accused of male oppression are now often claiming to have been victimized. 'All men are potential victims of sexual assault' was the conclusion of a study carried out in Memphis. In the UK, the Equal Opportunities Commission (EOC) now receives more complaints from men about job discrimination than it does from women.[53] It seems that every section of society is ready to claim some form of victimization. The all-pervasive sense of victimhood is the corollary of the sentiment that we are all at risk. The elevation of the victim has to be seen as an expression of the same process which leads to the diminishing of the subject. Many of the processes discussed previously have a direct bearing on the promotion of the victim. The process of individuation discussed in Chapter 3 along with the diminished sense of human potential has helped to weaken confidence in the relationships between people. The problematization of so many relationships has strengthened the sense of vulnerability. The perception of the elderly of younger generations provides an illustration of this trend. There is now considerable evidence which suggests that both in the USA and in the UK the elderly are actually afraid of young people. Such high levels of mistrust are clear symptoms of a wider mood which regards personal relations as potentially dangerous. The consciousness of being 'at risk' readily translates itself into the victim identity.

The potential for the emergence of a victim identity was contained in the process that helped consolidate the consciousness of risk. But the realization of this potential occurred under the specific circumstances of the 1980s. It is important to note that the politicization of the victim identity occurred in the 1980s. And it is the peculiar circumstances of the politicization of the victim identity that may help to clarify its current influence and power.

The cause of the modern victim was initially most closely associated with the right wing of the political spectrum. It is significant that in the 1960s, the issue of the victim became central to the US presidential campaign of the conservative Republican Barry Goldwater. In the 1964 election campaign, Goldwater made 'crime in the streets' part of his campaign. In subsequent years, right-wing American politicians made the issue of law and order a central plank of their manifestos. Their campaign promoted the defence of the victims of crime – particularly of street crime. Their appeal was to the so-called silent majority. This ill-defined term evoked the image of millions of ordinary American people who suffered in silence the inequities perpetuated by successive liberal democratic administrations. Long before the advocates of the abused pointed to the invisible and unacknowledged victim, the silent majority was in existence.

The association of the political right with the politicization of the victim is not merely of historical significance. Although most of the critics of victim culture are from the right, they rarely explore why the institutionalization of victim culture took off in the 1980s – the era of Reagan and Thatcher. It seems paradoxical that the decade known as the 'greedy eighties' was also the time when victims were discovered. Even liberal social scientists accept that the institutionalization of official support for victims took place under the reign of Conservative home secretaries in the UK. The *Victim's Charter*, published in 1990 by a British Conservative government, illustrates the importance which the political right has attached to the issue.[54]

However, the advocacy of the cause of the victim is by no means restricted to the political right. Many of the initiatives surrounding this issue were launched by people who identified themselves as feminists, leftists or liberals. During the 1960s and 1970s left-wing politics underwent a major transformation. The belief in social change and experimentation was undermined by events. During this period many of the left's allies, whom it regarded as agents of change, began to be seen as victims. The literature on the working class illustrates this shift. Workers, who were hitherto portrayed as a powerful force of change, were increasingly represented as victims of forces beyond their control. A parallel process was in evidence in the women's movement. In the late 1960s and early 1970s, feminists argued vehemently against the representation of women as victims. By the late 1970s, this perspective was fundamentally revised. Campaigns now stressed the woman victim – battered, violated, raped. Indeed, the perception that all women were always at risk emerged at this period.

The shift towards the victim in left-wing and feminist discourse reflected disenchantment with people as subjects of change. More and more people came to be regarded as being in need of 'help' or 'empowerment'. Most of the new ideas about victimhood came from this quarter. Unlike traditional conservative contributors, who treated individuals as victims of evil, feminist and leftist writers portrayed them as victims of the system or of patriarchy. But although there were differences in the interpretation of aspects of the problem, there was a shared assumption that people are victims.

The common assumptions of left and right are well illustrated by the question of crime. While the focus of left-wing concern was on the marginalized victims of crime, the main cause of the right was law and order. Both of these concerns became fused in a new broad-based sympathy for the victim. One of the consequences of this is that a political climate has been created in which defending people from victimization has become everyone's point of reference. This reorientation has had a major impact on the character of trade unionism, for example. Trade unions in the UK seek to protect their members from bullying and harassment rather to reform society. In the past workers used to complain that they suffered from poor pay and conditions, long hours and fear of redundancy. Today, they complain of stress, which surveys confirm has reached epidemic proportions in the workplace. The appearance of stress syndrome at work is a sure sign that the potential militant trade unionist has been turned into a helpless victim.

The transformation of the politics of the workplace is symptomatic of the changing contours of political life. The politicization of childhood is probably the clearest manifestation of this trend. The result is a synthesis of traditional conservative authoritarianism with leftist intrusion into the affairs of the individual. This synthesis helps explain why the politics of the culture of abuse has such a resonance across the entire political spectrum.

Notes

1. Ambert, A.M. (1994) 'A Qualitative Study of Peer Abuse and Its Effects', *Journal of Marriage and the Family*, February, p. 120.

2. See Granfield, M. (1996) 'The Molester Within', *New York Times Homepage*, June.

3. Gelles, R.J. and Conte, J.R. (1990) 'Domestic Violence and Sexual Abuse of Children: A Review of Research in the Eighties', *Journal of Marriage and the Family*, vol. 52, p. 1045.

4. For a devastating critique of the CanPan report see Fekete, J. (1994) *Moral Panic: Biopolitics Rising* (Montreal/Toronto: Robert Davies Publishing).

5. Cited in Taylor, G. (1993) 'Challenges from the Margins', in Clarke, J. (ed.) *A Crisis in Care? Challenges to Social Work?* (London: Sage), p. 132.

6. Anthony, G. and Watkeys, J. (1991) 'False Allegations in Child Sexual Abuse: The Pattern of Referral in an Area Where Reporting is Not Mandatory', *Children and Society*, vol. 5, no. 2, p. 120.

7. Casement, P. (1994) 'The Wish Not to Know', in Sinason, V. (ed.) *Treating Survivors of Satanist Abuse* (London: Routledge), p. 24.

8. See, for example, the British trade union MSF's pamphlet (1995) on workplace bullying, p. 3.

9. See, for example, Chapter 8 of the Code of Conduct of Leeds University Union.

10. Pritchard, J. (1995) *The Abuse of Older People: A Training Manual for Detection and Prevention* (London: JKP), p. 27.

11. Social Services Inspectorate (1993) *Social Services Inspectorate Guidelines. 'No Longer Afraid'* (London: HMSO), p. 3.

12. Action on Elder Abuse (1995) *Everybody's Business! Taking Action on Elder Abuse* (London: AEA), p. 3.

13. Olweus, D. (1994) 'Annotation: Bullying at School: Basic Facts and Effects of a School Based Intervention Program', *Journal of Child Psychology and Psychiatry and Allied Disciplines*, vol. 35, no. 7, p. 1173. Also see Smith, P. and Sharp, S. (eds) (1991) *School Bullying: Insights and Perspectives* (London: Routledge), p. 16, for the centrality of name-calling in the bullying statistics, and 'Pupils Say Emotional Bullying the Worst', *Guardian*; 11 April 1996.

14. See 'School Heads Accused of Bullying Staff', *London Evening Standard*; 12 May 1996, and Adams, A. (1993) 'The Bullying Kind', *Managing Schools Today*, July, p. 23.

15. See MSF (1995), pp. 1–5. On shopfloor 'Hitlers', see Kossoff, J. (1995) *Time Out*; 20 September.

16. Labour Party (1995) *Peace at Home* (London: Labour Party), p. 2.

17. MacKinnon, C. (1989) *Toward a Feminist Theory of State* (Cambridge, MA: Harvard University Press), p. 146.

18. Hanmer, J. and Maynard, M. (1987) *Women, Violence and Social Control* (London: Macmillan Press), p. 2.

19. Fekete, *Moral Panic*, p. 74.

20. Kelly, L. (1987) 'Continuum of Sexual Violence', in Hanmer and Maynard, *Women, Violence and Social Control*, p. 59.

21. Giddens, A. (1992) *Modernity and Self Identity: Self and Society in the Late Modern Age* (Cambridge: Polity Press), p. 121.

22. Giddens, *Modernity and Self Identity*, p. 121.

23. See *Shorter Oxford Dictionary* (1965), p. 1834.

24. Kaminer, W. (1993) *I'm Dysfunctional, You're Dysfunctional: The Recovery Movement and Other Self-Help Fashions* (Reading, MA: Addison-Wesley Publishing Company), p. 12.

25. See Tofler, I., Stryer, B., Micheli, L. and Herman, L. (1996) 'Physical and Emotional Problems of Elite Female Gymnasts', *New England Journal of Medicine*, vol. 335, no. 4.

26. Coward, R. (1989) *The Whole Truth: The Myth of Alternative Health* (London: Faber and Faber), pp. 102–3.

27. Morgan, J. and Zedner, L. (1992) *Child Victims: Crime Impact and Criminal Jusice* (Oxford: Clarendon Paperbacks), p. 183.

28. Morgan, J. and Zedner, L. (1994) 'Peer Rejection Places Children at Immediate, Long Term Behavioural Risk' in *Brown University Child and Adolescent Behavior Letter*, August.

29. Smith, D., Pearce, L., Pringle, M. and Caplan, R. (1995) 'Adults with a History of Child Sexual Abuse: Evaluation of a Pilot Therapy Service', *British Medical Journal*, vol. 310, p. 1177.

30. Bennett, G. and Kingston, P. (1993) *Elder Abuse: Concept, Theories and Intervention* (London: Chapman and Hall), p. 32.

31. Gulbenkian Foundation Commission (1995) *Children's Violence: Report of the Gulbenkian Foundation Commission* (London: Calouste Gulbenkian Foundation), p. 14.

32. Gulbenkian Foundation Commission, *Children's Violence*, pp. 11–12, 56–9.

33. Gulbenkian Foundation Commission, *Children's Violence*, p. 40.

34. Gulbenkian Foundation Commission, *Children's Violence*, p. 62.

35. See *Hackney Gazette*; 4 April 1996.

36. Kaminer, *I'm Dysfunctional*, p. 26.

37. Cited in Morgan and Zedner, *Child Victims*, p. 159.

38. Figures derived from Cunningham (1995), p. 1.

39. Nelson-Jones, R. (1994) *The Theory and Practice of Counselling Psychology* (London: Cassell), p. 507.

40. See Easton, S. and Van Laar, D. (1995) 'Experiences of Lecturers Helping Distressed Students in Higher Education', *British Journal of Guidance and Counselling*, vol. 23, no. 2, p. 173.

41. Sykes, C. (1992) *A Nation of Victims: The Decay of the American Character* (New York: St Martin's Press), p. 14.

42. Goodman, A. (1994) 'Diagnosis and Treatment of Sexual Addiction', *Journal of Sex and Marital Therapy*, vol. 19, no. 3.

43. See 'Children Obsessed with Computer Games Show Symptoms of Addiction', *Alcoholism and Drug Abuse Weekly*; 10 March 1994.

44. 'Compulsive Shopping "Real Illness"', *Guardian*; 6 October 1996; and Baker, L. (1995) 'Food Addiction Deserves to Be Taken Just as Seriously as Alcoholism', *Addiction Letter*, July.

45. *Ibid.*

46. See Goodman (1994), and Azhar, M. and Varma, S. (1995) 'Response of Clomipramine in Sexual Addiction', *European Psychiatry*, vol. 10, no. 5.

47. Kaminer, *I'm Dysfunctional*, pp. 9–13.

48. *British Medical Journal*; 10 February 1996, p. 377.

49. Morgan and Zedner, *Child Victims*, p. 73.

50. Rock, P. (1990) *Helping Victims of Crime* (Oxford: Clarendon Press), p. 87.

51. Morgan and Zedner, *Child Victims*, p. 22.

52. Gulbenkian Foundation Commission, *Children's Violence*, p. 255.

53. Lipscomb, G., Muram, G., Speck, D. and Mercer, P. (1992) 'Male Victims of Sexual Assault', *Journal of the American Medical Association*, vol. 267, no. 22.

54. Rock, *Helping Victims of Crime*.

CHAPTER 5

A World of Risky Strangers

The idea that we should err on the side of caution has been codified as the precautionary principle, and enshrined in numerous international agreements as the guide to environmental management. Those who uphold this principle assert that because of the impossibility of predicting the effect of human action on the environment it is best to be cautious about the introduction of technologies. This perspective is based on the belief that we do not possess enough knowledge of future outcomes. Uncertainty about the effects of human action provides the main rationale for the precautionary principle. Simply stated, the objective of this principle is 'the avoidance of unnecessary risk by playing safe'.[1]

Although the precautionary principle has emerged in the field of environmental management, it expresses an approach to the uncertain future which dominates other aspects of life. Uncertainty about the future – including that of the environment – does not exist in isolation from the mood and reaction of society to other matters. As previous chapters have suggested, although uncertainty has acquired a sense of material palpability in relation to the issue of the environment, the sources of this sentiment are actually existential. The idea that society gains by playing it safe also guides social and political life. Whether the subject be new technologies or sex, caution is presented as a prudent measure in an uncertain world.

The correlation of uncertainty with the future of the world strongly influences behaviour between people. Such sentiments are inspired by a lack of clarity about the terms on which relationships are built. A lack of fixity in fundamental relationships is but one important source of uncertainty. The idea of playing safe appears to make sense to people who are unclear about the best way of proceeding with an encounter. And it is not just personal relationships which are affected by the principle of caution; health and sexuality are increasingly judged from the standpoint of the principle of precaution.

Taking precautions is not in itself a novel phenomenon. People have always used their common sense to protect themselves from potential hazards. There have always been some individuals who are particularly cautious and devote their energies to shielding themselves and their families from dangers. However, such attempts to gain security should not be confused with developments in contemporary society. Today, caution has become institutionalized to cover every aspect of life. This institutionalization is often interpreted technically – as a responsible way of minimizing risk. It can also be seen as a way of regulating the increasingly unpredictable outcomes of human relations. The promotion of caution is based on the presentiment that even hitherto unproblematic relations between people are now fraught with tension. That means that the range of experiences whose outcome can not be automatically perceived has expanded. The perspective of unknown unknowns also informs perceptions of personal relations.

An interesting illustration of the growth of uncertainty in human relations is provided by the contemporary tension between young and old. Generational conflicts, e.g. the 'generational gap' of the postwar era, are not particularly novel. The rebellious youth has been a constant theme of literature for centuries. However, today the relationship between generations has acquired a more troublesome dimension. It is not just a question of youthful rebellion against the older generations but of a tangible sense of fear among the elderly. Surveys show that many old people are actually scared of children and teenagers. In an era where terms like 'granny dumping' and 'granny bashing' have gained currency, it is not surprising that the threat of violence specifically aimed at the old preoccupies the elderly. Some writers on the ageing of the population have speculated about the possibility of intergenerational conflict over resources. It has been suggested that the growth in the number of old people now represents an increasing burden on the young. The OECD has argued that such conflict over resources 'may put intergenerational solidarity – a concept on which all public retirement provisions are based – at risk'.[2]

The possible weakening of intergenerational solidarity has implications that go way beyond the issue of pension provision for the retired. The erosion of such solidarity must have an impact on the conduct of interpersonal relations. If old people are portrayed as a burden on society, with no useful contribution to make, it is unlikely that the young will regard them with interest. Instead of being a source of authority or wisdom they will be seen at best as an irrelevance and at worst as objects of scorn. In this relationship of uncertainty, children do not necessarily treat the old with 'respect'. For the elderly, the relationship of uncertainty is experienced as the heightening of their sense of vulnerability and insecurity. Not knowing what is expected of them and what they can demand of others, they are often strangers in their own home and in their own community. Sheltered accommodation, boasting the latest in security devices, indicates how personal security has become an issue for the elderly. It seems that for many elderly people, the streets are inhabited by risky strangers.

The effects of the institutionalization of caution form the subject of this chapter. This process is fuelled by our estrangement from others. Not only are more people seen as strangers but they also seen as potentially threatening to our security. That is why it is better to play safe. A lifestyle influenced by the value of caution is one that is subject to new limits and restraints. It holds back social experimentation and strengthens concern about personal security.

A world of strangers

There can be many sources of uncertain relationships, but one of their most common causes is a lack of clarity about the rules of engagement. Discussion on issues like harassment implicitly indicates a degree of uncertainty about what is permissible and what is not. A lack of clarity about what is expected of people within a range of relations is also a source of tension. Old people, who realize that they can no longer enjoy automatic deference, do not know what to expect from younger strangers who they encounter. Do they still have the right to reprimand a troublesome child who they overhear swearing on the bus? However, the elderly uncertain of their role are by no means the exception today. No section of society is immune to the lack of clarity concerning where they stand in relation to others.

Growing uncertainty about human relationships has strengthened the conviction that anything can happen. Events like high rates of divorce and sudden loss of a secure career have created a climate where people expect the unexpected. Consequently, there is a tendency in society to seize on the exceptional, extreme and abhorrent acts as confirmation of the kind of diseased world that we inhabit. The media's fascination with the serial killer reflects the sentiment that we are now prey to some extraordinarily perverted and sick individuals. Such sentiments even attach themselves to children. In the UK a small number of violent acts by children have received an extraordinary amount of publicity. The killing of James Bulger by two other children in 1993 provided the occasion for a major media panic about the meaning of childhood. The media did not merely exaggerate the scale of violence facing British children, but also raised questions about the state of childhood. The media stressed that it was children who perpetrated the crime.

The questions raised about child violence around the Bulger case expressed the uncertainty about human relationships in a particularly intense form. 'What has happened to children' was the question under consideration. After the trial of the child culprits, *The Sunday Times* reflected that we will 'never be able to look at our children in the same way again'. It added, 'all over the country, parents are viewing their sons in a new and disturbing light'.[3] This response self-consciously raised the issue of 'do we know what our children are up to?' The panic around this murder was interesting for what it revealed about society's anxieties about children. Suddenly sentiments that had existed under the surface acquired a tangible form. The fear of not being in control – i.e. of children being out of control – was vindicated by this one highly publicized event. This reaction did not mean that most parents feared that their children were murderers in the making. What it reflected was a sense of estrangement – 'do we really know them?'

The author, who lives in the sleepy Kent seaside village of Conyer, received a leaflet (see opposite) through his door in October 1995. This rather imaginative text – children throwing away hard drugs along with their used condoms – inadvertently reveals the profound anxieties of its authors. It suggests that, even in a small community like Conyer, where everyone knows everyone else by sight, the children inhabit a world which the adults neither know nor understand. For the 'Concerned Residents of Conyer', their children are strangers and they experience local teenagers as menacing. It seems that in this peaceful, if estranged, community, anything can happen. An impenetrable barrier seems to separate the generations. This is clearly a community that does not know itself.

That anything can happen can be affirmed by the most rare and exceptional experience. In comparison to the past, children today are relatively safe. During the years 1983–93, 57 children were killed by strangers in the UK – an average of five a year. The loss of life of any child is a tragedy – but when one considers that there are 12 million children in the UK, the risk of murder by a stranger is statistically negligible. And yet, because of a wider sense of insecurity, society continually warns children to be scared of strangers. Campaigns are

Dear residents

Hallowe'en is almost upon us again bringing with it the problems of 'Trick or Treat'. Concerns have been raised by residents about the children leading to a request that you discourage your children from taking part in 'Trick or Treat' and allowing them to be knocking on doors late at night.

Concerns have also been expressed about the telephone box at the corner of The Moorings being used as a meeting place by large groups of teenagers. Within the last few days, needles, hard drugs, used condoms and empty bottles and cans have been found littered around the telephone box. The police have been informed.

- **Do you know where your child is when he or she goes out to play?**

- **Are you aware that your child may be taking drugs and/or alcohol?**

- **What would you do if your child fell onto used needles?**

From Concerned Residents of Conyer.

mounted with the explicit objective of inculcating in young children a mistrust of people they do not know. 'Stranger danger' helps turn the unthinkable into an all too frequent threat that preys on our imagination.

Whatever the situation, the tendency is to imagine the worst. That is why a relatively small number of child murders could be interpreted to mean that all children are at risk. The corollary of this concern for children is the belief that there are many strangers out there, who are capable of unspeakable deeds. Such expectations, reinforced by sensationalist accounts of a handful of violent crimes, have provided the foundation for a permanent sense of anxiety about the safety of children. At times, the image presented is that of children being under siege from violent strangers. The *Good Housekeeping* 'Childsafe Campaign' provides a good example of how the media dealt with the 'crisis of child safety':

> *Our mission is to make Great Britain a country where we don't have to fear the moment a toddler is out of sight, where teenagers can enjoy themselves without the worry of attack, where it is not necessary to travel inside a locked car for fear of assault or walk in terror in case a joyrider causes havoc, where children can go to school without the risk of violence and rape from their classmates.*[4]

The message contained in this declaration is that parents should fear the moment when a toddler is out of sight, that teenagers are sensible to worry about a physical attack and that it is necessary to travel in a locked car. The rest of the world is represented as a human jungle where violence consumes the child.

It is not just children, but literally newborn babies, who are at risk from strangers. A couple of highly publicized cases where newborn babies were stolen from the hospital by seriously disturbed women helped to turn baby wards into low-level security wings. The intense level of media attention paid to the rare instances of baby-snatching has contributed to widespread demands for hospital security. Consequently, the exercise of vigilance has become part of the ritual of postnatal care. Indeed, one of the first pieces of information provided for expectant parents concerns the security arrangements made for the protection of their babies. Concerned parents are now routinely told to demand to see the ID card and the photograph of anyone who picks up their babies. Such measures are strongly supported by parents, fearful that baby-snatchers lurking in hospital wards constitute a very real risk to their babies.

The institutionalization of security measures against baby-snatching is symptomatic of the temper of our times. Isolated acts of baby-snatching are by no means novel occurrences, but by focusing attention on this act, yet another potential danger has been conveyed to parents: they have been warned and are now expected to exercise caution. Every stranger they encounter on the hospital ward should now be assessed from the point of view of their baby's security. The cumulative effect of this process is that although newborn babies are not in any greater danger from strangers than before, parents are educated to worry about their offspring's security as they emerge from the womb.

The intrusion of the issue of policing into the proceedings of maternity wards is part of a wider process influencing relationships in society. Social life, with all of its complications and tensions, is increasingly having to cope with the continuous reformulation of ordinary experience as dangerous. Thus an unexceptional act like visiting the family doctor can now have security implications. Recently, the British medical press has drawn attention to the problem of 'patient violence'. Doctors can now call up a helpline, attend a workshop or read leaflets on the problem of patient violence. It is not clear whether patient violence is really on the increase or whether health professionals just feel more vulnerable. The definition of the danger is often imprecise and relates to the difficulty that doctors have in gaining patients' confidence in an increasingly disorienting system of health. One doctor warned that the 'strain put on the doctor–patient relationship by aggressive and demanding patients could lead to incidents of "surgery rage"'.[5] The characterization of a strained relationship as 'surgery rage' exemplifies the tendency to associate problematic encounters with a security agenda. And although 'surgery rage' has not yet acquired the status of 'road rage' or some other widely acclaimed public risk, it is only a matter of time before some tragic incident at a medical centre gives it a major media profile.

It is not just maternity wards and doctors' surgeries which have suddenly become dangerous places. Most social encounters and experiences now require a careful vetting of strangers. Following a long-established practice in the USA, the management of British nurseries and schools is increasingly subject to the exigencies of security concerns. Children are more and more socialized to regard strangers as one of life's many threats. Institutes of higher education carry on where schools leave off. A leaflet published by the National Union of Students' Women's Campaign titled 'Women's Safety in the Home' offers 48 tips on home security. Its message is that anyone can be a danger:

> All too often, attacks on women occur in the victim's own homes. In many of these cases, there is no forced entry by the assailant into the home. It is vital to practice caution when letting anyone – either strangers or acquaintances – into your home.[6]

The advice is absolutely clear; everyone - stranger or acquaintance - needs to be treated with caution. That acquaintances may be strangers in masquerade is the subtext of the leaflet.

The extension of security concerns into areas hitherto untouched by the fear of danger has been widely commented on. Platitudes to the effect that 'we live in a violent society' are often used to explain these developments. But whether society is indeed more violent than it was in the past and whether there has been an increase in the danger to the individual is far from clear. It is certainly the case that many of the most widely feared dangers have the character of an overreaction. Often statistically insignificant occurrences, like the harming of a baby on a maternity ward, stimulate nationwide anxiety and fear. The pervasive character of such reactions suggests that they are produced by factors that are to some extent separate from the specific events which generated them. It may well be that the demand for the institutionalization of security in new spheres of social life may be the result of basic existential insecurities.

Concern with security can also be interpreted as the outcome of a tendency towards the problematization of everyday life. Many basic relationships have lost their clarity regarding what can and what cannot be taken for granted. Of course human relationships have always been fluid and subject to modification, but what is new about today is not so much that relationships are changing, but that these relations are less mediated than previously. Thus the discussion of patient violence often misses the fundamental issue, which is that the doctor–patient relationship itself can no longer be taken for granted. It is interesting to note that the issue of *BMA News Review* which carried the warning about surgery rage also carried an advertisement for the BMA Stress Counselling Service for Doctors! Clearly, doctors not only fear their patients but are also uncertain about their role and themselves. They are as estranged from themselves as they are from those looking for their diagnosis.

The estrangement of doctors from their patients is paralleled by the reaction of British schoolteachers to their pupils. Teachers have gone on strike in Nottingham to force a school to get rid of a disruptive pupil. Instead of questions being asked about why teachers could not control a 13-year-old child, educators applauded the strike in April 1996. The NASUWT, the main union at the centre of the strike, appears to believe that schoolchildren represent a physical danger to beleaguered teachers. In its 1989 pamphlet, *Discipline in Schools*, the NASUWT writes of a general moral decline, claiming that children exhibit 'lower standards of acceptable behaviour' due to the 'aggressive, selfish, materialistic and violent society' that we live in. The implications of this assessment of children for the traditional teacher–pupil relationship are of course far-reaching. And, increasingly, the burden of responsibility for the loss of authority in the classroom is placed on the backs of children rather than of teachers.

Uncertainty about a variety of encounters has led to an increase in the numbers of strangers. The pattern whereby parents do not know their children, or doctors their patients, recurs in a variety of social situations. However, there is more to this process of estrangement, for what we anticipate when we encounter strangers are not pleasant surprises but some undefinable quality of danger. Thus strangers are not only people we do not know, but also those who we cannot trust. The principle of caution becomes the appropriate response to the ambiguities thrown up by our encounters with strangers.

Precautionary principle in childhood

It is in the sphere of children's lives that the institutionalization of caution has had the most far-reaching effect. During the past twenty years, concern with the safety of children has become a constant subject of discussion. Children are portrayed as permanently at risk from danger. Even a relatively balanced account of 'children at risk' regards childhood as a 'uniquely dangerous time of life'.[7] In Britain and the USA, concern for the security of children has led to a major reorganization of the childhood experience. Childhood activities such as roaming about with friends or walking to and from school are becoming increasingly rare experiences. There is now a well-established consensus that children should not be left on their own. Middle-class children in particular are now subject to constant adult policing.

It is paradoxical that the emergence of the intellectual fashion for children's rights coincides with the continuous erosion of the freedom that children have to play with each other. A well-documented study of children's mobility clearly illustrates this erosion of freedom. The study was based on two surveys – one carried out in 1971 and the other in 1990 – and showed a marked decline in the amount of activities that engaged the energies of junior school children during the weekend. The proportion of children who were allowed to cross roads on their own had also decreased. In 1971, nearly three-quarters of junior school children were allowed to cross the road on their own. This proportion had fallen to a half by 1990. However, the most dramatic changes involved the explosion of parental supervision. Between 1971 and 1990 the proportion of children taken to school by car had quadrupled. The authors of the study also estimated that during the twenty years between the two surveys, the number of activities that children undertook on their own was nearly halved.[8]

The fear of allowing children to roam on their own has acquired obsessional proportions. These fears are seldom oriented towards accidents at home and on the roads – the most important causes of injury and death to children. It is the danger of the stranger preying on vulnerable children which influences parental action. Various schemes have been devised to keep children busy after school hours – under adult supervision of course. Surveys indicate that children spend less time outdoors than did their parents' generation. Indeed, the concept of unsupervised children's activity - which used to be called play – is now interpreted as, by definition, a risk. Those who question the merits of the constant supervision of children are sometimes accused of reckless parenting. In some communities, parents who allow their children to walk to school unsupervised often become the subject of local gossip. Parental responsibility is increasingly associated with the willingness to supervise and chaperone children.

The restriction of children's mobility has predictable consequences for their development. Numerous reports on children's health have warned about the negative consequences of their sedentary lives. For example, a recently published three-year research project on children's heartbeats has alarmed British medical experts. The report indicated that most children did little exercise. It also noted that many of the games that used to be passed on from one generation to another are no longer played by children.[9] Other reports have linked a decline in British children's fitness to the decrease in the amount of time they spend walking and cycling. The First National Travel Survey demonstrated a fall of about 20 per cent in annual distance walked and 27 per cent in distance cycled between 1985 and 1993. The possible link between this decline in physical activity and the increasing trend towards obesity, particularly in girls, has been noted in the medical press.[10]

There have also been a number of articles and reports in the British media which have drawn attention to the high level of parental anxiety about children's safety. A survey by Barnardo's, the UK's largest children's charity, titled *Playing It Safe*, expressed strong concern about the erosion of children's mobility. It observed that anxiety over children's safety has reached 'unprecedented levels' to the 'detriment of parents and children'. It concluded that the restriction of children's mobility 'is clearly not good for children's development and independence'.[11]

The recognition by Barnardo's and other agencies that the reorganization of childhood around the principle of caution has a debilitating effect on children's health and development is a step in the right direction. Although such reports often usefully question the consequences of the reorganization of childhood, they often share its premise. The promotion of children's safety as an end in itself is virtually never questioned. This is not surprising, since even free spirits do not want to be accused of putting their or other children's lives at risk. When, during the course of a conversation amongst parents, someone remarks that 'we live in another world', its reference to the prevalence of unspecified dangers is clearly understood by all. Such sentiments, which now have the character of common sense, ensure that the significance attached to the 'protection' of children predominates.

The implications of reorganizing childhood around the precautionary principle are rarely explored in detail. The consequences of the loss of freedom for the quality of childhood have become a subject of public concern. And yet unsupervised activities are crucial experiences for child development. Some of the most character-forming childhood experiences occur in peer-group situations, free from adult supervision. Such unsupervised opportunities have allowed children to make mistakes, to learn from them and to acquire important social skills. The element of interaction between peers in unstructured and unregulated circumstances allows children to gain important lessons about personal relationships. The current emphasis on children's environments which are structured and supervised is unlikely to stimulate initiative and enterprise. But probably the greatest casualty of this totalitarian regime of safety is the development of children's potential. Playing, imagining and even getting into trouble contribute to that unique sense of adventure which has helped society forge ahead. A society that loses that sense of adventure and ambition does so at its peril, and yet that is precisely a possible outcome of a state of affairs where socializing children consists, above all, of inculcating fears in them.

There has been little discussion and even less research on the consequences of artificially shielding children from coming into contact with strangers. The possibility that the attempt to protect children from risk may actually make them less likely to be able to cope with the unexpected is rarely entertained. As children's lives become increasingly mediated through adults, the question worth asking is 'how much are they able to learn for themselves?' Some school texts offer advice to children about how to be streetwise, but experience suggests that those who are indeed streetwise did not learn that skill from a book. It is difficult to imagine how a child can become streetwise without being allowed on the streets. It may well be the case that those children whose lives have been conducted under constant adult supervision are peculiarly ill-suited to handle the problems thrown up by everyday life.

The consequences of educating children to fear strangers are also rarely placed under scrutiny. The equation of adult strangers with danger does little to protect the child. However, it provides an early lesson in cynicism about human nature. A recent Home Office video for schools, *Think Bubble*, offers a list of 'grown-ups you can trust' – police officer, security guard, shop assistant, mum with a pram. But everyone else personifies danger. The video advises children to run if any such stranger tries so much as to talk to them. In the same vein, a pamphlet published by KIDSCAPE, a campaign 'for children's safety', advises parents to teach their offspring that it is 'NEVER a good idea to talk to a stranger'. Such advice can help to consolidate anxiety and fear but it will do little to develop a child's sense of danger. If everybody is dangerous, children will not develop the ability to discriminate between friend and foe or how to spot trouble. The division of the world into people who can and cannot be trusted provides little guidance for the negotiation of the ambiguities of routine personal encounters.

Restraining childhood actually helps to extend the state of helpless or at least dependent immaturity. At what point does adult supervision cease to be necessary? And how do those who have been denied independent mobility learn to transcend their previous existence of dependency? Anecdotal evidence suggests that the loss of independence in childhood helps to prolong the phase where children find it difficult to take responsibility for themselves and for their actions. One manifestation of this process is the extension of the period of dependency on the parent.

There was a time when students applying for an undergraduate course would never dream of going with their parents to the university to be interviewed. In the 1960s and 1970s, most students associated going to universities with the idea of breaking away from their parents. Many would have been self-conscious and embarrassed to be seen in the company of adults on campus. During the past decade, a major change in practice has taken place. Students now arrive on campus to be interviewed with their parents. During the group discussions, it is the parents who dominate the discussion, while their offspring sit looking bemused. It is as if they are there to be handed over by their parents to another group of responsible adults.[12]

And even when students finally arrive on campus, they are still under the supervision of a parent. Not their biological parent, but the university in its new role of *in loco parentis*.

The assumption of the doctrine of *in loco parentis* by American and British universities is the logical consequence of the reorganization of childhood around the principle of caution. This doctrine, by which institutions of higher education were held to stand legally 'in place of the parents', influenced life on American campuses during the first part of the twentieth century. One of the outcomes of the student radicalism of the 1960s was to challenge this doctrine. According to one account:

following the turmoil of the 1960s and 1970s a broad consensus emerged among administrators at leading colleges and universities that students, even undergraduates, were adult consumers of education, capable of making their own life-style choices and of being responsible for the consequences.[13]

During this period campus life was unregulated. Students got on with their lives and regarded any attempt by campus authorities to regulate their social or political life as a gross infringement of their autonomy.

During the 1980s, the open and unregulated campus came under challenge. The shift from an open to a regulated campus was justified in the language of risk consciousness. Indeed, many of the panics which blew up in the wider society acquired a particularly intense form on campuses. Consequently, there was virtually no opposition to the campus authorities when they began to regulate the lives of students around the issue of health and safety. Whereas in the 1960s students rebelled against the paternalism of university authorities, in the 1980s, the regulation of campus life was accepted and often positively welcomed. The reorganization of campus life around the principle of caution is now an accomplished fact. Universities on both sides of the Atlantic are probably the most regulated public institutions. Codes of practices provide detailed guidance on the most intimate issues.

The reaction against the 1960s deregulation of university life has had important implications for the way in which the relationship between students and university authorities is perceived. Students are treated as not-quite-adults, who constantly need pastoral care and guidance. The very idea that students should be left to fend for themselves, to learn the habits of independence and self-reliance, has become antithetical to campus culture. Every area of student life has become problematized, and campus administrators boast about the quality of their support services. The frailty of the contemporary university student is assumed and therefore counselling is always on hand. Thus when a group of academics conducted a survey on sexual harassment on a campus in Pennsylvania, they informed the student respondents that if they experienced any distress from completing the survey, they were to get in touch with the university counselling centre.[14] Today, the idea that students should learn to cope with their distress has become distinctly eccentric.

The reorganization of campus life around the issue of health and safety reinforces the promotion of infantilism. Pedagogic techniques which may or may not be suitable for children have become fashionable amongst university educators. Lecturers who make students feel 'uncomfortable' or who pile on pressure are advised to adopt more enlightened techniques. The regulation of campus life, along with its message of caution, cannot but influence the experience of higher education. The effect of this process of prolonging the state of dependence is difficult to measure. In the case of the UK, this issue is further complicated by the fact that a growing proportion of undergraduates – 46 per cent in 1995 – now live at home with their parents. This shift from leaving home to go to university to staying with parents does not necessarily have long-term consequences. However, it is difficult to agree with Tony Higgins, the chairman of the Universities and Colleges Admissions Service, when he stated that 'perhaps it is as character-building to be living with parents between 19 and 22 as it is to go away'.[15]

Staying at home has become increasingly prevalent among young adults in general in the UK. According to a June 1996 survey by the research organization Mintel, more than half of 20–24-year-olds in the UK were still living at home with their parents. Press reaction to this report by Mintel tended to point the finger at economic factors. A standard reaction among critical commentators was to identify the new stay-at-home attitude among young people as a consequence of economic insecurity, caused by unemployment, low wages, the removal of welfare rights, cuts in student grants and so on. This one-sided economic analysis missed the point that, in previous times, many would have left the parental home precisely to escape from poverty and make their way in the world. People have often travelled around the globe in search of a job. Yet today, a large proportion of British youth reacts to the same economic problems by hiding away at home. Clearly there is something more than ordinary insecurity at work here – especially since those young people with decent jobs showed little inclination to fly the nest either.

One of the consequences of the operation of the principle of caution in childhood is the prolongation of the relation of dependence. It may even lead to a situation where it actually produces people who are less self-sufficent than in the past.. The paradox of the reorganization of contemporary childhood is that it extends the phase of parental dependency whilst truncating the important period of childish experimentation. All this is done in the name of protecting our children from undefined risks and risky strangers.

The most dangerous place in the world

The promotion of the value of safety is given intellectual coherence by the input of the academic community. Concern with safety, health, the environment, children and risk are integral to contemporary intellectual trends. However, those who write on these themes do not merely pronounce on their views, they also live by them. Thus the promotion of the value of caution is also pursued institutionally on American and British campuses. Academia practises what it preaches. As a result, campuses provide a fertile terrain for the breeding of panics.

Many of the most important studies on family and sexual violence have been based on surveys conducted with students on campus. This research has helped to create an association between university life (particularly in the USA) and sexual violence. The expectation that British universities are also a breeding ground for sexual violence is indicated by the following notice, in the May 1996 issue of *Network*, the newsletter of the British Sociological Association:

. . . pornography, street hassling, unwanted touching or staring, flashing . . .

Sexual Violence in Higher Education

Has it ever happened to you?

If you have experienced this, or know of someone who has, we would like to hear from you. We are conducting a national survey of students' experiences, as well as reviewing current policy and practice, and would like to talk to students in more detail about their experiences.

. . . obscene phone calls, coercive sex, threats and use of violence, rape . . .

The abstracting of a distinct 'student experience' and its linking to a variety of acts from staring to rape suggests that the outcome of this survey will be no great surprise. It will contribute to the growing prejudice which represents university life as an intensely dangerous experience.

It was during the late 1980s that campus crime was discovered in the USA. A small number of violent campus incidents provided the raw material for the construction of the image of the dangerous campus. American university authorities responded by monitoring and regulating the risks facing students. Campaigns were organized against the consumption of alcohol and of drugs. The new politics of regulation were oriented to keep outsiders outside of university property – dormitories and students' unions were closed to non-students on the grounds of preventing crime and limiting civil liability. However, the politics of regulation had more far-reaching effects in terms of their impact on the students themselves.

The new politics of regulation actively upheld the values of safety and responsibility. Restrictions on the consumption of alcohol are often justified on the grounds of curbing violence, sexism, racism or other forms of unacceptable behaviour. By linking the regulation of student behaviour to the wider question of violent crime, university authorities have managed to reorganize campus culture. Most surveys indicate that American students and academics are becoming increasingly worried about the problem of campus crime. The media have taken up this theme and have created the impression that campus crime is violent and getting more and more out of hand.[16]

On many campuses, educational crime prevention and safety pro-grammes are now mandatory. Hundreds of campuses have installed or updated emergency telephones or alarms. On many campuses, students are recruited to patrol and monitor the campus at night. Anti-crime initiatives are also flourishing on American campuses. Syracuse University has RAPE (Rape: Advocacy, Prevention and Education), SCARED (Students Concerned About Rape Education), CARE (Community Awareness for Residents through Education), and SAFE (Safety-Security Awareness for Employees). Several court decisions have addressed the issue of university liability to student victims of campus crime and have used the doctrine of foreseeability as the standard for establishing liability. The American Congress responded by passing the Crime Awareness and Campus Security Act of 1990, which mandates institutes of higher education to publicly report certain crime statistics and security policies. In this way 'campus crime' has joined the many newly constructed crimes of the 1980s.[17] And because it is now a 'distinct' crime, it may well attract an outburst of media publicity.

The fear of campus crime in the USA indicates more about the mood that prevails in the university milieu than about the growth of physical danger. Research suggests that perceptions of danger diverge sharply from the incidence of physical violence. In fact, the results of one study showed that campus rates of both violent crime and property crime have been falling, especially since 1985. Moreover, it showed that students were significantly safer on campus than in the cities and communities surrounding them.[18] Nevertheless, the idea that campuses are becoming more and more dangerous persists.

As with most American fashions, it was only a matter of time before the concern with campus crime was imported to the UK. During the 1990s campus safety has emerged as the main focus of student activity in the UK. Student newspapers began to report on the high incidence of crime. The Bristol university newspaper reported a survey carried out in Newcastle which indicated that 59 per cent of students suffered from crime. Similar findings were reported from other campuses.[19] Newspapers carried stories of how young teenage thugs could terrorize passive undergraduates in Cambridge, and the *Independent* ran a feature 'Easy marks for criminal classes'. The main theme of the article was that 'students are particularly vulnerable to crime'.[20] Following the pattern established in the USA, campus safety became a key issue in the UK.

In the UK the main promoters of campus safety are the students' unions. It is interesting to note how safety has replaced political and social campaigning on campuses. Students' unions are in the forefront of promoting sensitivity towards health and safety issues. Their publications provide advice on virtually every aspect of safety. For example, the 'Little Blue Book' given to every fresher on arrival at Oxford University reads like a cross between a medical and ethical manual. The blurb on its cover boasts that the 'Little Blue Book edited by students for students, provides clear and up to date information on contraception, abortion, sex-related diseases, drugs and other health matters'.[21] Other student union publications are devoted to the question of personal security. Students' unions advertise rape alarms and in some cases offer women-only minibuses at night.

Almost imperceptibly, students' unions have emerged as guardians of campus morality. A clear illustration of this trend was the student alcohol awareness campaign launched by the National Union of Students in September 1995. The NUS published *The Big Blue Book of Booze* to launch this event. Whereas in the past, getting drunk was perceived as an acceptable part of student life, today it is represented as an antisocial deviant activity. 'If alcohol were to be discovered today it would almost certainly be as illegal as heroin', warns the NUS in this publication. The message of safety, responsibility and restraint expresses the sentiments that are held to be virtuous by these young professional moralizers.

It is interesting to note that no one in the British media asked the question of what precipitated the student alcohol awareness campaign. Alcohol on campuses is not a novel phenomenon and no one even pretended to argue that there has been a increase in student alcoholism or alcohol-related deaths or diseases. So why has it become necessary to make students aware of alcohol? And why is it necessary to use scare tactics which equate the consumption of alcohol with that of heroin?

Protecting students from themselves seems as important as protecting them from others. The regulation of the life of university students represents an extension of the restraints imposed on the previous phase of childhood. Campuses provide a strange synthesis of articulate vulnerability. Here, extravagant claims about campus crime are expressed through sophisticated arguments about the problem of safety. Gradually, in terms of institutionalizing a prescribed form of behaviour, campus practices are beginning to resemble those of a religious community. On campus, no human relationship is allowed to evolve spontaneously and be left to chance. Detailed codes of conduct lay down guidelines about appropriate forms of behaviour between students and between teachers and students. Such carefully crafted codes of behaviour indicate that, here, everyone is a stranger and that therefore individual relations need to be conducted through clear rules and regulations.

In the name of enlightened campus opinion, curbs on behaviour and the regulation of personal life are justified and accepted. In the past such restraints were rationalized through an explicit moral code. This is not the case today. Advocates of the regulation of campus life justify their actions 'not in the name of a transcendent set of values, but because high risk behaviour is an irresponsible assault on the rights of others to health and safety'.[22] Consequently very few acts are self-consciously morally condemned. The issue is not the taking of drugs but whether or not this is done safely. Safe drinking or safe sex all convey the religion of self-limitation but in a secular form. This is an etiquette that does not denounce any specific mode of behaviour, except that of risk-taking and putting others at risk. In this way campuses can retain a reputation for free-thinking liberalism even as they institutionalize a regime of regulating behaviour.

The emergence of the issue of campus safety and the growing tendency to regulate interpersonal behaviour are bound up with perceptions of existential insecurity. Such perceptions reflect a sense of individual vulnerability, which is almost palpable on campuses. Contemporary intellectual trends reflect this heightened sense of self-estrangement. This is why universities are experienced as very dangerous places. Many of the contributions that have helped to normalize the tendency to panic are influenced by the estranged atmosphere of the university milieu.

Individual insecurity and social isolation are what helps stimulate the image of a world of risky strangers. Such anxieties invariably raise the question, 'who can you trust?', which is the subject of the next chapter.

Notes

1. See O'Riordan, T. and Cameron, J. (eds) (1994) *Interpreting the Precautionary Principle* (London: Earthscan), pp. 17–18.

2. Cited in Mullan (1996) *Deconstructing the Problem of Ageing* (London: unpublished manuscript), p. 27.

3. *The Sunday Times*, 28 November 1993.

4. Cited in Hay, C. (1995) 'Mobilization through Interpellation: James Bulger, Juvenile Crime and the Construction of a Moral Panic', *Social and Legal Studies*, vol. 4, p. 214.

5. *BMJ News Review*, 19 June 1996, p. 18.

6. 'Women's Safety in the Home', leaflet published by the NUS Women's Campaign, London, 1993.

7. Roberts, H., Smith, S. and Bryce, C. (1995) *Children at Risk? Safety as a Social Value* (Buckingham: Open University Press), p. 1.

8. Hillman, M., Adams, J. and Whiteleg (1990) *One False Move . . . A Study of Children's Independent Mobility* (London: PSI Publishing), pp. 43 and 87.

9. Cited in *The Sunday Times*, 17 March 1996.

10. See 'Why Are Fewer Children Walking to School?', *Medical Monitor*, 24 July 1996.

11. Barnardo's (1995) *Playing It Safe* (London: Barnardo's), pp. 3 and 22.

12. Interview with F. Furedi and others in the *Independent*, 5 December 1996.

13. Simon, J. (1994) 'In the Place of the Parent: Risk Management and the Government of Campus Life', *Social and Legal Studies*, vol. 3, p. 16.

14. See Cleary, J. *et al.* (1994) 'Sexual Harassment of College Students: Implications for Campus Health', *Journal of American College Health*, vol. 43, p. 11.

15. Cited in the *Guardian*, 9 August 1996.

16. See 'Fear Prompts Self-defense as Crime Comes to College', *New York Times*, 7 September 1994.

17. See Fisher, B. (1995) 'Crime and Fear on Campus', *Annals of the American Academy of Political and Social Science*, vol. 87, pp. 183–91.

18. See Volkwein, J., Szelest, J. and Lizotte, B. (1995) 'The Relationship of Campus Crime to Campus and Student Characteristics', *Research in Higher Education*, vol. 36, no. 6.

19. See *Epigram*; 25 January 1995.

20. See the *Independent*; 4 January 1996; for an account of what happened at Cambridge, see the *Daily Telegraph*; 6 August 1996.

21. The Little Blue Book Committee (1992).

22. Simon, (1994), p. 31.

CHAPTER 6

Who Can You Trust?

In a world of risky strangers, it is difficult to trust. Indeed, the fear of strangers and of risks is proportional to the decline of trust. Increasingly, relationships between people, even those who live in the same neighbourhood or community, are characterized by a lack of clarity about the expected form of behaviour. Under these circumstances, the question that is invariably posed is 'what can you trust them to do?' To describe this state of affairs, an American social scientist has with prescience coined the phrase 'neighbourhoods without neighbours'. This term refers to people who live next to each other and are close spatially but remain isolated from one another in other respects. If you do not know very much about your neighbours it is difficult to feel any affinity towards them. If you do not know what your neighbours do for a living, it is easy to imagine that they are up to no good. And if even the children of different families are not allowed out to spontaneously engage with each other, there is little common interest to build upon. This absence of common interest minimizes the role of mutual obligations amongst people inhabiting the same neighbourhood.

In Chapter 5 the damaging consequences of society's preoccupation with children's safety were discussed. There are many reasons for the obsessive manner in which society upholds the safety of children, but probably one of the most important factors in the rising tide of the adult supervision of children is the emergence of neighbourhoods without neighbours. In the UK and in the USA, parents cannot rely on adults in their community to assume a measure of responsibility for the collective socializing of their children. In such circumstances parents regard others not as potential allies in the education of their children, but either as indifferent passers-by or, worse still, as risky strangers. In societies where neighbours and other adults assume a degree of responsibility for keeping an eye on children, attitudes towards their safety are far less obsessive.

A comparative study of children's independent mobility in the UK and Germany concluded that there is far less parental supervision in the latter than in the former. German parents put far fewer restrictions on the independent mobility of their children at all age levels. According to the authors, one of the reasons why German parents are more likely than their British counterparts to allow their children out on their own is because they expect other adults to keep an eye on them. The study notes:

> German children out alone are much more under the general supervision of adults on the street whom parents know can and will, if necessary, act in loco parentis. In parks, on buses and trams, and en route to any destination, children will be observed and 'guided' if their behaviour falls short of the standard expected. This serves as a powerful control mechanism and undoubtedly generates a feeling of security for parents, and others who operate this mutual surveillance network.[1]

This sense of security which parents in Germany have regarding their children's independent activity is based on the expectation that other adults will do the right thing. This requires a level of trust, which is conspicuous by its absence in the Anglo-American context. In the UK and the USA, adults are not expected to reprimand other people's children. If they did, their efforts would most likely be met with hostility from the parents of the children concerned.

According to the American author Francis Fukuyama, 'trust is the expectation that arises within a community of regular, honest, and co-operative behaviour, based on commonly shared norms, on the part of other members of that community'.[2] Of course, such expectations are always qualified by misunderstanding and the fluidity of social arrangements. Moreover, elements of conflict continually restrict the range of relationships where trust expectations can be realistically pursued. Nevertheless, within most communities there exists a system of formal and, more importantly, informal understanding about what people can expect from each other. As the saying goes, there is even 'honour among thieves'.

One of the factors contributing to the growth in the number and variety of strangers has been the increasing lack of clarity of the terms on which people relate to each other. According to many commentators, such lack of clarity has led to the weakening of trust, which in turn has had profoundly destructive consequences for society. Fukuyama has observed that *the decline of trust and sociability in the United States is also evident in any number of changes in American society: the rise of violent crime and civil litigation; the breakdown of family structure; the decline of a wide range of intermediate social structures like neighbourhoods, churches, unions, clubs, and charities; and the general sense among Americans of a lack of shared values and community with those around them.*[3]

The other side of this process is social isolation, vulnerability and a heightened sense of being at risk.

Politicians have come to recognize that their political, ideological and moral links with the electorate are fragile. Traditional forms of party politics, political values and identities have little purchase on an evidently disenchanted public. Fewer and fewer people are prepared to vote, and fewer still are interested in getting involved in party politics. In the UK, membership of the major political parties has fallen by half since 1980. During the same period, political party membership in France has declined by two-thirds, and in Italy by 51 per cent. By comparison, the German figure looks good: total membership fell by only 9 percent, probably because of an influx of new recruits from the east.

The decline of party membership coincides with a wider disengagement from political life. Today, people's idealism and hopes are rarely invested in a belief in political change, and individuals rarely develop their identities through some form of political attachment. Thirty years ago, an individual might have identified herself as a Labour woman, whose outlook was shaped by her belief in a socialist future and whose relationships in the present were with a community that shared this broad view. In the same way, for many members of the Conservative Party, to be a Tory really meant something. It involved an important source of self-definition and involved participation in an active social network. Today the question of who you vote for is seen as barely significant, and self-identity is viewed far more in terms of individuals' lifestyles, cultural habits and personal experiences.

It is not just political institutions that are experiencing a decline in active support. British trade unions have been effectively destroyed as effective organizations of working-class solidarity. Official membership figures have declined from the 1979 peak of 13 million to under 7 million in 1996. The fall in union membership is only part of the story. Membership itself has lost any great significance – unions mean very little to the people they are meant to represent. For most people, their membership of a union does not have much impact on their self-identity.

The pattern of declining popular involvement is repeated in relation to virtually every public institution. The National Federation of Women's Institutes, the Mothers' Union and the National Union of Towns-women's Guilds have all seen their memberships fall by nearly half since 1971. The Red Cross Society, the British Legion, the RSPCA, the Guides and the Boy Scouts (though not the Cubs and the Brownies) have all suffered major falls in membership over the past twenty years. Not even relatively recently established organizations, like the Green Party, are immune from these trends. In passing, it is worth noting that the enduring popularity of the Cubs and Brownies has more to do with the increasing demand by parents for safe and supervised environments for their children than with anything else.

The general loss of trust in authority goes way beyond the decline in the membership of public organizations. During the past decade, some of the UK's most treasured institutions have experienced a loss of prestige. The welter of marital strife and scandal surrounding the monarchy has led to a widespread questioning of its role. The Church of England increasingly appears anachronistic or absurd, or often both. The BBC and the Civil Service have been ravaged by market forces and rancorous internal conflicts. The loss of authority of these institutions has been paralleled by the growth of cynicism, apathy and disbelief. The contempt in which politics and politicians are held by the public highlights this palpable sense of social malaise. This sentiment is eloquently captured in the popular American television series, *The X Files*. This programme, which peddles the idea that government is one big cover-up, has a message which is devastatingly straightforward: 'Trust no one'.

The loss of trust in authority does not merely pertain to the domains of politics, religion and culture. Many of the professions – e.g. doctors, scientists – have also lost prestige and authority. The explosion of litigation in the field of medicine indicates that the image of the trusting patient unquestioningly accepting the doctor's advice has been overtaken by events. Suspicion towards science is particularly intense. Instead of trusting the expert opinion of the scientist, many people are disposed to look for a hidden agenda.

Indeed, the loss of public trust in science is one of the most striking expressions of the general erosion of legitimacy and authority. A tendency to mistrust scientific claims has helped to fuel public unease about the consequences of technological developments. Many of the panics about environmental and health-related issues demonstrate an explicit rejection of the claims of scientists on the subject. Mistrust of science is one of the most visible elements in the growth of risk consciousness itself.

The exhaustion of public trust has become an important subject of discussion in recent years. Monographs written by academics have suggested that the weakening of trust relations constitutes one of the central problems facing Western societies. This literature certainly confirms that there is a relationship between the decline of trust and the growth of risk consciousness.[4] How does this relationship work itself out and what is the explanation for the exhaustion of relations of trust?

The question of expertise

Cynicism towards expertise, particularly that of science, is often presented as one of the most important contributing factors to the development of risk consciousness. Suspicion concerning the claims of science is certainly widespread. The theme of scientists going beyond acceptable limits, explored in films like *Jurassic Park*, finds a ready resonance in society. The media representation of science reflects a clearly discernible shift from a positive evaluative tone to one that is increasingly critical, if not hostile. One of the ironies of our times is that while society is more dependent on science and technology than ever before, it is also more suspicious of their consequences.

Suspicion of science is explained in a number of different ways. Those who believe that this suspicion has good causes suggest that it is based on the awareness of technological development and its potentially destructive impact. Thus the German sociologist Ulrich Beck argues that risk consciousness has emerged 'against a continuing barrage of scientific denial, and is still suppressed by it'. And he adds that 'science has become the protector of a global contamination of people and nature'.[5] From this standpoint, science is to be not only mistrusted but also condemned. Here, Beck affirms the wisdom of not trusting science rather than analysing its emergence. This view may correspond to aspects of the public mistrust of science but it does not explain it. For Beck, this needs little explanation because risk consciousness is self-evidently linked to the failures of science.

Other writers emphasize the very growth of expert systems as the main contributing factor to the general mistrust of expertise. Some argue that the growing specialization of expertise contributes to the growth of unintended consequences. One of these consequences is the fragmentation of expert knowledge, which in turn makes it difficult for people to have access to reliable knowledge. It is suggested that people's faith in science is further undermined by public disputes between experts.[6] Others argue that with the tremendous increase in information, society becomes overloaded with the facts and people inevitably find it difficult to know what to believe.

The main problem with the discussion on the weakening of trust in expert systems is the tendency to explain this process in its own terms. But the crisis of public confidence in science is unlikely to be the outcome of a dynamic that is internal to itself. Confidence in any institution is shaped by a variety of influences, many of which are generated by forces which operate over society as a whole. The emphasis in the decline of trust in expert systems is quite misplaced in a situation where *all* forms of authority are liable to be questioned. The exhaustion of trust relations may well exist independently of any particular type of activity. It influences the interaction between neighbours as much as it impacts on the relationship between people and experts.

In any case, the public mistrust of science should not be confused with a general weakening of confidence or reliance on expertise. It is possible to argue that society's relationship to expertise is more ambiguous than most authors suggest. It appears that some forms of expertise are more mistrusted then others. In this respect, the strong anxieties provoked by the human genome project are worthy of note. This international programme, aimed at first mapping, and then sequencing, all of the genes in the human genome has met with a very mixed public reaction. Despite the promise that this research holds out for the better understanding and treatment of genetic disease, many commentators warned that this project was nothing short of playing God. Research into biotechnology and reproductive technology is also often criticized on the grounds of its 'unnatural' consequences.

Hostility to scientific research is invariably expressed in the vocabulary of the precautionary principle and always warns of the danger of risks. It is based on the conviction that human intervention in nature can only be for the worse. Critics of genetics and reproductive technology affirm their general fear of the unknown and an instinctive dislike of tampering with nature. Their hostility to scientific expertise is particularly focused on the most path-breaking, novel and adventurous initiatives. Such initiatives provoke a hostile reaction precisely because they are novel and therefore encroach upon the unknown. Since the unknown is by definition a dangerous country, innovative science becomes a threat.

The hostile reaction towards path-breaking science – science that extends the boundaries of the human imagination – suggests that what is at issue is not a general mistrust of expert systems but rather of particular types of expertise. Evidence suggests that the focus of society's suspicion is experimentation and innovation. This suspicion, which is well established in relation to the field of social and political experimentation, is also directed against scientific innovation. On the other hand, the expertise which is critical of experimentation is automatically assured of a positive hearing. Thus scientists who counsel caution and who call for self-limitation are seldom mistrusted. For example, environmental scientists are not exposed to the kind of mistrust that their colleagues experience in the field of embryology. The recent dispute between Shell and Greenpeace indicates that certain types of expert can always count on public confidence. In 1995, when Shell tried to dump the Brent Spar oil platform in the Atlantic Ocean, the environmental group Greenpeace launched an international campaign to stop it. Greenpeace sought to back its campaign with the argument that the dumping of Brent Spar at sea could cause unforeseen damage. This view was virtually unanimously accepted by the media. Under pressure from public hostility, Shell gave up its plan and abandoned its project. The speed with which the battle lines were drawn and the swift humiliation of Shell indicated the strength of public trust in Greenpeace's science. Greenpeace's claims were later exposed as misleading, and the organization had to apologize for getting its facts wrong. However, given society's worship of caution, such 'mistakes' are unlikely to diminish the public's trust of those who warn of the danger of tampering with nature.

Society's selective relationship with expertise is also shown by the emergence of a variety of new and influential experts. The past two decades have seen the consolidation of a distinct contemporary form of expertise. It is an expertise that is characteristic of a society that lacks confidence about its future direction. This new expertise flourishes on uncertainty and on the lack of clarity in many of the basic relations between people. The new expertise preaches the message that no one should be expected to cope with the uncertainties of life and that everyone is entitled to benefit from the skills of professional advisers. In the past, the provision of such advice was the monopoly of religious figures. Today, advice and guidance has been transformed into an expertise that is highly specialized and institutionalized.

This new expertise works at all levels of society. The world of business and industry has seen the phenomenal growth of the field of consultancy. The advice of outside consultants is now widely solicited on a variety of matters which were traditionally seen as the provenance of management. A cynical view of this new practice is that management now calls on consultants to take decisions for which it does not want to be held accountable. The rise of the consultant reflects both a lack of confidence of management in itself and the weakening of trust relations within the organization.

Another expert who clearly reflects the mood of the time is the facilitator. The use of facilitators to chair meetings and to manage group interactions reflects the general belief that, left on their own, people are not able to deal with each other. In many organizations, it is believed that an expert facilitator is called for to co-ordinate the interaction of colleagues. The growth of this expertise is a symptom of the growing sense of estrangement, where the most fundamental forms of human interaction are represented as requiring a difficult skill which only highly trained experts possess.

The weakening of taken-for-granted relations and of trust is clearly paralleled by the professionalization of everyday life. The professionalization of everyday life has undermined routine relations and has flourished on account of the weakening of fundamental human bonds. Consequently, areas of human activity which people learned as they went along are being increasingly reassigned to experts. This development is particularly striking in the professionalization of parenting. Experts now provide 'education for fatherhood' and run workshops and classes in parenting. Such experts continually emphasize the 'difficulties' and the complicated 'skills' required of parents. The transformation of parenting from a routine expectation of adulthood to a skill indicates the low estimation in which people are seen. What humanity has coped with since the beginning of time now requires the certification of experts.

The professionalization of everyday life can also be seen in the astounding growth of counselling. Counselling has become institutionalized in British society. These new experts advise people on virtually every aspect of life. Some of the areas where counselling has become well established are indicated below.

Counselling for what?

Abuse	Illness
Alcohol	Intercultural and race
Bullying	Men's groups
Career counselling and guidance	Old age
	One-parent families
Childline and child help	Phobias
Couples and marriages	Pregnancy and abortion
Co-counselling	Rape
Crisis	Redundancy and unemployment
Death and bereavement	
Disability	Religious
Drop-in centres	Schoolchildren
Drugs	Self-mutilation
Eating disorders	Sexual dysfunction
Feminist therapy	Singles and divorce
Fertility treatment	Trauma and disaster
Gambling	Victim support
Gay and lesbian	Winning the lottery
HIV and AIDS	Youth

It is worth noting that, despite the absence of any serious empirical evidence regarding the efficacy of counselling, there is no serious questioning of its growing influence.

The professionalization of everyday life has important implications for human relations. It helps to establish a new source of expert authority to which the parties of a relationship can refer for advice. Such counselling does not merely assist but actually alters the relationship. For example, how do parents parent, if their children are encouraged to take problems to counsellors in their school? According to a discussion of the counselling service in Canterbury and Thanet Health Authority, children of any age can have confidential access to counsellors in their schools.[7] In such circumstances, where children's problems are shared with experts rather than their parents, parents by definition become one of a number of competing sources of authority. The implications of such a development are straightforward. The complex relationship between parent and child becomes mediated through expert opinion. As the idea that 'parent knows best' gives way to the conviction that the welfare of the child is best articulated by a professional expert, parenting becomes increasingly mystified.

The transformation of human relationships through their professionalization creates a steady demand for expertise. The professionalization of everyday life creates its own demand for more counsellors and other experts. This happens because the new experts justify their role on the grounds that 'people need their help'. In this way, they at once emphasize their special skills and highlight the lack of competence of ordinary people to deal with their affairs. Although such experts always claim to 'empower' their clients, their every action has the effect of reinforcing people's lack of confidence in themselves.

Professional helpers are rarely aware how their 'helping' contradicts their claim to empower. For example, a recently published report advocating the setting up of self-help groups in the UK minimizes the tension between professional intervention and self-help. 'While autonomy is the hallmark of self help groups, their autonomy as well as their effectiveness may depend on receiving support from outside', noted the author of the report. The possibility that the concept of autonomy may sit uneasily with dependence on professional help is dismissed with the statement that these groups' 'autonomy may depend on receiving appropriate support'. The premise of this approach is that potential members of self-help groups are like children who need to be confident so that they can become confident adults. That is why the author of the report assigns a central role to the facilitator of the group. Although, she argues, some groups require 'facilitators more than others', they all seem to need professional support.[8] The incompetence of potential recruits to self-help groups and, by definition, the necessity for a professional facilitator seems to be beyond question.

The incompetence of ordinary people is the fundamental premise for professional intervention in personal life. Sykes has noted how from the beginning 'the marketing of parental incompetence has set the tone for the larger marketing of therapeutic techniques'.[19] The starting point for all the new 'helping' professionals is the incompetence of their clients.

In many respects, counsellors resemble traditional priests who have encouraged and lived off human fears for centuries. Such expertise thrives on the idea that people cannot be expected to cope on their own. It is interesting to note that the lack of confidence that people have about their ability to manage their affairs also extends to the church. In Britain, the Anglican Church now offers counselling to its priests about appropriate forms of behaviour with their women parishioners. That even spiritual leaders require counselling is a clear vindication of the claims of the new expertise.

The expansion of counselling is one of the clearest indications of not the decline but the ascendancy of expertise. Indeed there is little contradiction between the general decline of trust and the growing influence of expert systems. The erosion of trust can best be interpreted as the decline of trust in ourselves. This weakening of self-belief and the idea that we are capable of managing elementary relations between people has created a demand for experts. The growth of such expertise is proportional to the decline of belief in the problem-solving skills of people.

The influence of expertise is evident in all the areas which are bound up with existential security. The field of health offers an interesting illustration of the selective way in which expertise is regarded. Although there is a palpable sense of mistrust of the medical profession, there is also an unprecedented interest in health. Experts who can claim that their therapy is 'natural' or 'holistic' or is based on some 'ancient' practice have benefited from the decline of trust in medical science.

One of the main consequences of the professionalization of everyday life has been the growing public concern with health. There has been an ever-widening definition of health. It now includes areas of life which in the past lay outside conventional medicine. Alternative medicine and therapies flourish precisely because they claim to go beyond biomedicine. People trying to sell their expertise use the term holistic to draw attention to the all-embracive character of their skills. That means that everything – literally every form of behaviour – becomes medicalized. Thus today we routinely use terms like 'sexual health' to refer to matters that in the past were clearly seen as bound up with existential issues. This medicalization of behaviour in turn increases the demand for expertise.

It is in the field of sexuality that destructive consequences of the professionalization of everyday life become particularly evident. The proliferation of new 'information' about sex helps to create the impression that there is some mysterious skill or sexual knowledge which can be transmitted to the ignorant client. Experts continually proclaim their disappointment at the ignorance of their clients – especially of young males – and by implication advertise their indispensability to the maintenance of the sexual health of the nation. Sex education is now declared to be mandatory – the only responsible way of socializing the new generation – but practical information is obscured by excessive moralizing. The adult supervision of childhood acquires its most grotesque formulation in smug assumptions about the virtues of moral-based sex education. The idea that children should find out about sex on their own, and without professional guidance, is dismissed as hopelessly outdated by the new experts of sexual health. Some experts, who realize that children actually learn from each other, now seek to co-opt young people to run 'peer-to-peer' sex education as a means of controlling the flow of information.

The growth of new experts in the field of counselling and health does not necessarily mean that they are the automatic recipients of public trust. Nevertheless the influence of such expertise on individual action and behaviour is manifestly significant. One example – that of health promotion – demonstrates how the mobilization of expert opinion influences human behaviour.

According to the British government survey *Social Trends*, there have been marked changes over the past 30 years in the types of food eaten in households. They comment that 'doctors advise eating less fats containing saturated fatty acids, to avoid high levels of cholesterol in the blood and the risk of heart disease'. According to the report, this advice has had a major impact on household consumption: 'there has been a switch in household consumption from butter, firstly towards margarine and more recently to low and reduced fat spreads'. It noted that the 'average person drinks less milk today than in 1961'. Following expert advice, people are also eating less meat than previously. The consumption of meat has fallen steadily during the past 30 years. In 1992, each person ate, on average, under five ounces of beef and veal per week, only about half the amount consumed in 1961. Lamb and mutton consumption has fallen more sharply; the average amount consumed in 1992 had dropped to almost a third of the figure 30 years ago.[10]

What is remarkable is the authority which health experts now exercise over people's diet. The UK has not been known before for its observance of dietary laws. The Church of England never dictated what went on in the kitchen, as Islam or Judaism did. However, dietary customs now popular in Britain carry strong moral overtones. For example, people who eat meat in the presence of a vegetarian are often made to feel ashamed. Today, health experts can pronounce on the wisdom of eating this or that or avoiding a particular dish and can expect to influence people's behaviour. Clearly, trust in some types of expertise is still strong.

The differential response of society to expertise indicates a more ambiguous process than one would at first expect. There is intense suspicion of the expertise that is based around the advocacy of experimentation and innovation. The term 'experiment' no longer has merely a technical connotation. It is perceived as something that at the very least needs to be controlled or supervised by some public agency. Those who experiment are assumed to be irresponsible – unless they can prove otherwise. In contrast, expertise that is formed around the promotion of risk avoidance and of safety is likely to enjoy respect and authority. No one who counsels caution is ever likely to be accused of irresponsibility. Someone who forces the postponement of the trial of a new drug and thereby delays the production of a medicine which others desperately need is unlikely to be accused of putting life needlessly into jeopardy. The scientist in charge of the experiment, on the other hand, is likely to be charged with playing God.

Finally, mistrust produces its own experts. There is now a veritable army of consultants, facilitators and counsellors, whose fortunes depend on the continued erosion of trust relations. This expertise thrives on the belief that it is not right to trust yourself and others. Whatever their motives and aims – many of which are no doubt honourable – their cumulative effect is to weaken the capacity of humans to trust themselves.

Breakdown of community

Another argument used to explain the problem of trust is the growth of individualism and the breakdown of community. Commentators have remarked that the rise of individualism, especially in the 1980s, has been at the expense of sociability and civic-mindedness. Many key social problems, such as family breakdown and crime, are attributed to the intense sense of individualism, which is supposed to prevail in most communities. Such arguments are based on the assumption that if individual self-interest is allowed to develop unhindered, conflicts of interests will override relations of trust.

Many of the warnings concerning the destructive dynamic of individualism are based on the insights of nineteenth-century sociologists like Emile Durkheim. Durkheim argued that a society which was composed of isolated individuals pursuing their own narrow objectives could not survive for long. According to Durkheim, calculating individuals pursuing their self-interest undermined social solidarity. To overcome this danger, argued Durkheim, society required a morality of co-operation and a network of secondary institutions which bound people together.[11] Such secondary institutions – churches, co-operative societies, professional associations etc. – help to mediate the pursuit of self-interest by creating collective bonds.

Today, many observers argue that not only has individualism gone too far, but that with the erosion of secondary institutions the foundations for relations of trust have been badly damaged. This is the burden of the argument of Francis Fukuyama's work, *Trust*. According to Fukuyama, the USA is in danger of losing its 'art of association'. This ability to associate is based on the strength of commonly shared values. When such values are influential, it facilitates the subordination of individual interests to those of larger groups. This process leads to the consolidation of trust. Fukuyama contends that, today, individualism is less and less curbed by commonly shared values. He observed that the 'inherent tendency of rights-based liberalism to expand and multiply those rights against the authority of virtually all existing communities has been pushed towards its logical conclusion'.[12] As a result, the USA has experienced a decline of sociability. According to Fukuyama, the clearest manifestation of the erosion of relations of trust is the large amount of money devoted to keeping more than 1 per cent of the population behind bars and to employing an army of lawyers so that American people can sue each other. Both of these costs, 'which amount to a measurable percentage of gross domestic product annually, constitute a direct tax imposed by the breakdown of trust in society', writes Fukuyama.[13]

Fukuyama's thesis roughly coincides with the consensus that the main task facing Western societies is the rescuing of the community and the establishment of a new relationship between it and the pursuit of individual self-interest. This communitarian consensus regards the 1980s as the decade when the situation got out of hand. It is commonplace today to look back upon the 1980s as a decade of greed that went too far. The popular version of this argument is exemplified in Oliver Stone's caricature of the acquisitive trader Gordon Gekko in the film *Wall Street*, who proclaims to an audience of shareholders that 'Greed is good'. This culture of greed, which ignored the destructive consequences of unrestrained egoism, is held responsible for the breakdown of elementary forms of social solidarity and the weakening of trust.

There is little doubt that the 1980s saw an acceleration in the disintegration of social solidarity and of communities. During this period, virtually all forms of collective institutions became weakened. There is little doubt that as relationships that had bound people together lost their salience, the sentiment of trust suffered. There is also little doubt that the process of individuation has contributed to the consolidation of the consciousness of risk. But the recognition of the strength of individuation should not be confused with the alleged ascendancy of individualism. Individuation, which involves the release of individuals from pre-existing obligations and institutions, does not automatically lead to the ascendancy of the individual. Thus the weakening of community and relations of trust is not necessarily the consequence of the rise of an unrestrained individualism.

The central paradox of the 1980s is that the attempt by the Reagan and Thatcher regimes to promote the individual actually had the effect of undermining individuals. These governments were far more successful in breaking trade unions and in destroying other forms of solidarities than in liberating the individual entrepreneur. This is because once social solidarities were dismembered, individuals were left isolated and vulnerable. The confidence that collective identity generated in the past was dissipated. Instead, individuals came to experience circumstances as forces beyond their control.

Individuation without a parallel process of reintegration into some new social network can contribute to the creation of an atmosphere of mistrust. In particular it has the effect of altering the interactions between people. Where once neighbours and colleagues might have been seen as friends and allies, today they are more likely to be perceived as competitors and as potential threats. Of course people are not really at war with each other. The incidence of crime, warring neighbours and harassment at work is much exaggerated. However, once the familiarity of a common endeavour and outlook is undermined, things begin to look different. Other people start to look like strangers instead of friends.

The decline in solidarity has not been paralleled by the emergence of a confident culture of individualism. Despite all the discussion devoted to the problem of individualism, these confident egotistical individuals are conspicuous by their absence. The process of individuation has not produced a culture of confident individualism, because of society's attitude towards change, experimentation and the future. British schools have begun to stigmatize competitive sports, and single-minded ambition is often portrayed as a symptom of some illness. At a time when society is suffering from a failure of nerve, individuation has the tendency to weaken ambition and, in particular, the disposition to take risks. Thus the erosion of relations of trust has coincided with the process of individuation but *not* with the growth of individualism.

Those who bemoan the contemporary era as that of the egotistical individual actually ignore one of the central features of our times. The decline of old collectivities – trade unions, local communities and political associations – has not given rise to active, outgoing individualism. It has become fashionable to describe society today as one which is uniquely individual. However, such descriptions fail to account for the significant anti-individual trends that dominate culture. The philosophy of the 'caring nineties', with its emphasis upon people showing caution, concern and restraint for the good of the community, is often presented as an antidote to the 'greedy eighties'. One of the most fashionable themes of contemporary political discourse is to attack the selfishness and the egoism of the yuppie culture, and to uphold a romanticized 'community' over self-centred individualism. It has become fashionable to criticize 'fat cats' on high salaries and conspicuous consumption. Such themes are sustained by the philosophy of caution, which criticizes those who go too far and thereby put others at risk.

Instead of the confident individual, today's society flatters the victim or the survivor. The influence of the principle of self-limitation ensures that individuals as much as the community are in need of repair. The widely held misconception about the ascendancy of the individual is entirely understandable. The growth of individuation and the weakening of solidarity has helped create an impression of an atomized existence – where unrestrained egoism sweeps everything before it. But this impression is only half true, for the highly fragmented individual is actually held back and restrained by a society whose main demand is that of caution and which cannot accommodate itself to the spirit of experimentation. Thus the distinct feature of society today is not the unprecedented flowering of the individual but the weakening both of a sense of collectivity and of individual aspiration.

When you can't trust yourself

The decline of trust can only be understood within the context of the fundamental changes influencing Western societies. It is ironic that societies which not so long ago celebrated their triumph over the Soviet

Union are now so deeply affected by a pervasive sense of social malaise. As noted previously, society is gripped by a profound sense of new limits as to what is possible. An intense consciousness of environmental limits is complemented by widespread concern about the possible side-effects of any new initiative, and the pervasive sense of risk extends from a suspicion of science to an anxiety about strangers.

The prevailing suspicion of experimentation and the continuous exhortation to exercise caution reflect an unprecedented level of self-doubt amongst those who run society. A lack of faith in the efficacy of human intervention has become a defining feature of modern society. The absence of a confident individualism is bound up with these trends. If human action is ineffective or is likely to lead to destructive outcomes, confidence in the individual becomes difficult to sustain. It is this perception of human action which has influenced attitudes towards the individual. Doubts about the efficacy of human intervention reveal a pessimistic perspective on humanity. Little significance is attached to the transformative potential of action. Implicitly there is a deeply held rejection of the idea of a self-determining agent.

The issue of who you can trust cannot be separated from what constitutes one of the defining features of contemporary social and political life, which is *the diminished importance attached to subjectivity*. Today's culture of limits ascribes a minimal role to the subject – to effective human action. In such circumstances, individualism acquires a meaning that is quite specific to a culture which counsels limits and caution. What emerges is an individualism focused on survival rather than on the drive to realize potential. Moreover, this leads to an outlook where individuals are perceived as victims of their circumstances rather than as makers of their destiny. The defining feature of the subject becomes its passive side. Thus, the subject is distanced from the future and has no role in the shaping of this far-away place.

The diminished importance attached to subjectivity is bound up with the tendency to question the scope available for individual action. There is little room for the pretensions of the hero. Instead, people are perceived through an entirely different prism. Society feels far more comfortable with losers than with winners. Those who have learned to live with their limits are the new role models. Someone like Christopher Reeve, the ex-Superman actor, disabled in a tragic accident, but who has survived rather than given up, personifies the role models of the 1990s. (To his credit, Reeve has steadfastly refused to revel in the survivor status which has been thrust upon him.) This shift from the hero to the survivor illustrates a new modest subjectivity in the making.

A diminished subject has as its premise a misanthropic view of the world. It is a world inhabited by survivors and damaged people, who know only too well the force of human destruction. Such negative sentiments about people inform the problem of trust, for the breakdown of relations of trust represents a statement about what society thinks of people. Ultimately, the problem of trust is very much about not being able to trust ourselves.

The premise of the problem of trust is that people are actually not worthy of it. How can adults be trusted to look after children in a society where abuse is seen to be routine? When carried to their logical outcome, such sentiments constitute a condemnation of the human species. It is not surprising, therefore, that humanism – a human-centred worldview – has come under increasing attack in recent years. For example, anyone who today affirms the superiority of human reason over animal instinct risks being accused of promoting a variety of speciesism, and the sentiment which contends that people are worse than animals is not entirely marginal to contemporary culture.

Once the problem of trust is seen in the context of the decline of subjectivity, then it becomes possible to extract that which is distinct to contemporary society. Many societies in the past have experienced conflict and the collapse of co-operation and trust. In the 1960s and 1970s, industrial relations experts continually complained about the lack of trust between labour and capital. However, the problem they referred to was very different to that which exists today. The weakness of trust between employees and employers did not signify that social solidarity as such was feeble. Although the relation between employers and unions was fraught with tension, within both sides of industry there existed a sense of solidarity. In this situation the weakening of trust in one particular relationship coexisted with a strong sense of solidarity in other spheres.

Today, the problem of trust is not restricted to one or a number of distinct relationships. It is not merely a question of workers not trusting their employers. The situation has reached the point where colleagues regard each other as potential enemies and where neighbours are perceived as threatening. Thus, in contrast to the past, the problem of trust exists within a setting where at all levels of society there is a manifest lack of confidence about the working of society.

Those who merely point to the loss of faith in expertise and authority tend to overlook a more significant development, which is that those who are in authority also do not trust themselves. Those who run the leading institutions of society have not remained immune from the workings of the wider processes discussed in the previous chapters. The conviction that there is something fundamentally wrong with human intervention afflicts all sections of society. Many scientists are increasingly concerned about the consequences of their achievements. For example, those engaged on research in the areas of genetics and assisted reproduction are increasingly reluctant to take responsibility for their own actions, preferring to invite some external agency to regulate their work. In many areas of clinical medicine, decisions once taken by doctors in consultation with their patients are now referred to ethical committees, or even to the courts and the media.

Doubts about the efficacy of human intervention are widespread among business people and managers. Many of them seek to pass the responsibility for the most elementary decisions to specialist advisers and consultants. When directors encounter difficulties, their instinct is to call in a public relations expert to advise them on the niceties of 'ethical' management.

The general failure of nerve encourages an evasion of responsibility at every level of society. Just as managers are afraid to manage, so teachers often seem reluctant to teach and parents appear unsure how to rear their children. Counselling, helplines and other forms of professional intervention in everyday life are expressions of the prevailing sense of helplessness which also do much to reinforce it. The secret of the problem of trust is the belief that we are so pathetic that we cannot trust ourselves. In recent years this belief has helped to shape a new morality based on the themes of mistrusting people, exercising caution and avoiding risk. This new etiquette – sometimes inappropriately labelled as political correctness – is the subject of the next chapter.

Notes

1. Hillman, M., Adams, J. and Whiteleg, J. (1990) *One False Move . . . A Study of Children's Independent Mobility* (London: PSI Publishing), p. 84.

2. Fukuyama, F. (1995) *Trust: The Social Virtues and the Creation of Prosperity* (London: Hamish Hamilton), p. 26.

3. Fukuyama, *Trust*, pp. 10–11.

4. For a useful overview of the discussion on trust, see Misztal, B. (1996) *Trust in Modern Societies* (Oxford: Polity Press).

5. Beck, U. (1992) *Risk Society* (London: Sage), p. 70.

6. See Lubbe, H. (1993) 'Security: Risk Perception in the Civilization Process', in Bayerische Ruck (ed.) *Risk is a Construct: Perceptions and Risk Perception* (Munich: Knesebeck).

7. Klinefelter, P. (1994) 'A School Counselling Service', *Counselling*, August.

8. Wann, M. (1995) *Building Social Capital: Self Help in a Twenty-first Century Welfare State* (London: IPPR), pp. iv, 70–2.

9. Sykes, C. (1992) *A Nation of Victims: The Decay of the American Character* (New York: St Martin's Press), p. 43.

10. *Social Trends* (1994), p. 98.

11. See Durkheim, E. (1964) *The Division of Labour in Society* (New York: Free Press).

12. Fukuyama, *Trust*, p. 10.

13. Fukuyama, *Trust*, p. 11.

CHAPTER 7

The New Etiquette

The fear of taking risks and the transformation of safety into one of the main virtues of society has been the principal theme of this book. This worship of safety has influenced attitudes towards all aspects of life. It has fostered an inclination to continually exaggerate the problems facing society, which in turn has encouraged a cautious and anxious outlook. The disposition to perceive one's existence as being at risk has had a discernible effect on the conduct of life. It has served to modify action and interaction between people. The disposition to panic, the remarkable dread of strangers and the feebleness of relations of trust have all had important implications for everyday life. These trends have also altered the way in which people regard each other. Through the prism of the culture of abuse, people have been rediscovered as sad and damaged individuals in need of professional guidance. From this emerges the diminished subject; ineffective individuals and collectivities with low expectations. Increasingly, we feel more comfortable with seeing people as victims of their circumstances rather than as authors of their lives. The outcome of these developments is a worldview which equates the good life with self-limitation and risk aversion.

Unlike most other accounts of the growth of risk consciousness, I question the attempt to link its development to technological advance or the growth of environmental hazards. The growth of risk consciousness is proportional to the decline of what are often called traditional values. The weakening of these values is clearly connected to the fragile consensus that prevails on the basic questions facing people. Many commentators have noted the absence of agreement on even some of the fundamental issues facing society. Ideas about what constitutes an appropriate form of family life or what is acceptable as opposed to criminal behaviour are continually contested. Such disagreements about the elementary conduct of behaviour in the USA have been characterized as 'culture wars'. The term culture war pertains above all to the sphere of moral behaviour. This politicization of morality has major implications for the maintenance of social solidarity. According to one well-known American commentator, 'there is no longer an intellectually responsible ruling idea of Americanism, a fully acceptable formulation of this justificatory national purpose'.[1]

In the UK too, some of the fundamental questions concerning what it means to be British are under review. For example, there is a running controversy over what kinds of values schools should teach their pupils. This became an issue in January 1996, when Dr Nick Tate, the government's chief curriculum adviser, told a conference that school pupils must be given a firm moral lead. Tate argued for more teaching time to be devoted to the teaching of traditional values so that children could learn to distinguish between what is right and what is wrong. This plea for more moral lessons in the classrooms was dismissed by the liberal media. An editorial in the *Independent* declared that society was no less moral than in the past and added that students were 'far too sophisticated to swallow simplifications of subjects such as sexuality and marriage'.[2] In this exchange the lack of common ground on some of the most elementary questions of human behaviour was clearly exposed.

Major differences of view on what to teach children indicate a lack of consensus on even elementary values. This feebleness of shared values contributes to the creation of an atmosphere of ambiguity and doubt. When even the more fundamental questions are far from clear-cut, basic decisions about life appear increasingly risky.

The relationship between the weakening of shared values and the growth of risk consciousness is not simply that of cause and effect. The emergence of a sense of risk helps to provide a provisional solution to the problem of social cohesion. The consciousness of risk carries with itself its own morality. It is a prescriptive and intrusive morality. It demands that individuals subject themselves to the core value of safety. It encourages behaviour to be cautious and self-limiting. At the same time, it condemns those who put others at risk. Its impact on everyday life is far-reaching. Even personal habits regarding sexuality and the consumption of food and alcohol are continually inspected from the perspective of safety.

The emergence of risk consciousness is paralleled by the erosion of traditional forms of morality. In Anglo-American societies, moral statements often appear to have the form of a plea. 'We must bring back traditional values' is the frequently repeated refrain. It often has the character of a warning about what will happen to society if it does not find its moral bearings. Such statements, usually by religious leaders or conservative publicists, usually have an old-fashioned air. In contemporary culture, traditional values and morality have an anachronistic image. That is why most mainstream opinion-makers go out of their way to emphasize that they are not making a moral judgement when they comment on particular issues.

'Why has moral discourse become unfashionable?' asks one leading American observer. In line with most adherents of traditional morality, he blames intellectuals and their view that morality has no basis in science.[3] It is true that the contemporary intelligentsia is uncomfortable with traditional morality, but to blame intellectuals for the state of moral discourse is to blame the messenger for the bad news. The reason why moral discourse has become so unfashionable is that it has lost the capacity to influence the diverse sections of society. Attempts to promote the 'values we share' always come up against the reality of heterogeneous aspirations and lifestyles. Successive attempts by British Conservative and American Republican politicians to 'return' to family values have only served to expose a lack of consensus on the basics.

Those who uphold traditional morality are clearly on the defensive. Indeed, it is difficult to formulate ideals and models that can relate to all sections of society. Many traditional values have been recast in negative terms. Key traditional institutions like the family are denounced as instruments of patriarchal domination. Appeals to the community sound hollow when factories close down, forcing people out of work, or when big out-of-town shopping malls force small shops out of business on the high street. For many people, the community is an elusive vision rather than a fact of life. For those who are committed to traditional morality, the world resembles a kind of high-technology Sodom and Gomorrah. In her eloquent denunciation of moral decline, Gertrude Himmelfarb wrote that 'as deviancy is normalised, so the normal becomes deviant'. For Himmelfarb, the representation of the nuclear family as a site of abuse and the legitimization of illegitimacy exemplifies a reversal of values about what is right and what is wrong.[4] Traditional morality has, so to speak, lost the moral high ground. Although it survives, it does so amongst the least influential sections of society. The so-called opinion-makers in politics, the media and academia are wholly distanced from it. For the younger generations, it often has the appearance of a distant historical ideal.

The marginalization of traditional morality does not mean that society is without any system of values. On the contrary, the space left by the marginalization of traditional morality has been filled by the system of values and notions of conduct associated with risk consciousness. What has emerged is a new etiquette for regulating the interactions between people. It is to this etiquette that we now turn.

The new etiquette

One of the paradoxes of this new etiquette is that it self-consciously proclaims itself to be value free. Indeed, the term 'non-judgemental' is one of its leading working concepts. The lack of direct attachment of this new etiquette to a system of values is at least in part a product of its own internal instability. A worldview which is based on an inflated sense of risk, and which seeks to reconcile people to the life of uncertainty, cannot provide certainties and absolute truths. This is illustrated in the practice of risk management. Alcohol can be pronounced to be a major health risk, but wine can be declared to be a useful prophylactic against heart attack. Even such fundamental tenets of public health promotion as the close association between blood cholesterol levels and cardiovascular diseases have been called into question. It is precisely the very absence of certainty that underwrites the message of caution. In turn the message of caution justifies itself through the continuous inflation of risks.

The new etiquette of caution has used the technical language of risk management to distance itself from explicit moral judgements. For example, many of its values are promoted through the neutral discourse of health and safety promotion. It is not surprising that some commentators have drawn parallels between the current imperative of health and religion. According to one medical sociologist, 'healthiness' has replaced 'Godliness' as a standard of proper living. She noted that in this 'secular age, focusing upon one's diet and other lifestyle choices has become an alternative to prayer and righteous living in providing a means of making sense of life and death'.[5] While perhaps this comparison between the functions of lifestyle promotion and religion is rather forced, there can be little doubt about the importance of health awareness in the regulation of individual life.

The core values of the new etiquette, such as caution, self-restraint and responsible behaviour, are rarely advocated through an explicit moral discourse. Instead, these values are transmitted through associating activities and experiences with the calculus of risk. For example, the new etiquette eschews any overt moral orientation on the subject of sex. It does not stigmatize any sexual activity *per se*. It is non-judgemental and has no misgivings about any particular sexual orientation. That is why, superficially, sex education appears to have an open, almost anything-goes, character.

In reality, sex is no less subject to moralizing than before, but this takes place through the appropriation of sex into the risk calculus. Questions concerning the risks of a particular form of sex inexorably leads to the conceptualization of 'risky sex'. The moralistic undertones of 'safe sex' or 'responsible sex' are apparent in any serious discussion of the subject. However, the warnings are always delivered in a highly medicalized tone. For example, a discussion of teenage sex in the *British Medical Journal* warned about the risks in purely medical terms. 'The scale of morbidity associated with under age sex is sobering and suggests that for many teenagers, sexual activity is far from appropriate' was the conclusion of this study.[6] The technical language adopted by this study is illustrative of a studied distancing from the making of value judgements. Under-age sex is neither condemned nor criticized. The author merely suggests that for 'many teenagers' – by no means all – sexual activity is 'far from appropriate'. These words are carefully crafted. Teenage sex is not undesirable or morally wrong – it is just not 'appropriate'!

Those of the older generation, who were exposed to explicit moral strictures, will note that the same warnings about the dangers of sex are now recycled through the discourse of risk. The new etiquette of sexuality has its own hierarchy of what is allowable and what is not. Because many of the practices which were once condemned are now accepted, it appears as a far more tolerant sexual etiquette than that which prevailed in the past. For example, homosexuality and masturbation are no longer denounced as immoral. Indeed, many sex educators actively promote masturbation as a 'safe' and valid form of sexuality. At the same time, there is a tendency to regard penetrative sex as risky and not at all desirable. The dividing line today is not between practices that are normal or abnormal, or moral or immoral, but between sex that is safe and sex that is unsafe. Through the safe–unsafe couplet, sex becomes subject to a moral agenda that is no less intrusive than in the past. Whereas young women were once told that good girls did not go all the way, today they are made aware that responsible girls exercise caution.

It is through the emergence of HIV infection and AIDS that the association between risk and sex has become intensified. However, once health is defined from the standpoint of risk, behaviour in general and not just in the domain of sexuality becomes subject to a new moral agenda. Researchers argue that the practices advised for safe sex ought to be considered for other forms of communicable diseases. Many diseases are much more contagious than HIV – so should society insist, for example, that those who suffer from influenza should desist from coming into contact with others? 'What moral responsibilities does a person have towards her colleagues if she believes that she has contracted a cold or flu?', asked two leading figures in medical ethics.[7] Clearly, notions of blame, morality and obligation are bound up with notions of health risks.

The prescriptive consequences of the etiquette constructed around risk consciousness have been widely commented on. The stigmatization of smoking shows that what is at issue here is an effective power of regulation. The immorality of risk-taking behaviour is justified on the grounds that an individual's action should not have consequences for other people. Thus smoking is condemned because of what it does to those involuntarily exposed to it. Since any individual action is bound to have some consequence – direct or indirect – on others, there is always further scope for regulation. According to some advocates of a risk-oriented morality, those who expose themselves to risk-taking are spreading the responsibility for their behaviour onto everyone else, 'including of course those individual taxpayers who abstain' from taking risks.[8] Sociologists who advocate risk consciousness also define problems in terms of individual action. 'That one person's risky behaviour becomes a danger to others', wrote Luhman, is 'among the fundamental problems of modern society'.[9] Such a perspective implicitly contains the demand for the regulation of individual action.

The tendency to regulate individual behaviour has from time to time provoked the indignation of people. Articles have appeared in the media which have condemned 'food fascism' and the different initiatives which are designed to influence and alter lifestyle. Some writers, especially those from the right, have denounced health activists on the grounds that they undermine 'freedom, responsibility and self-determination'.[10] Such criticisms usually have the character of a reaction rather than of a coherent interpretation of the phenomenon of lifestyle regulation. Critics of the new etiquette tend to react to its intrusive consequences and rarely engage with its premise.

One reason why criticism of the new etiquette tends to be shallow is that it is not perceived as a system of values, with its own implicit rules for individual behaviour. Yet that is precisely what the new etiquette is all about. In the name of personal health and safety, many of us are willing to accept the kind of strictures that would seem intrusive or moralistic if they came from a traditional figure of authority.

Another reason why the new etiquette is rarely conceptualized as a coherent entity is that it emerged unannounced. The morality of caution evolved in a makeshift and haphazard fashion. Since it evolved in bits and pieces, it never claimed for itself the status of a body of ideas and was rarely perceived as such. Nevertheless, since the 1970s, the morality of caution has steadily gained influence. Many of the new issues of the past two decades – the environment, AIDS, the culture of abuse – helped to crystallize the outlook of the new etiquette.

That this etiquette evolved unannounced can be seen retrospectively in relation to the 1980s. This was the decade of Reagan and Thatcher – an era ostensibly of free enterprise, rugged individualism and conservative morality. And yet this was precisely the period when all the different elements of the new etiquette flourished. This is the decade of caution, the normalization of abuse, of AIDS, of the flourishing of risk consciousness and of the massive increase in the professionalization and the regulation of everyday life. One important analysis of risk has asked 'what has caused this rapid and enormous increase in regulatory activity' in the UK in the 1980s. The author added: 'it is ironic that it has taken place under a Conservative Government ostensibly committed to market forces and the liberation of the entrepreneurial spirit'.[11]

The growth of risk aversion and regulation under free-market political regimes devoted to a different orientation points to the strength of the forces which brought them about. It indicates that despite the opposition of successive governments a new form of social regulation has successfully evolved. That must mean that there are powerful forces within the structures of society which are responsible for the ascendancy of the new etiquette. It also points to the failure of the conservative political regimes of the 1980s to consolidate their own moral authority.

The growth of momentum behind the new etiquette during the Reagan–Thatcher era was a source of frustration to many adherents of these regimes. Intuitively, they appeared to recognize that, despite their electoral success, values and practices which they despised were flourishing. Many of the practices, which became prominent and in some cases incorporated into public policy during the 1980s, had the effect of demoralizing partisans of the right. These were the regulatory instruments that evolved in relation to the environment, health, safety and personal behaviour. But what infuriated them more than anything was the apparent ease with which the new etiquette succeeded in marginalizing traditional morality. Their reaction to these developments eventually exploded into the controversy about 'political correctness'.

The highly charged debate about political correctness had the unfortunate tendency to confuse the issues at stake. This was an extremely superficial discussion which rarely engaged with the underlying influences that gave strength to what has been called political correctness. Instead, criticisms concentrated almost exclusively on some of the consequences of these tendencies – particularly as they related to American campuses. In the public mind, political correctness became bound up with campus controversies about speech codes, sexual harassment and the issue of race. Articles debated the rights and wrongs of censorship, the issue of multiculturalism and the disparaging of so-called Western culture.

Opponents of political correctness have found it difficult to articulate what they identified as the focus of their scorn. In most cases, the object of their concern was what they perceived to be an intolerant rejection of Western values. Often, the spread of these ideas was explained as the consequence of the action of what traditionalist writers have called 'a new class of intellectuals'.[12] Such contributions were oblivious to the wider trends, of which campus speech codes are only a small part. This failure to comprehend the success of the new etiquette is not merely a failure of the intellect. Possibly, the awareness that their own values had lost the battle for moral authority may have made traditionalists reluctant to confront the new reality.

The sociology of political correctness

Political correctness (PC) is a subject that no serious academic is supposed to write about. Of course, nobody is really 'politically correct'. The term probably originated as a light-hearted joke. Later, conservatives transformed it into a term of abuse with which to caricature the actions and behaviour of American liberals and leftists. However, the way in which this term took off on both sides of the Atlantic indicates that, as with all successful caricatures, it touches a raw nerve. That raw nerve is the widespread, if inarticulate, public resentment against attempts to regulate and restrict the autonomy of the individual.

One reason why this is such a troublesome topic is the confused manner in which the controversy around PC evolved. Many of the early attacks on PC had the character of a passionate rant. Those hostile to PC clearly resented the ascendancy of ideas and practices which ran counter to their beliefs. That these ideas were flourishing at the time when conservative regimes were enjoying significant electoral support helped create the impression that the rise of PC was the work of a tiny minority of unrepresentative malcontents. The term PC was used by the right to embrace virtually any development that it did not like. It combined traditional hostility to the changes in the position of women and black people with a rejection of the intrusive speech codes and practices associated with the new etiquette. This lack of precision about what was specific to PC contributed to a climate of confusion concerning what the argument was about.

The association of PC with so many features of changing American institutional and cultural production meant that traditionalists did not have to spell out the content of the term PC. Neither did they have to consider the failure of their way of life as being in some sense linked to the success of the phenomenon they detested. In turn, many liberals and leftists reacted by denying the very existence of PC. One interesting analysis of the debate has accused left-wing commentators of being 'unwilling to grant the right of existence to PC phenomena, even in the face of alarming evidence to the contrary'.[13] Denial of the existence of PC, or dismissal of it as a right-wing fabrication, still characterizes the response of liberal and leftist academics. Some are prepared to accept that it exists, but argue that it is a marginal and extremely rare phenomenon.

Nevertheless the new etiquette has spread to all sections of society. Even hard-nosed capitalist firms have adopted many of its practices. Most major firms have enacted their own codes of conduct on harassment and bullying. They have also gone out of their way to shed their 1980s image of greedy capitalists. Instead, terms like 'ethical capitalism' are bandied about, as firms boast of all the attempts they have made to go green and to have a dialogue with all of their stakeholders. Caring capitalism uses terms like 'sustainable development' and 'people-centred approach' to emphasize its self-restraint.

The confusing state of the discussion around PC is not helped by the rhetorical flourishes that surround it. The focus on its most extreme and ludicrous manifestations detracts from understanding the main features of this development. What is interesting about PC is not the well-rehearsed intellectual condemnation of middle-class, white, male power, or its relativist epistemology. These are superficial and relatively eccentric expressions of more important trends. The campus variety of PC may well turn out to be its least significant manifestation. What is important about PC is that it offers a new etiquette for the conduct of life. It is, above all, a moralizing project.

As noted before, this new etiquette has contributed to the reorganization of human relationships in a variety of different situations. One widely identified symptom is the important way in which language has changed. Changes in language do not merely point to new values but also to the ambiguities in life. Is the cat still a pet or has it become an 'animal companion'? Do you call your spouse your wife (or husband) or your partner? The preferred term indicates an attitude both to your relationship and also to the way that you want that relationship to be perceived. The ambiguities brought out in language testify to some unresolved tensions at the level of behaviour. Lack of clarity about behaviour is linked to the rather feeble consensus that exists regarding systems of values. This problematic consensus can be seen in relation to the bitter debates on issues like family life, the relation between adults and children, education and sex.

The new etiquette provides an alternative way of regulating human conduct. Its emphasis on responsible behaviour always contains an implied threat to intrude into the domain of personal life. Ironically, it is its moralizing impulse which gives it the dynamic to intrude, and it is the failure of traditional morality which gives the new etiquette an air of confident authority. This is an authoritarian morality that believes that it has the right to judge, censor and punish. Paradoxically, it presents itself as non-judgemental and as the protector of the powerless. This commitment to protect us from ourselves extends into areas which were previously left untouched by authoritarians. For example, in 1995, a British television advertisement for Dime chocolate bars was banned because it incited people to gorge food. Under the new rules prescribed by the Independent Television Commission, advertising must not 'encourage or condone excessive consumption of any food'.[14] This may be a trivial issue, but once the regulation of the quantity of chocolate consumption comes to constitute a legitimate ground for censorship, what else will be censored? The 'not in front of the children' element of traditional morality is here recycled in a far more paternalistic and censorious manner.

In passing, it is worth noting the double standard immanent in the new etiquette. Outwardly, it expresses an open and non-judgemental attitude towards the different lifestyles. For example its practitioners often criticize conventional morality for stigmatizing so-called deviant subcultures. It denounces attacks on lone-parent families as outdated attempts to impose Victorian morality. But, at the same time, those who uphold the new etiquette have no inhibitions about practising their own moralizing. People who take risks and those whose form of behaviour is too masculine or too assertive can expect to be lectured on their need to become aware.

In terms of its practice, the new etiquette is probably more interventionist than traditional forms of morality. The past two decades have been marked by a relentless expansion of new methods of social regulation. Countless new rules have been enacted by the state and implemented within private organizations. These authoritarian initiatives are often justified with liberal, sometimes left-wing rhetoric. The most elementary aspects of lifestyle are subject to moral pronouncements. For example everything that pregnant women do – the food they eat, their drinking habits, whether or not they smoke – is subject to public intrusion. One important consequence of this development has been the blurring of the distinction between the private and public spheres. This frenzy of regulation sometimes resembles the rituals of control that characterized pre-capitalist societies. An illustration of this return to past forms of regulation is the growing acceptance in the UK and the USA of the principle that parents should be made responsible for crimes committed by their children.

Many of the instruments of regulation associated with the new etiquette of safety do not appear at all authoritarian. Such policies are justified through the claim to empower, support and respect their object of intervention. PC provides a new language with which to express traditional moral themes concerning the regulation of human conduct. Public intervention in private life often assumes 'helpful' and 'supportive' forms. When people lose their jobs, there are plenty of professionals available to advise them on how to cope with unemployment. A large number of professionals are employed to provide advice on a variety of issues. A cynic might argue that it is easier to give helpful advice than provide opportunities for employment, and many professionals turn out to be less than sympathetic when their helpful advice is ignored.

A variety of devices, from health campaigns to counselling, have become the mechanism through which the state is recasting its ability to control society. The new mechanisms of 'support' are actually an encroachment on individual autonomy. In the first instance, they represent a method of controlling people's lives. Encouraging people to look for professional advice instead of exercising initiative also helps to breed a climate of passivity; a situation where a relation of dependency is established between the individual and the professional helper.

This dynamic behind the new etiquette can be seen in the way in which institutions of traditional morality have crumbled and given way to the practices of the new etiquette. No institution seems to be immune to the influence of this new morality. The Anglican Church, a core institution of English tradition, clearly illustrates this trend. Over the past decade, the traditionalists inside this church have been in full retreat. Defeated over the issue of accepting women to serve as priests, it is only a matter of time before traditionalists will also have to accept openly gay clergy. The church also has problems in upholding the virtues of marriage. Though it has long accepted married clergy, in 1994 it had to come to terms with a minister who had married for the third time after his second divorce. A report to the Synod in 1995 approved cohabitation as a prelude to marriage.

The rout of the traditionalists inside the Church of England has been paralleled by its declining influence over society as a whole. The desperation of this church to gain a measure of influence among the young was forcefully demonstrated by the scandal that surrounded the Nine O'clock Service (NOS) in Sheffield during August 1995. The NOS was an initiative associated with a young vicar, Christopher Brain. Brain sought to synthesize rave culture with the Christian service in order to appeal to the young. His service, which attracted a cult following among the young, combined ancient Christian symbolism with new age mysticism, environmental awareness and rave culture. For the leaders of the Church, the popularity of this venture helped to overcome their own revulsion at this opportunist mix of practices. However, a scandal erupted around the personality of Reverend Brain. Accused of sexually abusing some of the women members of his flock, he was forced to resign his ministry. At the time most of the media attention focused on the charismatic personality of Brain, but a far more fundamental issue was the sense of malaise inside the Church of England. The reliance of the church on elements of youth culture and show business indicated its own lack of belief in itself and its mission.

The reaction of the Church of England to its growing isolation from society has been to grudgingly accommodate the new etiquette. The way in which the church reacted to the scandal surrounding Brain clearly illustrated this tendency to accommodate. Following well-established PC practices on campus, the Church of England issued a new 'Code of Ministerial Practice'. For the first time, the church laid down a conduct of behaviour for its priests. Following the PC tradition, the Code of Ministerial Practice provided instructions on the minutiae of human behaviour. The code urges clergy not to meet young women late at night, not to drink while working and not to sit too close to parishioners when offering solace or advice. The code warns priests to use 'appropriate bodily posture'. It also offers useful tips on 'the arrangement of lighting and furniture' and about where to sit when visited by a parishioner.[15] This code, with its anticipation of clerical misbehaviour, represents an acknowledgement of moral defeat. By treating vicars as potential abusers, the Church of England has acknowledged that it has no claim to unquestioned moral authority. Moreover, it has also accepted that a PC code of conduct is more relevant to its internal regime than its own conventions for the conduct of human behaviour.

The accommodation of the Church of England to the new etiquette is part of a wider pattern evident throughout society. The case of the Girl Guides provides some useful insights into the pattern of this accommodation.[16] In recent years the Guides has experienced a steady decline in membership. It is now less a youth organization than a play group for the very young. In an attempt to appeal to young girls, the Guides has tried to modernize its image. The original philosophy of the Guides expressed a fervent commitment to the British Empire and to traditional moral values. Since these values and practices run counter to the spirit of our times, the Guides has been forced to overhaul its image. In its Vision Statement, the Guide Association tries to take a stand on morality. It promises to provide a unique 'environment of fun, friendship and adventure underpinned by spiritual and moral values'. As Jenny Bristow argued, the question is, what are the moral values that can be seen as relevant today?

The three absolute principles on which membership of the Guides has always been based – loyalty to God, the Queen and the nation – are institutions which no longer enjoy unquestioned authority, so the Guides has made the appropriate changes. For example the old oath to 'do my duty to God' was replaced by the more subtle promise to 'love my God', which, as the new *Guide Handbook* reveals, is designed to accommodate everyone from a Zen Buddhist to an atheist. When it comes to 'serving the Queen', the girls are told to feel sorry for her, because 'it can't be very nice to be watched everywhere you go, even on holiday!'; and patriotism is reduced to the idea that 'we can find out about our country, its history and customs, so we can tell other people about it'. What was once a simple oath, summed up in three words, now takes three tortuous pages of the handbook to explain.

The apologetic reorientation of the Guides indicates the problem that traditionalists have in upholding tradition. Increasingly, they are forced to reorganize around uncertainties implicit in most relations. Even organizations like the military and the police are influenced by these trends. Many of the tensions between men and women and between differences in sexual orientation are revisited in these institutions. New codes and policies on these matters now inform the operation of these services in the UK.

The announcement in August 1995 by David Alton, a leading anti-abortionist MP, that he would not run for Parliament in the next election symbolizes the dilemma of traditional moralists. Alton claimed that he was disillusioned with PC and his inability to bring a moral agenda into British politics.[17] The problem of upholding a principled traditionalist stance is shown by Alton's own record. Alton, and the anti-choice lobby that he personifies, have sought to accommodate to the prevailing climate by modifying their traditional arguments against abortion. They rarely argue in public that abortion is wrong *per se*. Instead, they point to the 'ethical issues' raised by new technology and try to win support by keying into the widespread public reaction against tampering with nature. Another adaptation of anti-abortionists to the present climate is their attempt to recast the issue as one of abuse against the victim, the fetus. Since they are so willing to go down the PC road, it is not surprising that they cannot set a traditionalist agenda. This accommodation to the new etiquette by traditionalists on one of the most fundamental issues that defines their very identity indicates how the balance has shifted on the plane of morality.

Incidentally, Alton's claim regarding the absence of a moral agenda in the UK represents a misreading of the situation. The very PC that he attacks is totally saturated with moralism. It is interesting to note that on many issues, traditional morality and that of the new etiquette run parallel to each other, whilst on others they actually converge. The synthesis of these two trends of morality will be considered in the final section of this chapter.

The moralist imperative

Alton's statement concerning the absence of a moral agenda in the UK is particularly surprising since issues that are closely bound up with morality have dominated politics during the past twenty-five years. The debate on lone parents, questions to do with abortion, adoption and IVF treatments, and the controversy over crime are only some of the many moral themes that have dominated British politics in recent years. Indeed, it can be argued that during this period it is the social agenda which has lost out to the moral one. This response is not surprising, since whenever society is in trouble it begins to moralize. The main themes of this book – risk consciousness, the culture of abuse, the fear of strangers, the erosion of relations of trust – reflect this moralizing imperative.

Alton's confusion about the state of the moral dynamic in the UK is understandable since he seems to recognize morality only when it appears in its traditional form. This confusion, which is shared by most traditionalists, is further compounded by their failure to understand why their own brand of morality is in decline and why alternative versions are ascendant. The source of this confusion is very much bound up with the difficulty that they have in dealing with the relationship between the individual and community. Alton's confusion about the current state of morality is by no means confined to him or to his traditionalist co-thinkers. Radical promoters of the new etiquette can only see morality if it is wearing a dog collar (significantly, a practice eschewed by many modern vicars).

Although the right wing of the political spectrum is conventionally identified with the individual, this has been a rather troublesome relationship. In many situations, conservatives and even liberals regard a strongly developed individualism as a threat to the community. Even those who uphold free enterprise and the free market are sometimes repelled by the destructive consequences of the unhindered pursuit of individual self-interest. It is in this vein that many academics are reassessing their interpretation of Adam Smith. In the 1970s and 1980s, Smith, the author of *The Wealth of Nations*, was hailed as the first and the greatest free-market guru. In the 1990s, however, Smith was reinvented as a moral philosopher, the author of *The Theory of Moral Sentiments*, and the guardian angel of responsible, caring capitalism.

Whenever strong social divisions emerge and communal bonds appear feeble, support for the spirit of individualism diminishes. It is interesting to note that many conservatives denounce the trends associated with PC on the grounds that they represent a demonstration of the 'Me' generation of the 1960s. Traditionalists often denounce their opponents as egotistical. Thus women who have abortions are 'selfish'. From a traditionalist perspective, the decline of the 'spirit of the community' is due to the growth of individualism. This view even informs the writings of more liberal communitarian thinkers like Amitai Etzioni. As against the 1980s 'celebrations of the self', Etzioni argues that the time has come for emphasizing the 'we', the 'values we share'.[18] More conservative American writers go a step further and actually blame the loss of their moral authority on the belief that 'autonomous individuals can freely choose, or will their moral life'.[19]

The notion advanced by radical proponents of the new etiquette that it reflects the emergence of a more autonomous individual is based on a fundamental misconception of the dominant trend of our times – the decline of subjectivity. Many of the practices of the new morality are concerned with restraining or limiting individual aspirations. Popular culture and the media project an image of people as damaged and incapable. Despite their rhetoric, the advocates of the new morality are as influenced by the feebleness of individual initiative as the most conservative promoters of the community.

The confusion about the relationship between the rise of the new etiquette and the individual is actually an understandable one, for the main reason why traditional values have lost their purchase on society is that they have not been able to relate to social processes bound up with the growing individuation of capitalist societies. The tendency towards fragmentation – growing social divisions, changing relations at the level of family life, etc. – has created an environment which is inhospitable to traditional morality. The atomization of social life and the growing sense of privatization have made it difficult to appeal to the community. Many traditionalists confuse this privatized and isolated individual with the cult of the individual. In fact, human beings who are atomized and whose bonds with others are weak are unlikely to have an elevated sense of individual aspiration. The weakening of social cohesion means, ironically, the diminishing of the sense of individual autonomy. Individuals are unlikely to transcend the mood of caution that afflicts a society that is uneasy with itself.

The reason why the new etiquette has succeeded where traditional morality has failed is that it directly relates to the atomized individual and tries to make sense of the experience of isolated alienation. The consciousness of risk carries with it its own morality. It shifts the burden of responsibility for society's problems onto the plane of the individual. Most of the evils that prevail are increasingly located on the level of interpersonal behaviour. Thus violence has been systematically individualized. Violence has become associated with the acts of out-of-control individuals – the bullies of this world. It is rarely conceptualized as the conscious projection of social power. The regulation of individual behaviour that follows is further justified in the language of risk. The values of risk aversion, not putting others at risk, the need to protect people from risky individuals, and the necessity for regulating behaviour at the level of individual relations, all work towards the creation of an etiquette which is no less moralizing than its traditional cousins.

The main difference between the new etiquette and traditional morality is its individualistic orientation. It does not attempt to provide a single answer to the existential problems facing humanity. It recognizes that traditional morality cannot cope with existing social divisions and offers a relativist morality oriented towards making sense of the process of individuation. Consequently, the new etiquette does not hold up one particular lifestyle as a model for society as a whole. It actually makes a virtue of social fragmentation and declares that every identity is equally worthy of respect. It does not explicitly criticize any lifestyle. It rejects the attempt to uphold one form of the family and instead prefers the plural 'families'.

The reason why the new etiquette may provide a provisional solution to the problem of social cohesion is that it relates directly to the contemporary experience of individuation. Its solution is to offer a morality that is based on the experience of the isolated individual. Instead of attempting to reintegrate the individual into a wider community, it seeks to make some moral sense of the different fragments of society. Giddens, who eloquently expresses this standpoint, argues that today all moral questions in some way involve choices about lifestyle. In this way, morality does not directly demand a commitment to society but to a lifestyle. Indeed the project of the self provides the fundamental dynamic towards what Giddens calls a 'fundamental impetus towards a remoralising of daily life'.[20]

The relativistic orientation of the new etiquette constitutes both its strength and its weakness. Its strength is that, unlike traditional morality, it can relate to the process of individuation. By acknowledging the legitimacy of all forms of lifestyle, it avoids the question of how to demand a common commitment. At the same time, by subjecting everyone to the demands of low expectations and restraint, it possesses a powerful instrument of social regulation. The weakness of the new etiquette is that, because it avoids the big question of social cohesion, every new question opens another debate about values and ethics. The lack of consensus about a system of values creates an imperative towards moralizing. That is why areas of life which were hitherto considered unproblematic have become a matter of public interest.

Consider the example of IVF. Initially, assisted conception was opposed by a handful of traditionalists, who were worried that it would encourage women to have children outside marriage and family. However, because of the benefits this technology brought to infertile couples, this treatment was generally accepted by the public. In recent times, IVF has again become a subject of controversy. So-called ethical dilemmas over IVF are conventionally explained as the outcome of new reproductive technology. In fact, these debates are a product of the moralizing imperative. They reflect the wider anxieties about parenting and family life. But whereas the right to parent is rarely contested in cases of natural conception, a different approach can be adopted when conception is artificial. Under the guise of the ethical problems surrounding IVF, a debate about the problems surrounding parenting is taking place.

One of the flaws of the new etiquette is that it relies on an extremely negative interpretation of what constitutes humanity. Most religions and moral codes have tended to denigrate the human potential. Representations of humans as evil beings who would be punished by an omnipotent God(s) reappear in one form or another in all human systems. But for all their mystifications, many of these systems recognized the special quality of human beings and were often human-centred. Today, the anti-humanist orientation of the new etiquette is one of its defining features. The exaggeration of problems and risks is only matched by the denigration of the problem-solving potential of people. On the basis of such a negative representation of people, it is difficult to motivate or inspire society.

The unexpected synthesis

The success of the new etiquette cannot be explained as being entirely due to its own work. Its success was ultimately realized through a synthesis with elements of traditional morality. Many of the key features of the new etiquette – the worship of safety, the emphasis on restraint and limitation – are fully consistent with the basic tenets of traditional conservatism. The precautionary principle, with its rejection of experimentation, was, at least in outline, first formulated by nineteenth-century conservative philosophers. Not all features of the new etiquette could be synthesized into a wider conservative outlook, but many elements could be and were integrated into this outlook and thereby accelerated its general acceptance.

The most important area for this unexpected synthesis is that of sexuality. Most traditionalists regarded the so-called sexual revolution of the 1960s with horror. The acceptance of couples living with each other outside of marriage, the popularity of sexual experimentation and the very idea of recreational sex had the effect of undermining conventional morality. This was an area where conventional morality was in full retreat by the end of the 1970s.

Where conventional morality failed, the new etiquette succeeded. Since the early 1980s, sexuality has been recast in a more conservative mould. Many of the core ideas of the new etiquette have the effect of problematizing sex. Sex has been increasingly associated with being at risk. The idea of sex as fun now competes with views which emphasize the problems of harassment and abuse. The reinvention of sex as a profoundly risky affair is inextricably linked to ideas about human beings as damaged and of men as being innately violent. The equation of masculinity with male violence and the representation of penetrative sex as a mild form of rape have created a climate where recreational sex is increasingly dismissed as irresponsible.

The present puritanical climate could not have been achieved through traditional puritanical means. Consider the example of oral contraceptive pills. Traditionalists have always hated the pill because it decoupled sex from reproduction. They denounced the pill for encouraging sex without responsibility. Such arguments have had little impact on society and millions of women opted for this form of contraception. But whereas the traditional arguments failed to find any resonance, those of the new etiquette have made many women think twice before using the pill. Through using the discourse of risk, raising alarm about its long-term side-effects and stigmatizing the taking of hormones, the pill has become increasingly problematized. Traditionalists who have been forced to compromise and accept the reality of 'family planning clinics' have been only too happy to adopt the new medicalized arguments against the pill. It is not the traditionalists but those who uphold the new etiquette who succeeded in introducing caution into sex. Moreover, through the popularization of the culture of abuse, the need for regulating sexual relations has become widely accepted. The new codes of behaviour on sexual etiquette, which have been institutionalized throughout society, have the effect of controlling interpersonal conduct.

Today's condemnation of masculinity helps to recycle nineteenth-century images of virtuous womanhood adrift in a sea of predatory males. Today's helpful advice to women has dangerous parallels with the old moral codes which decreed that decent girls should not drink or talk to strangers. It is not surprising that many conventional moralists have been pleased by this sexual counter-revolution. They are absolutely delighted when liberal writers declare that we now realize that the 1960s had gone too far. Claims that a lot of people were damaged by the 1960s confirm the religious conviction that those who sin will be punished.

The contemporary moralizing about sexual restraint is based on the premise that human beings are degraded people. In specialist literature, sex and sexuality are seen to be driven by dark and evil passions. The image of the dark side of the family points to a situation where people are capable of anything. The metaphors of the dark side, hidden and invisible, help us to expand our imagination regarding the countless forms of depravity that people practise on each other. According to one psychiatrist wedded to this image of sexuality, the many evils 'despite being widespread, remained unnamed and invisible, a tribute to how fully integrated they were into the fabric of social life'.[21] The effect of this naming of the unnameable is to normalize abuse and to perpetuate new fears about sex.

The high point of the unexpected synthesis between conventional moralizers and proponents of the new etiquette was over the issue of AIDS. In many respects, the emergence of the AIDS issue can be seen as the defining moment of this unexpected synthesis. AIDS came as a godsend to all moralists. Initially, it was the right-wing moralists who sought to take the initiative. They characterized AIDS as a gay plague and presented this disease as rightful punishment for immoral behaviour. In the AIDS literature, this attempt to create an anti-gay moral panic is still presented as the dominant theme around the issue. But in reality, the anti-gay representation of AIDS soon ran out of steam. Proponents of the new etiquette succeeded in redefining AIDS. It was argued that AIDS was not just a disease which afflicted gays – 'everyone was at risk'. This argument soon triumphed, and on both sides of the Atlantic the main moral lesson that was drawn was the need for safe sex. The safe-sex campaign was not addressed to any one section of society. Everyone, heterosexual and homosexual, was instructed to practise safe sex.

AIDS awareness and 'safer sex' have become models of the synthesis between traditional and new forms of morality. Even those who are bitterly hostile to PC have a positive regard for the AIDS industry. Charles Sykes is pleased because AIDS has made it possible to restore sexual responsibility. He hopes that 'holding people responsible for their behaviour means restoring social stigmas that shrink the zone of acceptable conduct'.[22] The importance of AIDS in helping to create an atmosphere of sexual responsibility is recognized universally.

Like nineteenth-century Jesuit priests, who terrorized young boys by telling them that masturbation would make them blind, public health advocates transmit scare stories about AIDS that seek to restrain and limit people's activity. The only difference is that AIDS awareness represents the issue of morality as that of personal safety. But in both cases, the traditional prudish rejection of sex as fun is justified on the grounds that it has the 'most profound consequences'. AIDS awareness gives an alternative secular, medical form to old-fashioned moralizing.

The sexual counter-revolution of the 1980s and 1990s is a product of the convergence of traditional morality and the new etiquette. The potency of this synthesis is shown by the important changes that have occurred at the level of individual behaviour and in the establishment of a new moral climate. The impact of these changes goes way beyond the realm of sexuality. The very idea of experimentation in any shape or form has come to be associated with irresponsible behaviour. At least temporarily, the principle of caution has triumphed over the pioneering spirit of adventure and discovery.

Notes

1. Pfaff, W. (1990) *Barbarian Sentiments: How the American Century Ends* (New York: The Noonday Press), p. 185.

2. *Independent*; 15 January 1996.

3. Wilson, J. (1993) *The Moral Sense* (New York: The Free Press), p. viii.

4. Himmelfarb, G. (1994) 'A Demoralized Society: The British/American Experience', *The Public Interest*, Fall, p. 66.

5. Lupton, D. (1995) *The Imperative of Health: Public Health and the Regulated Body* (London: Sage), p. 4.

6. Stuart-Smith, S. (1996) 'Teenage Sex', *British Medical Journal*, 17 February, p. 312.

7. Harris, J. and Holm, S. (1995) 'Is There a Moral Obligation Not to Infect Others?', *British Medical Journal*, 4 November, p. 312.

8. Leiss, W. and Chociolko, C. (1994) *Risk and Responsibility* (Montreal: McGill-Queen's University Press), p. 11.

9. Luhman, N. (1993) *Risk: A Sociological Theory* (New York: Walter de Gruyter), p. 147.

10. See Anderson, D. (1991) 'The Health Activists: Educators or Propagandists?' in Berger, P. (ed.) *Health, Lifestyle and Environment – Counteracting the Panic* (London: Social Affairs Unit), pp. 45–6.

11. Adams, J. (1995) *Risk* (London: UCL Press), p. 206.

12. See the special issue of *Partisan Review*, vol. 60, no. 4, 1993, on 'The Politics of Political Correctness'. In this publication, virtually all the contributors have this narrow, formal reading of what constitutes political correctness.

13. See Bush, H. K. (1995) 'A Brief History of PC, with Annotated Bibliography', *American Studies International*, vol. 33, no. 1, p. 45.

14. Cited in the *Daily Telegraph*; 2 February 1995.

15. Cited in *The Sunday Times*; 27 August 1995.

16. This section on the Guides is based on the excellent article 'Guiding Principles' by Jenny Bristow in *Living Marxism*, September 1996.

17. Cited in the *Guardian*; 1 August 1995.

18. Etzioni, A. (1993) *The Spirit of Community: Rights, Responsibilities and the Communitarian Agenda* (New York: Crown Publishers), p. 25.

19. Wilson, *The Moral Sense*, p. 250.

20. Giddens, A. (1991) *Modernity and Self Identity: Self and Society in the Late Modern Age* (Cambridge: Polity Press), pp. 225–6.

21. Rutter, P. (1989) *Sex in the Forbidden Zone* (London: Routledge), p. 23.

22. Sykes, C. (1992) *A Nation of Victims: The Decay of the American Character* (New York: St Martin's Press), p. 246.

CHAPTER 8

Conclusions –
The Politics of Fear

Throughout this book, reference has been made to the significance of the diminished importance attached to subjectivity. This development is not only of crucial importance for understanding contemporary social and political life: it also provides an explanation for the development of the consciousness of risk and of the pervasive culture of abuse.

The perspective which underlines the diminished importance attached to subjectivity is one which is fundamentally sceptical about the effectiveness of human intervention. Such scepticism is reinforced by the sentiment which exaggerates the destructive outcomes of human action. The identification of people with pollution, abuse and environmental destruction makes it difficult to believe in a humanist worldview. The erosion of subjectivity means that society finds it difficult to demand respect for anything that is remotely a human creation. As a result, even the most respected institutions of the capitalist system such as markets and state and religious institutions are rarely promoted in positive terms.

Unfortunately, the growth of cynicism towards society's institutions benefits no one. Cynicism about politicians or any section of the elites does not on its own lead to any positive outcomes. In the absence of an alternative, such cynicism can lead to the conclusion that *any* form of human intervention is suspect. Cynical criticism does not strengthen critical thought. Rather, it can reinforce the view that there are no choices and that the limits of human effectiveness oblige us to accept our fate.

The absence of real choice is the message that is implicit in the many anxieties stimulated by society's obsession with risk. One can exercise caution but not choice. How could there be choice when the human agency is deemed to be so ineffective? The separation of human action from its desired outcome is one of the key tenets of risk thinking. The impossibility of predicting future outcomes – which is a thesis proposed by advocates of risk consciousness – leads to only one possible course of action: that of precaution.

The precautionary principle – be careful or else – assigns a minimalist role for the human agency. This is a fatalistic outlook, whose main aim is to warn rather than direct people. Since it tends to assume that people have already gone too far, it is not inclined to encourage any more voyages of discovery. The fatalistic sociology of the precautionary principle depicts people as essentially powerless to do very much more than to avoid taking risks.

The fatalistic mood is further reinforced by the whole culture of abuse. The normalization of relations of abuse and its presentation as an intergenerational disease has profound implications for the way we understand human beings. It presents people as essentially out of control over their lives. Incidents which may have happened to them as children seal their destiny. The view that incidents of abuse 'scar you for life' represents a modern variety of the old theme of predestination. It is no longer God that has preordained an individual's fate but the earthly act of human abuse.

The view that we are not fully in control of our actions is emphasized in the cycle of abuse theories. This separation of subjectivity from action further emphasizes the notion of the powerless and out-of-control individual. These days, the lack of relationship between consciousness and action is also argued for in the numerous biological theories that have become fashionable. The medicalization of behaviour continually expands the range of individual acts which are said to have a biological foundation. Rage and violent action by women are often explained as a result of some hormonal imbalance. Also, premenstrual tension is now held accountable for a variety of disturbing outcomes, and the association of masculinity with violence and of male sexuality with the impulse to degrade women help extend the biological foundation for human action.

Increasingly, biology combines with fatalism to produce a highly deterministic view of the human condition. Such explanations are flawed even within their own terms. Why is it that people *have* managed to overcome the limits of their hormones and genes and their childhood experiences and exercise a measure of control over their life? Why is it that many who experience a variety of abuses as children apparently grow up as reasonably aware, well-adjusted, non-abusive adults – usually without the benefit of expert intervention?

The answer to these questions is provided by the rich experiences of growing up, encountering new experiences and interacting with other people. It is through the influence of these social experiences that we become who we are.

Fatalism and biology combine to restrict the space in which human consciousness can be operational. They also call into question the social character of human action. One of the most far-reaching consequences of these forms of thinking is to obscure the social causation of many of the problems people face. Indeed, the tendency to focus on abusive relations has the effect of overlooking their social origins. Yet, people's behaviour is influenced by their social circumstance. Take the case of child abuse. Although childhood experiences may play a part, the adult experiences of economic insecurity, poverty, marital breakdown, community disintegration and the ways in which individuals respond to these pressures are arguably more important as conditions leading to the neglect and ill-treatment of children. Behind the people who are out of control lies a society that has also lost its way. The effect of concentrating on degraded people rather than on society is to abandon any hope of finding solutions. Why? Because it is only possible to conceive of effective intervention in relation to a social problem. After all, a problem created by humans ought to be subject to human solution. But the degraded person is not susceptible to effective intervention. Their state is caused by a moral flaw – and the only thing to be done is to punish and pray.

The main trends discussed in this text have the effect of accentuating the powerlessness of people. The perception of powerlessness is further reinforced by the erosion of social solidarity. The process of individuation and the weakening of relations of trust contribute to an intense sense of isolation. The attempts by society to artificially compensate for this isolation through self-help groups, help-lines and professional counselling do little to resolve the problem. Such initiatives seek to reconcile people to their experience of estrangement. They represent an accommodation to powerlessness.

It is ironic that the experience of individuation and the erosion of social solidarity is so often depicted in positive terms. Some politicians present life today as providing greater choice for people. Even the break-up of communities and the loss of a way of life are often presented as opportunities for choosing a new lifestyle. This impression is also conveyed in style magazines and the media, where the process of individuation is celebrated as providing people with the means for choosing new lifestyles. The presentation of estrangement as a positive choice is not confined to the media. Many academics argue that the freeing of individuals from their social ties is a creative process. From this standpoint, there is a growth rather than a diminishing of subjectivity. Two well-known British sociologists, Lash and Urry, claim to detect an 'increasingly significant *reflexive* human subjectivity'. They believe that the breakdown of trust in expert systems helps a 'critical reflexivity to develop'.[1] Unfortunately, social isolation does not stimulate critical thought. Individuals on their own are far more likely to be overwhelmed by a sense of insecurity than to have the confidence to develop critical thought.

Those who contend that people now possess greater choice than before misunderstand the fundamental processes at play. What has happened is that the weakening of social bonds has undermined the more or less predictable patterns of the past. Whether they like it or not, people have been 'freed' from many of the relations which linked individuals together in the past. So, in principle, people are free to choose their lifestyles and relations. But in the absence of new forms of social solidarities such freedom helps to intensify the sense of estrangement and of powerlessness. It is as if people must 'choose', whether they like it or not. There was a time when a life which consisted of this kind of choosing was just called survival. The tendency to endow estrangement with the positive quality of lifestyle choice represents an attempt at reconciliation with powerlessness.

The idea behind the reconciliation with powerlessness is not new. But in the past, the idea of 'Blessed are the meek for they shall inherit the earth' did not have the prominence that victimhood has today. Probably the clearest manifestation of the diminished significance attached to subjectivity is the contemporary celebration of power-lessness. Increasingly, the media derides those who have heroic pretensions. The new role models are those who can suffer. As one proponent of this shift in cultural taste remarked, 'risk-taking heroism has been increasingly replaced by stress-bearing heroism'.[2] Being able to take it, rather than doing something about it, aptly summarizes the mood of low expectations.

The corollary of 'stress-bearing heroism' is the ridicule directed at the aspiration of human control. People who try to exercise a measure of control over their lives are disparaged as control freaks. Professional counsellors characterize the belief in self-control as a 'perfectionist complex'. Women who try to plan their families or use reproductive technology are accused of wanting 'designer families' or 'designer babies'. Through the celebration of suffering, society legitimizes its fear of taking risks.

The politics of fear

A profound sense of powerlessness has encouraged an atmosphere where competing claims about dangers vie for the allegiance of the public. Take the debate around the risks associated with the MMR vaccine. Anti-vaccination activists have successfully preyed on parents' anxiety about their children's well-being. In turn, health officials have reacted by warning of the danger of an outbreak of an epidemic of measles if parents do not vaccinate their children. The debate about food has also been subject to competing claims about alleged risks. Opponents of genetically modified food have made all the running. Their label of 'Frankenstein food' has struck a chord with the public imagination. Their opponents have also joined in and adopted the politics of fear by promoting the idea that eating organic food is more dangerous than eating the conventional variety.[3] Sections of the child protection industry have helped create a sense of paranoia amongst parents with their warning of stranger-danger and the perils faced by children outdoors. In June 2001, the charity Child Accident Prevention Trust issued a report which correctly disputed the claim that child abduction was a serious risk facing parents. That was the good news. The bad news was that it substituted one scare story with its own. It warned that the risk of a child's accident was greatest at home. It stated that the greatest risk to every young child 'actually lies in their own home'. So parents are entitled to be paranoid but they need to be paranoid about the right dangers. These competing claims about which risks constitute the greatest danger continually reinforce public fears and anxiety.

The main beneficiaries of the politics of fear have been consumer activists. Consumer activism has succeeded in transforming food into one of the most high-profile political issues facing UK society. Although genetically modified (GM) foods have been the main target of a bitter environmentalist crusade, the entire food industry has been stigmatized by the claim that it puts profits before people's safety. Other industries have also come under attack from consumer lobbyists. In the past few years, cars, mobile phones, electric cables, the Internet, computer screens, plastic toys, airline travel and baby walkers have all been cast in the roles of unacceptable health risks.

Consumer activism has gained formidable respectability in the UK. The government is uniquely sensitive to lobbying by consumer advocacy groups. Faced with criticism from anti-GM food lobbyists, the Blair regime substantially modified its stance on the issue. Government ministers have sought to project themselves as the consumer's champion. In July 1999, Stephen Byers, then Secretary of State for Trade and Industry, launched a populist public relations campaign against inflated retail prices, remarking that many people 'feel they are living in "rip-off" Britain'. He painted a picture of a society where people are 'paying high prices for shoddy goods, with cheats being allowed to prosper and move with ease from one scam to another'.[4] Since the summer of 1999, the Office of Fair Trading has adopted the image of a crusading consumers' outfit. It is worth noting that the sensitivity of ministers to consumer lobbying stands in sharp contrast to the relative failure of more traditional interest groups like trade unions to win concessions from the government.

Consumer and environmentalist activism also enjoy an unprecedented degree of adulation in the media and public life. Campaigns against road building, live animal exports, the fast-food chain McDonald's and trials of GM foods are characteristically portrayed as heroic acts of responsible citizenship. Recently, the media depicted environmentalists who wrecked GM crop test sites as peoples' champions tackling giant American Goliaths. According to John Vidal, the environmental editor of the *Guardian*:

> the ecological-inspired critique of democracy is now exploding and the crop pullers should be seen as part of an international movement that, thanks to email and the web, watchdog groups and increasing networking, is throwing up new issues, philosophies, ethics, and legal arguments.[5]

This representation of environmental activists as intellectual innovators, who are providing a morally exhausted society with a priceless philosophical contribution, is rarely interrogated. At every turn, environmental activists are praised for their altruism, social responsibility and moral outlook.

The adoption of the cause of consumer activism by the contemporary UK political establishment raises interesting questions about its status as a movement. Consumer and environmental activists routinely attempt to portray themselves as disadvantaged radical outsiders who are continually battling against powerful vested interests. Environmental activists in particular claim that they represent a disenfranchised public who lack any significant access to the political system. However, judging by the highly positive representation of these 'outsiders' by the mainstream media, one could be forgiven for drawing the conclusion that this is very much a movement led by *insiders*.

Take the example of the campaign against GM foods. This campaign has been endowed with considerable respectability by Prince Charles, who declared that the 'genetic modification of crops is taking mankind into realms that belong to God, and to God alone'. Key institutions of the UK establishment, such as the Federation of Women's Institutes, have joined Greenpeace, the Consumers' Association and over 70 other consumer, environment and other groups in calling for a freeze on the development of GM crops. Far from being powerless outsiders, it is evident that campaigns such as this enjoy a privileged relationship with the people that matter in the UK. Consumer activism exercises considerable influence over the media and the intelligentsia and enjoys a mutually profitable relationship with the UK's political class.

The new insiders

Consumer and environmental groups, advocacy organizations and non-governmental organizations (NGOs) regularly participate in the New Labour government's network of review groups and task forces. Since May 1997, New Labour has launched hundreds of these government reviews. According to one account, this initiative 'has stretched the resources of even the most well-endowed pressure group as they strive to keep up with all the new opportunities'.[6] Organizations like the Consumers' Association have achieved a semi-official status and participate in dozens of consultative committees. Consumer organizations and advocacy groups are seen by officials and politicians as key allies in policy-making. The representatives of such groups are often presented as neutral experts, who express the interests of the public. They are usually portrayed as 'independent' and their legitimate public concerns are often favourably contrasted with the narrow vested interests of business and the unions.

The ascendancy of consumer activism in the UK, and its institutionalization near the heart of the political system, parallels important developments in the USA. A recently published study by Jeffrey Berry, *The New Liberalism: The Rising Power of Citizen Groups*, provides compelling evidence of the rise of the powerful and well-financed so-called citizen lobby groups in the USA. According to Berry, these groups have had a major impact in altering the US political agenda and in shaping the way that business is conducted on Capitol Hill. Berry contends that these groups express a brand of new liberalism which is oriented towards 'quality-of-life issues' such as consumer affairs, environmentalism and good government. Motivated by 'post-material values' (that is, by non-material concerns), these groups reflect, according to Berry, the affluence of US society.

Berry has noted that this rise of consumerism coincides with declining interest in the issues of economic equality and sympathy for the poor. According to Berry, the new liberalism appeals principally to an upper middle-class suburban constituency. As a result, it can access a level of funding not available to either labour advocates or promoters of right-wing populist causes, whose appeal is primarily to people of more modest means. He remarks that, paradoxically, 'it is the citizen groups of the right, and not of the left who are more attuned to the interests of those on the lower rungs of the economic ladder'.[7] Berry concedes that new liberalism's stress on quality-of-life issues 'has certainly left them open to the charge of elitism', but he believes that their 'post-materialist' politics represent the wave of the future.

Berry's research provides a detailed account of the influence of these groups on the legislative process. In the 1960s, most domestic economic and social legislation coming before House and Senate dealt with the allocation of economic resources, and only around a third of the bills dealt with quality-of-life issues such as consumer or environmental concerns. By 1991, this pattern was fundamentally altered. Something like 71 per cent of all congressional hearings that year took up legislation based around quality-of-life concerns, whilst economic issues occupied just 29 per cent of the domestic legislation. There is little doubt that in-depth research would also reveal a discernible shift by the UK Parliament towards quality-of-life concerns.

At least in part, the success of US liberal citizen groups is due to the considerable resources which they can access. It is worth noting that liberal citizen groups often convey the impression that they are poor Davids confronting the rich Goliaths of the conservative right. 'Liberals speak in terror of the resources available to the groups on the right', observes Berry. Yet, these appearances are deceptive since on Berry's three criteria – visibility, credibility and funding, 'the liberal lobbies are far better off than competing conservative groups'.[8] Many of these organizations possess considerable resources. Numerous environmental groups have budgets in the tens of millions of dollars and have large staffs of lawyers, PhDs and expert lobbyists. This network of affluent activists and lobbyists has succeeded in establishing an important position of authority comparable to that achieved by consumer activists in the UK. It is worth noting that Europe-wide advocacy groups also possess considerable financial muscle. They play an active role around the proceedings in Brussels. A 1996 survey found that European-wide interest advocacy groups 'tend to have more permanent staff and higher budgets than the more numerous business lobbying groups'.[9]

The association of citizen groups with economic and social privilege is also evident in the UK situation. A recent study extolling the virtues of these 'post-materialist' associations notes that 'for the most part, political activism and the associational life that sustains it have remained middle-class phenomena in Britain'.[10] This study paints a picture of a Britain where the network of voluntary associations cater to the needs of the affluent section of society. The author of the study observes that Britain is a 'nation divided between a well-connected and highly active group of citizens with generally prosperous lives and another set of citizens whose associational life and involvement in politics are very limited'.[11] Consumer activism remains very much an elite project and its claim to represent the forces of powerless outsiders is belied by its privileged social status.

There is little point in speculating about whether or not the leaders of consumer activism are cynical or actually believe their rhetoric about constituting a movement of disenfranchised outsiders. They probably possess the conviction that they represent a movement from below, which is not tainted by vested interest and is independent from the established political class. The belief that they are motivated by the public good informs their political style. It also invests their political project with all the sanctimony of selfless altruism. Whatever its motives, consumer activism has managed to project an image that contrasts favourably with the squalid reputation of party politics. It has succeeded in winning a reputation for its selflessness and its ability to 'rise above' disreputable adversarial politics. The claim that 'they are not doing this for themselves' and that they are not interested in material rewards is widely accepted by media commentators. Television and radio programmes regularly feature consumer activists in order to give 'independent comment'. This image also prevails in the USA. As Berry points out, 'citizen groups stand out, of course, because many of them are able to present themselves as free of self-interest, while business, labor, and professional groups are commonly perceived as having a selfish interest in the issues they pursue'.[12]

The intellectual advocates of consumer activism believe that this movement represents a dynamic constructive force, with a capacity to renew the political and social life of Western societies. The well-known German sociologist, Ulrich Beck, has argued forcefully that the 'sub-politics' of grassroots citizen groups possess the capacity to transform an exhausted political system in an enlightened direction.[13] Consumer activists and legal advocates claim that the growth of complaining and litigating represents a positive sign that people are standing up for themselves and refusing to defer to powerful institutions. Roger Smith, director of the Legal Action Group, argues that 'high litigation rates may well be a sign of an active citizenry, prepared to be vigilant as to their rights'.[14] Advocates of consumerist politics contend that their success is due to the fact that the public has become more educated, more informed and more insistent on upholding its rights.

Berry too, believes that the new liberalism represents the standpoint of an educated public that is more aware of its rights. He believes that the success of this movement is 'the mark of a system that is open, democratic, and responsive to its citizens'.[15] Maybe. However, in his enthusiasm for the new liberalism, Berry overlooks one very important development. The rise of citizen lobbying groups is paralleled by a major decline in the participation of the American people in the electoral process. It seems that citizen activism for a small minority is inextricably linked to the political disenfranchisement of large sections of American society. There is considerable evidence that consumer and legal activism are symptomatic not of active citizenry but of a far more disturbing process: an erosion of social trust and of civic and social engagement. Apathy and a decline in political participation, rather than a renaissance of citizen activism, appears to be the precondition for the growth of consumer politics. The coincidence of citizen activism with a disturbing decline in political participation throws serious doubt on the claim that the Western public has become unusually politically educated and socially aware.

Social disengagement

Popular mistrust of authority is confirmed by the growing alienation of people from the system of elections. American-style voting apathy has become a fact of life in the New Europe, where a significant proportion of the electorate believes that voting is a waste of time. The low turnout of voters affects the authority of governments who are keenly sensitive to the erosion of their legitimacy.

Rather than renewing the political mandate, every election threatens to become an embarrassing reminder of the political wasteland that we inhabit. Apathy is no longer an adequate term of description for the steady erosion of the public's involvement in the political life of the US. In almost every presidential election since 1960, voter participation has steadily declined – from 62.5 percent of the electorate in 1960 to 50.1 per cent in 1988. During the election in 1996, only 49 per cent of the voting-age population bothered to cast their ballots – the lowest turn out since 1924. The election in 2000 continued this pattern, with only about 50 per cent of registered voters participating. The alienation of the public from the political process was particularly striking in relation to the election of 2000. Unlike the election of 1996, where the outcome was seen to be a foregone conclusion, the contest in 2000 was the most open for decades. Yet the number of Americans who voted was roughly the same as in 1996. According to the Committee for the Study of the American Electorate, the cumulative effect of voter disengagement during the past 30 years is that today, '25 million Americans who used to vote no longer do so'. Yet voter participation in presidential elections appears positively high compared to the ballots cast for candidates running for a seat in the House of Representatives. These have averaged around 35 per cent in the 1990s.

In the aftermath of 9/11, media pundits speculated that this tragic event and the sense of patriotism to which it gave rise might increase political participation. However, it soon became evident that not even such a major event could disrupt the pre-existing pattern of disengagement. The first 18 primaries prior to 5 July 2002 saw 'not just low turnout, but record low turnout – with only eight per cent of Democrats and seven per cent of Republicans going to the polls'.[16] At least during the November 2004 Presidential elections, the steady decline in the turnout of voters was halted. Voter turnout was 6.4 per cent higher than in 2000. However it is worth noting that 78 million Americans who were eligible to vote stayed at home, and only 30.8 per cent of eligible voters cast their ballot for the winner, President Bush.[17]

European commentators should not feel smug about the passivity of the American electorate. In Britain, the facts speak for themselves. It is worth recalling that back in 1997, New Labour was backed by only 31 per cent of those qualified to vote. Voter turnout at this election was the lowest for 80 years. Even the much-hyped public relations campaign surrounding devolution in Scotland and Wales failed to engage the public's interest. Voter participation in these 'history-making' elections in 1999 indicated that the public regarded devolution as another stage-managed event. Only 46 per cent of the Welsh electorate voted, while in Scotland, a high-profile media campaign designed to promote voter participation led to a turnout of 59 per cent, less than two-thirds. On the same day, polling booths in England were empty, with only 29 per cent of registered voters turning out for the 6 May local elections. The June 1999 UK elections to the European parliament brought a turnout of 23 per cent – and in one Sunderland polling station, only 15 people turned up out of the 1,000 entitled to vote. In the 2001 General Election, apathy emerged as the dominant issue under debate – and the turnout was an all-time low of 59 per cent. Tony Blair was returned to office with the backing of just 24 per cent of the electorate. He achieved the same feat in 2005 with the votes of only 22 per cent of those eligible to vote.

One of the most disturbing manifestations of the process of disengagement is that young people are even less inclined to vote than their elders. For example, during the 2001 general elections in Britain, the Electoral Commission estimated the turnout rate for 18–24 year olds at only 39 per cent – down 27 per cent from the 1997 elections. As Weinstein notes, 'as well as being less likely to vote in elections when compared with older age cohorts, young people have consistently fewer memberships of formal groups of various kinds, express less interest in politics and are much less likely to offer a party political identification'.[18] An interesting study of electoral behaviour in Canada confirms the finding that the turnout of young people at elections is about 20 points lower then that of their elders. This generational dynamic is underpinned by attitudes that regard the act of voting as not a particularly important one.[19]

The steady decline of voter participation is directly linked to a much wider process. Lack of participation provides a clear index of dis-illusionment and public mistrust in the existing political system. Surveys of American public attitudes indicate that approval of the government has steadily declined in recent decades. Whereas in 1958, over 75 per cent of the American people trusted their government to do the right thing, only 28.2 per cent could express a similar sentiment in 1990. Since the beginning of this decade, trust in politicians has continued to decline. According to one study, between the mid-1960s and the mid-1990s the proportion of Americans who felt that 'the government is run by a few big interests looking out only for themselves' more than doubled to reach 76 per cent. In the same period, the number who believed that 'public officials don't care about what people think' increased from 36 per cent to 66 per cent.[20]

A major study carried out by the Brookings Institution in May 2002 found that not even the wave of patriotism that followed in the aftermath of 9/11 translated into a durable growth of trust in the US government. This survey showed that whereas in July 2001 only 29 per cent of Americans expressed a positive regard for their government, this figure almost doubled to 57 per cent in the aftermath of 11 September 2001. However, by May 2002, public trust in federal government had fallen back to 40 per cent, and experts felt that the opportunity for the reforging of a relationship of trust had already probably passed.[21]

Surveys in Europe point to a similar pattern. Studies carried out in the European Union indicate that around 45 per cent of the population is dissatisfied with the 'way that democracy works'. In Britain, surveys reveal a high level of public cynicism towards politicians. A Gallup poll conducted in April 1995 concluded that most people's opinion of Members of Parliament was 'low' or 'very low'. A decade previously, only a third of people adopted this view. According to another survey, carried out in 1994, only 24 per cent of the population believed that the British government places the national interest above their party interests.[22] Politicians consistently come at the bottom of the list of professions that the public trusts. A survey published by the ICM in June 1999 found that only 10 per cent of the respondents stated that they trust politicians a lot, 65 per cent a little, and 25 per cent not at all.[23] A study carried out by the BBC in February 2002 indicated that many people under the age of 45 regarded politicians as 'crooks', 'liars' and a 'waste of time'.[24]

During the 1990s, the erosion of public trust was reflected in a national mood of suspicion towards the political system itself. What emerged was a brand of anti-politics, a cynical dismissal of the elected politician and an obsession with sleaze and corruption in Westminster and Washington. The Clinton era was one of permanent scandal; and controversy surrounded the manner of Bush's election, only to be followed by a series of corporate scandals culminating in the Enron collapse. In 2005, allegations of financial misconduct against Tom DeLay, Republican leader in the House of Representatives called into question the moral agenda he promoted as a voice of the so-called religious right.

New Labour's success at portraying the Conservatives as a party of sleaze was crucial to its electoral success of 1997 – but the New Labour government quickly found that it was not immune to the politics of scandal. A spate of minor scandals involving Labour MPs and ministers followed the 1997 election victory, and the issue of sleaze continued to haunt the government through 1998, as successive ministers were forced to resign. The suspicion that surrounds the manner in which Blair and Bush handled intelligence and information concerning weapons of mass destruction in Iraq is instructive in this respect. Instead of a principled opposition to the war, critics of Blair and Bush prefer to look for scandals and pontificate about conspiracies and cover ups. Similar patterns are at work on the European continent. In Germany, charges of financial misdemeanour by the formerly governing Christian Democratic Union (CDU) surfaced soon after its defeat in 1998. This resulted in a scandal that rocked German politics for the best part of three years, from which conservative parties never recovered. In recent years scandal has become a regular feature of German political life, the most recent being the alleged illicit emoluments received by members of the German parliament.

The question of trust

In reality, consumer activism is symptomatic of a profound process of atomization that dominates UK society and politics. In the past, consumer activism was not flattered with the description of social activism. It was characterized as what it still is – professional lobbying. Charities and advocacy organizations were often involved in the honourable business of raising public awareness of important social issues. Through briefing opinion-makers within the media and in political life, they sought to influence officialdom and parliament. Often their work possessed considerable merit. However, these organizations did not see themselves as constituting a movement. Their prime objective was to gain the ear of the powers, without any aspirations to be a popular movement. Nor did they often claim to be the voice of the people. They were in the business of advocating their own sectional opinions, and their aim was to gain a wider audience among influential opinion-makers. This was a self-consciously top-down approach which rarely sought to mobilize people beyond the dominant network of opinion-makers, officials, politicians and other professionals.

Today, consumer and environmental organizations have adopted a more ambitious profile for themselves. This shift is most strikingly illustrated in the transformation of consumer advocacy. Consumer groups have moved from being fringe organizations, whose main aim was the comparative testing of products, to become a powerful lobby that is widely portrayed as representing the voice, views and aspirations of the general public in their role as consumers of commodities and services. Consequently, an organization like the Consumers' Association now claims a representative role for itself. Unlike immodest environmental activists who claim to speak on behalf of the people, the Consumers' Association has a more restrained conception of its representative role. It makes a distinction between 'citizen interests' and more short-term and narrower 'consumer interests', and modestly claims itself to be the voice of the consumer rather than of the British people.[25] Nevertheless, this shift from lobbying to a representative status reflects an important expansion in the role of consumerism.

There is little doubt that the growth of consumer activism is bound up with the decline of traditional forms of political participation and social engagement. The question worth probing is whether this trend is merely a symptom of social disengagement, or whether consumer activism also reinforces the disengagement of the British public from political life.

The growing respect accorded to consumer activism is proportional to the decline of public trust in conventional authority. For better or worse, no institutions, not even the churches, are immune from growing public suspicion.[26] Widespread disenchantment with conventional institutions has created an opening for new, alternative forms of authority. The main beneficiary of this process has been consumer activists. Consumerism has been able to tap into widespread public disillusionment with politicians and traditional institutions, and to claim a role for itself as a credible source of authority. Consumerism is driven by the widespread perception that it is not possible to believe the words of politicians, business people, scientists and other traditional authority figures. It clearly reflects the politics of mistrust and fear. Consumer organizations recognize that the growth of their influence is rooted in the expansion of public mistrust. The Consumers' Association, for example, justifies its case for consumer representation on the grounds of 'low levels of consumer trust in the decision making process'.[27]

Since the status of consumer activism is so much bound up with prevailing perceptions of mistrust, it is inevitable that many of its leaders find it difficult to resist the temptation of manipulating this mood for their own ends. Jeffrey Berry concludes that citizen action groups in the USA have won considerable credibility because 'they have skilfully exploited the public's distrust of interest groups in general and business in particular'.[28] Exploiting public mistrust is an understandable response from activists, whose authority depends on the maintenance of suspicion towards formal institutions of authority. That is why the promotion of public mistrust is the message of consumer activism.

Contemporary society is hospitable to claims that a wide variety of dangers and risks are threatening society. Alarmist warnings about unprecedented threats continually fuel the perception of mistrust. Panics about children's safety, various forms of abuse, new technology, health and food products have become routine. Such panics can be of short duration. For example, the explosion of mass hysteria in Belgium in June 1999 regarding anxieties about health risks associated with Coca-Cola led to the withdrawal of 30 million cans and bottles. But within a few weeks it became evident that this particular panic was all in the mind, and that was the end of it. Other panics, for example over 'satanic ritual abuse', can influence people's actions for a much longer period. One of the distinguishing features of society today is that panics tend to follow one another in quick succession and attach themselves to an ever-growing range of subjects. This atmosphere of fear has created a situation where warnings about the possible risks of a new technology are far more likely to be believed than the reassurance of an expert authority. In these circumstances, the mood of 'better safe than sorry' provides consumer activists with considerable opportunities.

It would be wrong to suggest that the consumer activists set out dishonestly to exploit people's fears and mistrust. In most cases, they genuinely believe that politicians, business people, scientists and other professionals regularly cover up the truth. Environmental and consumer activists have deep-seated convictions that new products and technologies are likely to be unsafe and that they must make society aware of the multitude of dangers it faces. Their activities are born out of this conviction, and they believe that their insights entitle them to spread the gospel of mistrust. Encouraging people to fear, mistrust, complain and litigate is seen as a socially responsible act. Consequently, consumer advocates do not merely reflect the existing state of mistrust: they play an active role in educating people to believe the worst in most circumstances. They do not simply articulate the complaints of the powerless, but also attempt to extend the constituency of potential complainers.

Every healthy society benefits from scepticism and the refusal to accept unearned authority. And, no doubt, there are good reasons why so many traditional institutions have experienced a decline of their status. In many cases they bear direct responsibility for the erosion of their authority. However, whilst critically questioning the relevance of these institutions is an exercise in democratic accountability, an uncritical celebration of mistrust can only help to breed passive cynicism. Cynicism leads nowhere, certainly not to political renewal. Since consumer activism thrives on mistrust, it is difficult to understand how it can contribute to the kind of political renewal claimed for it by its intellectual supporters. Such a standpoint draws succour from the failure of the existing political institutions rather than from a constructive vision of how society should be run. Its authority rests on undermining trust in competing institutions rather than on its own accomplishments.

An oligarchical network

Social disengagement founded on the culture of fear represents the foundations of consumer activism. The erosion of civic solidarity and the growth of individuation has created a climate where shopping appears to have more meaning than democratic participation. And, precisely because professional politicians appear discredited, lobbyists can demand a new role for themselves. Consequently a space has opened up for the activities of advocacy groups, charities and non-governmental organizations to act as the voice of the people. No longer subservient lobbyists, they can claim the role of representatives of popular interest. For an otherwise isolated political class, advocacy groups provide an important point of contact with the so-called public. What New Labour strategists call the 'politics of inclusion' usually means bringing on board the representatives of a vast number of advocacy groups. 'Those who used to shout the loudest now find themselves invited in for tea and biscuits while their wildest ideas are given a polite hearing', observes Alan Travis, the *Guardian's* home affairs editor.[29] Campaigners are consulted and made to feel that they have some influence over the outcome of policy-making.

The new cosy relationship benefits politician and campaigner alike. What consumer activists gain is a privileged access to key official institutions. Many of them have been integrated into the network of consultative committees that the government uses to test out its policies. Many lobbyists have been directly co-opted into parliament, where they constitute a significant portion of the new generation of MPs. The political class also profits from this symbiotic relationship. Their deliberation with advocacy groups helps create the impression that genuine consultation has taken place. As long as political lethargy continues to prevail, consumer activism will be accorded a special status by officialdom. Why? Because the activism of the civic lobbyist allows the UK's political class to retain a semblance of accountability.

During the past decade, successive governments have actively encouraged volunteering and have increasingly sought to use non-governmental organizations to deliver services. In recent years, NGOs have become more and more integrated into the delivery of foreign aid whilst charities and advocacy groups have been given new opportunities to play an active role in the provision of social services. Official support for consumer activism is based on the belief that these organizations have a special privileged access to the public. Politicians and officials hope that their association with advocacy groups will endow their policy-making with greater credibility. Official patronage of advocacy groups represents an attempt to mitigate the effects of the loss of legitimacy previously enjoyed by the political class.

Consumer activism is the activism of small numbers of professional advocates in pursuit of a bewildering variety of causes. It is the activism of traditional pressure-group politics. But in the absence of a healthy political environment, such pressure-group politics are able to acquire unprecedented momentum and gain considerable public profile. During the last two decades or so, the network of UK advocacy organizations has evolved a division of labour between respectable lobbying organizations like the Consumers' Association, and campaigning organizations like Friends of the Earth as well as formally unaffiliated protestors. Protests over issues like animal experimentation and road-building are important for helping to transform the image of pressure-group politics into that of dynamic organizations that can claim the status of a movement. Whereas in the past, many voluntary organizations and charities preferred to keep a low profile, the maintenance of an active image today lends weight to the authority of an advocacy organization.

The activism of consumer politics should not be confused with the activism sought by traditional social movements in the past. Unlike traditional social movements, lobbying groups are not interested in mobilizing popular support *per se*. Campaigns organized by consumer activists are primarily media events designed to gain the maximum publicity. These campaigns are essentially public relations exercises oriented towards stimulating the interest of the media. The significance which advocacy groups, NGOs and campaigning groups attach to publicity is motivated by the realization that their influence is intimately linked to their public profile. Indeed, it is their ability to gain profile which determines the degree of influence they can exercise over officialdom. Consequently, the machinery of consumer activism is single-mindedly oriented towards gaining publicity through the media. A large active membership is quite unnecessary for an organization devoted towards oiling the network wheels of Britain's political oligarchy. Contacts in the media and friends in influential places are far more important than thousands of active supporters. Even when consumer activists take direct action, what counts is the presence of the television cameras. There is little point in protesting or demonstrating if it does not gain publicity for the group concerned. From this perspective, an act is deemed to be effective if it makes the news. It does not matter whether anything has been achieved on the ground, publicity is all that counts. The typical Greenpeace stunt involving a small core of professional protestors, whose appearance is carefully crafted for the maximum dramatic effect, is emblematic of the political theatre of consumer activism.

For its part, the media uncritically embraces the consumer activists. They are the good guys. Unlike politicians, they are not tainted by corruption or self-interest. They are typically portrayed as altruistic idealists, whose motives are beyond reproach. The media's celebration of consumer activism reflects a wider establishment consensus about the semi-official status of this movement. In all but name, the leadership of this informal network of NGOs has become integrated into the new establishment. As Kevin Dunion, the Scottish director of Friends of the Earth, boasted after becoming the first eco-warrior to receive an OBE, 'There is now an alternative establishment that is being listened to.' He added that he was 'very pleased that Prince Charles made the presentation as he is a fellow environmentalist'.[30] This 'alternative establishment' extends from the British aristocracy to representatives of 'Cool Britannia' in the media.

On any day of the week, the media will interview lobbyists concerned with the interests of consumers, single parents, the disabled, children and a variety of other groups. The interviewer will often refer to these individuals as representatives of the consumer or of the single parent. There is an automatic assumption that the head of a particular advocacy group has the moral authority to speak on behalf of everyone he or she claims to represent. The question of, say, exactly how the Consumers' Association gained the right to speak on behalf of millions of British consumers is rarely posed. Were they elected by these consumers? Did they gain their mandate from heaven? I know that I am a consumer. I also know that, although the Consumers'

Association speaks on my behalf, I have never been consulted about my opinions on consumer subjects.

The emergence of a new oligarchy of semi-official organizations, which have not been elected by the public but which claim to represent its voice, raises some disturbing questions about democratic accountability.

The small issue of democracy

As part of the UK oligarchy, consumer activists have a mandate to promote their cause through means not usually available to other movements. Anyone who recalls how protesting miners were treated by the police during the 1985 strike will be struck by the gentle camaraderie that the forces of law and order have adopted against protests organized by consumer activists. Anti-road protesters and demonstrators against live animal exports never had to contend with the level of repression experienced by the miners. I have seen hunt saboteurs, who have spat at and physically attacked their opponents, treated by the police as if they were naughty children. And anti-GM food protestors who destroy the hard work of others are often portrayed as if they have divine right on their side, since they exist on a higher moral plane than the rest of society.

There was a time when direct action and protest was systematically denounced as subversive by the media. As a 1960s student activist, I do not recall newspaper articles commenting favourably on our direct action. Denounced as 'dirty scum', radical activists were portrayed as a threat to society. Contrast this typical media reaction to 1960s direct action with the way consumer activists are portrayed today. Anti-road protestors are treated with the kind of indulgence that one usually reserves for one's grandchildren, with a Swampy-type character portrayed as some kind of underground Mother Teresa.

There is a fundamental difference between the honourable tradition of direct action and the media-driven protest of consumer activism. The aim of direct action was to mobilize people in order to shift the balance of power in society. Consumer activism is not about people gaining power for themselves. It is about 'empowering them' through the benevolent acts of others. It involves small groups of activists who see themselves as acting on people's behalf. The principal aim of this sort of initiative is not popular mobilization, but the exercise of influence over the media and significant people in the political oligarchy.

Consumer activism is not only highly respectable. It also has a semi-official mandate to break the law. Anti-GM foods protestors are often represented as idealistic young people who are acting on our behalf. As part of the UK political oligarchy, they have the kind of freedom to protest that is usually denied to ordinary mortals. When Lord Melchett, the aristocratic leader of Greenpeace, was recently arrested for criminal damage and theft, he was genuinely shocked by his treatment. As far as he was concerned, his action was a 'direct expression of "people's power"'. As the self-appointed voice of the British people, Greenpeace represents its action as an exercise in 'active citizenship' which 'keeps democracy healthy and responsive'.

Melchett, like many other leading consumer activists, possesses a highly elitist notion of democracy. They are driven by the conviction that, if they believe that something is wrong, then waiting for an unresponsive political system to do something about it is a luxury that society cannot afford. Professional environmental protestors assume that they have the moral authority to take matters into their own hands, since they are acting on behalf of The People. They believe that their unique philosophical insights entitle them to act in accordance with their ideology, irrespective of its legal implications. Stokely Webster, another protestor involved in destroying GM crops, explained her involvement in the following terms:

> I was doing a PhD in environmental ethics before I joined environmental groups and eventually the Greenpeace staff this year. I was asked if I wanted to join the direct action against the government's GM crop in Norfolk and I had no hesitation. It was open and accountable, the clear intention was to stop imminent pollution.[31]

Webster's explanation of her role is symptomatic of a profoundly elitist notion of accountability. Her claim that her action resulting in the destruction of other people's work was 'open and accountable' represents an exercise in linguistic acrobatics. Who was she open and accountable to? To her colleagues working at Greenpeace? To some wider protest movement? The British people? In reality, these questions need not even be posed by protestors whose 'clear intention was to stop imminent pollution'. From the standpoint of professional protestors, honourable intentions provide a moral licence to do whatever they think is necessary.

One of the key arguments used by consumer activists to justify their mandate to break the law is that the UK political system is not really democratic and that it is unresponsive to the demands of ordinary people. Doug Parr, the campaign director of Greenpeace UK, argues that the public have made their views on GM foods absolutely clear and that his organization is merely acting on the expressed will of the people. So how does Parr know that Greenpeace has a democratic warrant to break the law? It appears that people's fears about GM food 'come up time and again in focus groups'. For Parr, the focus group, a traditional instrument of market research, represents an arena for the expression of popular will. Another barometer used by the campaign director of Greenpeace to gauge the will of the people is their shopping habits. 'When Greenpeace "decontaminated" a farm-scale trial it was acting on behalf of people whose views were not being represented', writes Parr. Why? Because 'the public had already demonstrated its views very strongly by forcing GM foods off the supermarket shelves'.[32] Consumer suspicion towards GM foods is represented as an act akin to casting a vote in a ballot box. Presumably, if people stopped eating cornflakes and forced this cereal off the shelves of supermarkets, protestors would feel that they were entitled to wreck the plant that was producing such unwanted pollutants.

Parr also claims that protestors have acted on behalf of people whose views are otherwise not represented. How does he know? From focus groups? From market research into people's shopping habits? For a self-appointed representative of the public, the conviction of righteousness is sufficient to justify action. It appears that the consumerist critique of parliamentary democracy is driven by the motive of providing protestors with a *carte blanche* to break the law. George Monbiot, a leading media environmentalist campaigner, contends that disruptive protest is a civic duty. Why? Because 'parliament is incompletely representative'. 'It tends to concentrate on the concerns of target voters and powerful institutions, rather than those of the poor, the vulnerable or the unborn', writes Monbiot.[33] By dragging in even the unborn, Monbiot is able to construct a formidable constituency, whose voice is ignored by parliament. In turn, the claim to be able to speak on behalf of people not yet born expresses the kind of supernatural powers that ordinary politicians manifestly lack.

There is little doubt that UK democracy is imperfect and generally subject to vested interest. Most people have little say over the way that society is conducted and the political oligarchy possesses interests which often contradict what's good for society as a whole. Nevertheless, people at least have a formal right to elect representatives to speak on their behalf. Whatever the defects of parliamentary democracy, it does invite people to vote for individuals and parties that reflect their preference. This political system also allows people – albeit infrequently – to get rid of politicians who have lost the support of the electorate. Paradoxically, this system of defective democracy is far superior to the so-called active citizenship advocated by Greenpeace. Why? An elected politician and party at least have a mandate to speak on behalf of the public. In contrast, Lord Melchett can only speak for his colleagues, who gave him his post as executive director of Greenpeace. The issue here is not whether consumer activists are right or wrong about a particular subject. The point is that they are entitled to speak only for themselves and no one else. Lord Melchett can no more claim to speak on my behalf than the director of the Consumers' Association. In contrast, my MP – with whom I disagree on virtually every subject – has at least the right to claim to be my representative.

In reality, the consumerist critique of representative democracy is fundamentally an anti-democratic one. It is based on the premise that unelected individuals who possess a lofty moral purpose have a greater right to act on the public's behalf than politicians elected through an imperfect political process. Environmentalist campaigners, who derive their mandate from a self-selected network of advocacy groups, represent a far narrower constituency than does an elected politician. Judging by its record, the response of consumer activism to the genuine problem of democratic accountability is to avoid it altogether in favour of opting for interest-group lobbying.

The anti-democratic ethos of many consumer activists is clearly demonstrated in their opportunistic and self-serving attitude towards the law. Activists reserve the right both to break the law when it suits them and to use it when it serves their purpose. Monbiot claims that the law serves the interest of the rich and often discriminates against the poor.[34] Traditionally, this was a compelling argument used to demand greater democracy. However, today, consumer activists and their friends in the legal profession are likely to spend far more time using the law than demanding the expansion of democratic representation. Increasingly, campaigners seek to advance their cause through the courts rather than the political system. They appear to have a greater faith in an unelected judiciary than in parliament.

The problem with consumer activism is not only its anti-democratic ethos. Consumer activism thrives on the apathy of the British public. It elevates the role of the professional activist and transforms politics into a system of lobbying and oligarchical networking. Although it is not responsible for the social disengagement that prevails in society, it helps to perpetuate this state of affairs by contributing towards the further professionalization of political life. The result is a form of oligarchic politics that is far more restrictive than the old imperfect parliamentary democracy. It is the politics of fear in action.[35]

Notes

1. Lash, S. and Urry, J. (1994) *Economics of Signs and Space* (London: Sage), pp. 3–4.

2. R. Coward, 'Search for the Hero inside Us', *Guardian*; 19 February 1996.

3. 'Organic Food Isn't Good for You, and He Can Prove It', *The Sunday Times*; 12 August 2001.

4. 'A Fair Deal for Consumers, a Fair Deal for Business', press release; 22 July 1999, Department of Trade and Industry.

5. J. Vidal, 'Seeds of Dissent', *Guardian*; 17 August 1999.

6. A. Travis, 'The Camelot Effect', *Guardian*; 19 May 1999.

7. Berry, J. M. (1999) *The New Liberalism: The Rising Power of Citizen Groups* (Washington, DC: Brookings Institution Press).

8. J. M. Berry, 'A Look at Liberalism's Transformation', *Washington Post*; 11 July 1999.

9. Rabkin, J. and Sheehan, J. (1999) *Global Greens, Global Governance* (London: Institute of Economic Affairs), p. 10.

10. Hall, P. (1999) 'Social Capital in Britain', *British Journal of Political Science*, vol. 29, no. 3, p. 455.

11. *Ibid.*, p. 455.

12. Berry, *The New Liberalism*, p. 133.

13. This argument is outlined in a series of articles in Beck, U. (1998) *Democracy without Enemies* (Cambridge: Polity Press).

14. Smith, R. (1997) *Justice: Redressing the Balance* (London: Legal Action Group), p. 9.

15. Berry, *The New Liberalism*, p. 170.

16. See Seth Gitell, 'Apathy at the polls', *Boston Phoenix*; 4 December 2002.

17. See the *Washington Post*; 14 January 2005.

18. Mark Weinstein, 'Political Activity and Youth in Britain', in Todd, M.J. & Taylor, G. (2004) (eds) *Democracy and Participation: Popular Protest and New Social Movements* (London: Merlin Press) p. 189.

19. Blais, A., Gildengil, E., Nevitte, N. and Nadeau, R. (2004) 'Where Does Turnout Decline Come From ?', *European Journal of Political Research*, vol. 43, pp. 227–8.

20. Study by Gary Orren is cited in Skocpol, T. (2003) *Diminishing Democracy – From Membership to Management in American Civic Life* (Norman: University of Oklahoma Press) pp. 245–6.

21. Mackenzie, G. and Labiner, J. (2001) *Opportunity Lost: the Decline of Trust and Confidence in Government After September 11* (Washington DC: Center for Public Services), pp. 2–3.

22. Curtice, J. and Jowell, R. 'The sceptical electorate', in Jowell, Curtice, Park, Brook and Ahrendt (1995), pp. 141 and 148.

23. Findings of the poll published in the *Guardian*; 8 June 1999.

24. 'Politics a "turn-off" for under 45s', *BBC News*; 28 February 2002.

25. Which? Online Campaign: *Policy Report, Consumer Representation, Executive Summary*, 1999, p. 1.

26. This development is analysed in this volume, Chapter 6.

27. Which? Online Campaign: *Policy Report, Consumer Representation*, p. 3.

28. Berry, *The New Liberalism*, p. 131.

29. A. Travis, 'The Camelot Effect', *Guardian*; 19 May 1999.

30. Cited in BBC ONLINE NETWORK; 7 July 1999.

31. Cited in the *Guardian*; 17 August 1999.

32. 'Seeds of a Political Revolution', *The Times*; 23 August 1999.

33. G. Monbiot, 'Disruptive Protest Is a Civic Duty', *Guardian*; 19 August 1999.

34. *Ibid.*

35. See Furedi, F. (2005) *The Politics of Fear; Beyond Left and Right* (London: Continuum).

Bibliography

Action on Elder Abuse (1995) *Everybody's Business! Taking Action on Elder Abuse* (London: AEA).

Adams, J. (1995) *Risk* (London: UCL Press).

Barnardo's (1995) *Playing It Safe* (London: Barnardo's).

Bayerische Ruck (ed.) (1993) *Risk Is a Construct: Perceptions and Risk Perception* (Munich: Knesebeck).

Beck, U. (1992) *Risk Society: Towards a New Modernity* (London: Sage).

Beck, U. (1998) *Democracy without Enemies* (Cambridge: Polity Press).

Beck, U., Giddens, A. and Lash, S. (eds) (1994) *Reflexive Modernisation: Politics, Tradition and Aesthetics in the Modern Social Order* (Cambridge: Polity Press).

Bennett, G. and Kingston, P. (1993) *Elder Abuse: Concept, Theories and Intervention* (London: Chapman and Hall).

Berger, P. (ed.) (1991) *Health, Lifestyle and Environment − Counteracting the Panic* (London: Social Affairs Unit).

Berry, J. M. (1999) *The New Liberalism: The Rising Power of Citizen Groups* (Washington, DC: Brookings Institution Press).

Brown, P. (ed.) (1996) *State of the World 1996* (London: Earthscan).

Clarke, J. (ed.) (1993) *A Crisis in Care? Challenges to Social Work?* (London: Sage).

Community Care (1995) *Scare in the Community: Britain in a Moral Panic* (London: Reed Business Publishing).

Coward, R. (1989) *The Whole Truth: The Myth of Alternative Health* (London: Faber and Faber).

Cunningham, J. (1995) *Sociology of Counselling* (Glasgow: unpublished manuscript).

Douglas, M. (1992) *Risk and Blame: Essays in Cultural Theory* (London: Routledge).

Douglas, M. and Wildavsky, A. (1983) *Risk and Culture: An Essay on the Selection of Technological and Environmental Dangers* (Berkeley: University of California Press).

Durkheim, E. (1964) *The Division of Labour in Society* (New York: Free Press).

Erikson, K. (1994) *A New Species of Trouble: Explorations in Disaster, Trauma and Community* (New York: W.W. Norton & Company).

Etzioni, A. (1993) *The Spirit of Community: Rights, Responsibilities and the Communitarian Agenda* (New York: Crown Publishers).

Fekete, J. (1994) *Moral Panic: Biopolitics Rising* (Montreal/Toronto: Robert Davies Publishing).

Forward, S. (1990) *Toxic Parents: Overcoming the Legacy of Parental Abuse* (London: Bantam Press).

Fremlin, J. (1987) *Power Production: What Are the Risks?* (Oxford: Oxford University Press).

Fukuyama, F. (1995) *Trust: The Social Virtues and the Creation of Prosperity* (London: Hamish Hamilton).

Furedi, F. (1992) *Mythical Past, Elusive Future* (London: Pluto Press).

Garrett, L. (1995) *The Coming Plague: Newly Emerging Diseases in a World out of Balance* (London: Virago).

Giddens, A. (1991) *Modernity and Self Identity: Self and Society in the Late Modern Age* (Cambridge: Polity Press).

Giddens, A. (1998) *The Third Way: The New Renewal of Social Democracy* (Cambridge: Polity Press).

Gulbenkian Foundation Commission (1995) *Children's Violence: Report of the Gulbenkian Foundation Commission* (London: Calouste Gulbenkian Foundation).

Hanmer, J. and Maynard, M. (1987) *Women, Violence and Social Control* (London: Macmillan Press).

Hillman, M., Adams, J. and Whiteleg, J. (1990) *One False Move . . . A Study of Children's Independent Mobility* (London: PSI Publishing).

Horrocks, R. (1996) *Masculinity in Crisis* (London: Macmillan).

Jowell, R., Curtice, J., Park, A., Brook, L. and Ahrendt, D. (eds) (1995) *British Social Attitudes*, 12th report (Dartmouth: SCRR).

Kaminer, W. (1993) *I'm Dysfunctional, You're Dysfunctional: The Recovery Movement and Other Self-Help Fashions* (Reading, MA: Addison-Wesley Publishing Company).

Karlen, A. (1995) *Plague's Progress: A Social History of Man and Disease* (New York: Random House).

Kaufman, W. (1994) *No Turning Back: Dismantling the Fantasies of Environmental Thinking* (New York: Basic Books).

Kirsta, A. (1988) *Victims: Surviving the Aftermath of Violent Crime* (London: Century).

Krimsky, S. and Golding, D. (eds) (1992) *Social Theories of Risk* (Westport, CT: Praeger).

Labour Party (1995) *Peace at Home* (London: Labour Party).

Lamplugh, D. (1994) *Without Fear: The Key to Staying Safe* (Gwent: Old Bakehouse Publications).

Langford, W. (1999) *Revolutions of the Heart: Gender, Power and the Delusions of Love* (London: Routledge).

Lash, S. and Urry, J. (1994) *Economics of Signs and Space* (London: Sage).

Lash, S., Szerszynski, B. and Wynne, B. (eds) (1996) *Risk, Environment and Modernity: Towards a New Ecology* (London: Sage).

Leach, P. (1993) *Children First: What Society Must Do – and Is Not Doing – for Children Today* (London: Penguin).

Leiss, W. and Chociolko, C. (1994) *Risk and Responsibility* (Montreal: McGill-Queen's University Press).

Leslie, J. (1996) *The End of the World: The Science and Ethics of Human Extinction* (New York: Routledge).

Little Blue Book Committee (1992) *The Little Blue Book* (Oxford: Parchement Limited).

Luhman, N. (1993) *Risk: A Sociological Theory* (New York: Walter de Gruyter).

Lupton, D. (1995) *The Imperative of Health: Public Health and the Regulated Body* (London: Sage).

MacKinnon, C. A. (1989) *Toward a Feminist Theory of State* (Cambridge, MA: Harvard University Press).

Miles, R. (1994) *The Children We Deserve: Love and Hate in the Making of the Family* (London: HarperCollins).

Misztal, B. (1996) *Trust in Modern Societies* (Oxford: Polity Press).

Moore, M. (ed.) (1989) *Health Risks and the Press* (Washington, DC: Media Institute).

Morgan, J. and Zedner, L. (1992) *Child Victims: Crime Impact and Criminal Justice* (Oxford: Clarendon Paperbacks).

Mullan, P. (1996) *Deconstructing the Problem of Ageing* (London: unpublished manuscript).

Nelson-Jones, R. (1987) *The Theory and Practice of Counselling Psychology* (London: Cassell).

Olweus, D. (1993) *Bullying at School* (Oxford: Blackwell).

O'Riordan, T. and Cameron, J. (eds) (1994) *Interpreting the Precautionary Principle* (London: Earthscan).

Pfaff, W. (1990) *Barbarian Sentiments: How the American Century Ends* (New York: The Noonday Press).

Plant, M. and Plant, M. (1992) *Risk Takers: Alcohol, Drugs, Sex and Youth* (Routledge: London).

Preston, R. (1994) *The Hot Zone* (London: Corgi).

Pritchard, J. (1995) *The Abuse of Older People: A Training Manual for Detection and Prevention* (London: JKP).

Quick, A. (1991) *Unequal Risks: Accidents and Social Policy* (London: Socialist Health Association).

Rabkin, J. and Sheehan, J. (1999) *Global Greens, Global Governance* (London: Institute of Economic Affairs).

Roberts, H., Smith, S. and Bryce, C. (1995) *Children at Risk? Safety as a Social Value* (Buckingham: Open University Press).

Rock, P. (1990) *Helping Victims of Crime* (Oxford: Clarendon Press).

Rutter, P. (1989) *Sex in the Forbidden Zone* (London: Routledge).

Shrader-Frechette, K. (1991) *Risk and Rationality: Philosophical Foundations for Populist Reforms* (Berkeley: University of California Press).

Simon, J. (1995) *The State of Humanity* (Oxford: Blackwell).

Sinason, V. (ed.) (1994) *Treating Survivors of Satanist Abuse* (London: Routledge).

Singer, E. and Endreny, P. (1993) *Reporting on Risk: How the Mass Media Portray Accidents, Diseases, Disasters and Other Hazards* (New York: Russell Sage Foundation).

Smith, P. and Sharp, S. (eds) (1991) *School Bullying: Insights and Perspectives* (London: Routledge).

Smith, R. (1997) *Justice: Redressing the Balance* (London: Legal Action Group).

Social Services Inspectorate (1993) *Social Services Inspectorate Guidelines. 'No Longer Afraid'* (London: HMSO).

Sontag, S. (1990) *Illness and Its Metaphors* (London: Penguin).

Sykes, C. (1992) *A Nation of Victims: The Decay of the American Character* (New York: St Martin's Press).

Walklate, S. (1985) *Victimology: The Victims and the Criminal Justice Process* (London: Unwin Hyman).

Wann, M. (1995) *Building Social Capital: Self Help in a Twenty-first Century Welfare State* (London: IPPR).

Whiteley, P., Seyd, P. and Richardson, J. (1995) *True Blues: The Politics of Conservative Party Membership* (Oxford: Clarendon Press).

Wilson, J. (1993) *The Moral Sense* (New York: The Free Press).

Index

abortion 16, 166–7
abuse 48–9, 82, 86, 90
  cycle of 91–6, 176
  evidence for 84–5
  normalization of 79–91, 159, 172,
    176–7
  pathology of 92, 95–8
  see also children; women
Accident Line 12
accidents 8–9, 12–13
  non-recognition 9, 10–12, 13, 179
addictions 99–100, 101
advertising 162
advocacy groups 34, 181, 183, 191–2,
    193 *see also* consumer activism;
    environmental activism
AIDS (acquired immune deficiency
    syndrome) 33–4, 56, 157, 159,
    172–3
alcohol consumption in universities
    129–30
alcoholism 99
alienation 168, 184–7
Allison, Dorothy 83
Alton, David 166, 167
altruism 183
Ambert, Anne-Marie 49
America *see* United States
Angeli, Toni Marie 80–1
anxiety disorders 100
Apollo spacecraft 16
'at risk', concept of being 5, 27–8,
    76–7, 107, 153
Atkinson, Sheldon 81
attention deficit disorder 47, 100

authority, attitudes to 67, 135–40,
    150–1, 184–7, 189–91, 196
autonomy 142
  of risk 27–8, 71
aversion and avoidance of risk 2, 9–10,
    13, 15, 26, 53–4, 113, 153, 159,
    169 *see also* caution
awareness of risk 8, 25, 56–61, 63

baby-snatching 118
Baker, Jake 41
Balkan War Syndrome 23
Bangladesh 35
Bank, Russell 83
Barnardo's 122
BBC (British Broadcasting Corporation)
    136, 187
Beck, Ulrich 63, 71, 137, 184
Berliner, Lucy 84
Berry, Jeffrey 181–2, 183, 184, 189–90
Big Book of Booze, The 129
Bigelow, Jim 102
Bigelow, Kathryn 83
biological theories 176–7
Blair, Tony 186, 188
blame culture 10–12, 18
Boots the Chemist 81
Boy Scouts and Cubs 136
Brain, Christopher 164
Brent Spa oil platform 139
Bristow, Jenny 165
Britain *see* United Kingdom
British Legion 136
British Medical Association 97, 120

British Medical Journal (BMJ) 10–11, 13, 102, 157
British Sociological Association 127
Brookings Institution 187
Brookside 82
Brownies 136
BSE (bovine spongiform encephalopathy) 30, 64
Bulger, James 115–16
bullying 49, 86–7, 92, 105, 109, 161
  of teachers 87
Bush, George W. 185, 188
Byers, Stephen 180

Camelot 97
Canada 186
cancer 4, 30–1, 33, 44–5, 59
CanPan survey 84
Canterbury and Thanet Health Authority 141–2
Canvey Island (Essex) 19
capitalism 72, 74, 161, 167, 168, 175
Casement, Patrick 85
catastrophes 8–9, 16–20
  anticipation of 28–30, 34–5, 63
  non-recognition 9, 10–11
caution 8, 69, 75, 113–14, 119, 121–7, 138, 139, 148, 149, 154, 156, 159, 170–1, 176
  institutionalization of 114–15, 121
  see also aversion and avoidance of risk
Challenger space shuttle 16–17
change, experience of 67–8
Channel 4 television 83, 102
Channel Tunnel 38
charities 191
  named after victims 106
Child Accident Prevention Trust 179
children 7
  dangers facing 14, 31, 32–3, 39–41, 42, 45–6, 48–9, 54–6, 65, 76, 80–4, 87, 91, 92, 93–6, 104–5, 116–18, 176–7, 179
  generational gap 107, 114–15
  health 122, 179
  supervision of 121–5, 133–4, 141–2
  violence committed by 115–16, 120
Childsafe campaign 118
Christian Democratic Union (CDU) Party 188

Church of England 136, 142–3, 164–5
circumcision 102–3
Civil Service, British 136
CJD (Creutzfeldt-Jakob disease) 30
Cleveland 54–5
clomipramine 100
co-dependency 100
codes of conduct 6–7, 130, 161, 164–6
Committee on Safety of Medicines 59
community, breakdown of 4, 6, 18–19, 74, 116, 117, 134–5, 145–8, 155, 167–8
Community Care (periodical) 55
conkering 15
Conservative Party 108, 135, 155, 159
consultants 140, 151 *see also* 'experts'
consumer activism 179–84, 188–90, 191–6, 197–8
continuum of violence 89–90
contraceptive pills 59, 171
control 75–7 *see also* outcomes
Conyer (Kent) 116, 117
Coronation Street 82
counselling 72, 74, 96–8, 101, 125–6, 140–5, 151, 163–4, 178–9
Counselling, British Association for 97
crime 1–2
  fear of 1, 2–3, 5–7, 24, 31–2, 48, 106, 107, 129
  normalization 2, 3
  in universities 128–9
Crime Awareness and Campus Security Act (1990, USA) 128
crime complexes 3
Criminal Injuries Compensation Scheme 104
Cubs 136

damaged people 91–2, 150, 153, 168, 172
danger, preoccupation with 26, 28–35, 44 *see also* personal security
daring 10
deference 7
  raw fear and 8
DeLay, Tom 187
democracy 194–7
dependence
  on professional helpers 163–4
  of young people 121–7

dependent personality disorder 100
Diana, Princess of Wales 101–2
diarrhoea 35
diet 144–5
Dime chocolate bars 162
direct action 194–6, 197
disease 4, 29–31, 33–4, 35, 37, 44–6,
    56, 59, 157, 159, 172–3
Dixon, Jeremy 81
doctors, violence and 119, 120
domestic violence 76, 83–5, 87–8,
    92–6, 127
drink *see* food and drink
drinking water 15
drug-taking 116, 117, 128
Dunion, Kevin 193
Durkheim, Emile 145–6

Ebola 35
Edinburgh 96
egoism and egotism 146–7, 148, 167–8
elder abuse 49, 85–6, 93
elderly people 2, 6
    abuse of 49, 85–6, 93
    generational gap 107, 114–15
election apathy 135, 184–6
Electoral Commission 186
electro-magnetic fields 44–5
elitism 182, 183, 195, 197
empowerment 108, 142, 163, 194
endless risks 44
Endreny, P. 58
environmental activism 179, 180–2,
    188, 190, 193, 194–6, 197
environmental hazards 16, 17–19, 29,
    36, 37, 43–5, 79, 113, 153, 159
epidemics 29–31, 35, 37, 38, 44–5
Equal Opportunities Commission 106
Etzioni, Amitai 168
Ewald, François 8
exercise 34
experimentation (political, social and
    scientific) 13, 70–1, 115, 139, 145,
    149, 170, 173
'experts'
    perceptions of 35, 54–5, 96, 104, 181
    on safety 13–14, 15–16
    trust in 137–40, 143–5, 150–1, 178,
        189–90

facilitators 140, 142, 145
families 46–7, 48–9, 74, 75–6, 91, 101,
    105, 155 *see also* domestic violence;
    parenting
fatalism 5, 67, 94–5, 176–7
feminism 84, 88, 108 *see also* women
films 83, 137, 146
floods 17–19
food and drink, dangers from 15, 25,
    30, 99–100, 179, 180, 181, 190,
    194–6
food consumption patterns 144–5, 162
Foreign Affairs (periodical) 44
Forward, Susan 46
fragmentation of society 74–5, 167–8,
    169 *see also* social solidarity and
    isolation
free-floating dynamic 4–5, 8, 28
French, Marilyn 83
Fukuyama, Francis 134, 146
future, the 113
    fears about 25–6, 43, 44, 68–9, 73
    knowledge of 64
    see also outcomes; speculation

Gaitskill, Mary 83
Gallup 187
Garland, David 3, 8
Garrett, Laurie 29
generational gap 107, 114–15.
genetic engineering 42, 151
genetically modified (GM) food 179,
    180, 181, 194–6
Germany 134, 135, 188
Giddens, Anthony 63, 90, 169
Girl Guides 136, 165–6
Gladwell, Malcolm 37
global warming 29
Goldberg, Dr Ivan 41
Goldwater, Barry 107
Good Housekeeping (magazine) 118
'good lies' 34, 173
'good risks' 26
Gray, John 64
Greece 58
Green Party 136
Greenpeace 34, 139, 193, 195–6, 197
Guardian 18, 29, 33–4, 75, 82, 102,
    173, 191
Gulbenkian Foundation 93–4, 105

INDEX

INDEX

Hackney 48–9

Hackney Gazette 95

Haggerty, T. 7

Hanmer, Jalna 88–9

Harper's (magazine) 83

hazards 4–5, 16, 25, 27, 28, 35, 61, 62, 63, 64, 65 *see also* environmental hazards

see also illness

Health Education Authority 45

health promotion 27, 30–1, 33–4, 45–6, 59, 143, 144, 156, 163

Higgins, Tony 126

Hillsborough disaster 101

Himmelfarb, Gertrude 155

HIV (human immunodeficiency virus) 157–8

Hobbes, Thomas 7, 9–10

Home Office 33, 124

human relationships 47–50, 66–7, 71, 79, 83–4, 87–91, 108, 113, 114–15, 120, 123, 130–1, 162

humanity, disenchantment with 12, 36–7, 77, 91, 107–8, 148–51, 170, 175–6

illness 4, 11, 29–31, 33–4, 35, 37, 38, 44–6, 48, 56, 57–8, 59, 157, 159, 172–3

Imperial Cancer Research Fund 59

Independent 129, 154

Independent Television Commission 162

Internet 14, 41–2, 83

IVF (*in vitro* fertilization) 39–41, 170

Johnson, Samuel 26

Jowell, Tessa 3

Kaminer, Wendy 91, 96, 100

Karlen, Arno 29–30

KIDSCAPE 124

Koss, Mary 88, 89

Labour Party 41–2, 88, 135, 180, 181, 185, 186, 187–8, 191

Lancet, The 59

Landau, Ruth 39–41

Lash, S. 178

Lawson, Mark 33–4

Leach, Penelope 32

Leslie, John 29

'Little Blue Book, The' 129

Luhman, Niklas 62, 64, 70, 158

Lynch, Frederick 47

Lynmouth (Devon) 17, 19

MacDonald, Heather 56

MacKinnon, Catherine 88

Madonna 83

208

manufactured risks 35–6, 64
manufacturing of fear 56–7
masturbation 157
Maxim (magazine) 102
Maynard, Mary 88–9
media, the 16, 18–19, 24, 45, 58–60,
  68, 81, 82–3, 102–3, 115–16, 122,
  129, 130, 137, 177–8, 180–1, 183,
  192–3, 194
Medical Monitor (periodical) 49
medicalization of behaviour 98–101,
  143, 157, 176
Melchett, Lord Peter 195, 197
Memphis 106
Miles, Rosalind 32
Mintel 73, 126
military forces 166
misanthropy 81–2, 85, 91, 149
MMR (measles, mumps and rubella)
  vaccine 179
mobile phones 3
modernization 63–4 *see also* technology
  and technological advance
monarchy, British 17–18, 136
Monbiot, George 196, 197
moral values 154–73 *passim*
moralizing imperative 167, 170
Morgan, J. 104–5
Mothers' Union 136
mountain climbing 15
Ms (magazine) 88
MSF (Manufacturing, Science and
  Finance) Union 87
Murder One 82–3

NASA (National Aeronautics and Space
  Administration) 17
NASUWT (National Association of
  Schoolmasters Union of Women
  Teachers) 120
national lottery winners 97
National Union of Students 119,
  129–30
NATO troops, Balkan War Syndrome
  23
natural and unnatural risks 35–7, 64
Nature (periodical) 43–4
neighbours 19, 147
  'neighbourhoods without neighbours'
  6, 133

new disorders and addictions 47–8,
  98–100
New England Journal of Medicine 91
new liberalism 181–3, 184
new morality 76, 151, 168, 172
newly discovered hazards 63
NGOs (non-governmental
  organizations) 181, 191, 192, 193
Nine O'clock Service 164
non-judgemental attitudes 157, 163
norms of behaviour 75–6, 133–4
NSPCC (National Society for the
  Prevention of Cruelty to Children)
  82
nuclear energy 24, 34
nurseries 14

OECD (Organization for Economic
  Cooperation and Development)
  114
Ohio 32
Olympic Games 91
opinion polls 68
outcomes, lack of knowledge or control
  of 69–72, 113, 176

Paddington rail crash 23
panic 53–8, 190
  definition of 53
parenting 14, 39–41, 46, 55–6, 75, 76,
  80–1, 93–4, 121–5, 126, 142,
  162–3, 170
  training in 97, 140
Parkin, David 7, 8
Parr, Doug 195–6
pastimes 15
pathology of abuse 92, 95–8
patients, violence committed by 120
Pearson, Geoffrey 55
peer abuse 49, 80
peer pressure 7
perceptions of risk *see* risk consciousness
personal security 2–3, 13–16, 31–2,
  115, 119–20, 128–9
photographic laboratories 80–1
plagues 29–30, 31, 37
police force 166, 194
political correctness (PC) 151, 160–6,
  173
political democracy 196–7

political experimentation 70–1
political participation 74, 129, 180,
    181–2, 183, 191–2
politicians
    disenchantment with 184–8
    mistrust of 186–7, 190, 191
    superfluity of 187
politicization 1–2, 18, 107–8, 109, 154
pollution 43–5, 62
    of people by people 46–7, 50, 79,
    90–1, 106, 175
post-materialism 182, 183
post-traumatic stress disorder 18, 48, 98,
    103
precautionary principle 8, 69, 113, 138,
    170–1, 176
    applied to young people 121–7
Preston, Richard 37
problematization 66, 105, 125, 171
professionalization of everyday life
    140–4, 159
professions, attitudes to 136
Proulx, E. Annie 83
Public Interest (periodical) 55–6
public transport 14, 23

quality-of-life issues 182

RAC (Royal Automobile Club) 47
rail travel 14, 23
rape 49, 84, 88–9, 118, 171
Reagan, Ronald 108, 147, 159
Red Cross 136
Rees, Professor John 45
Reeve, Christopher 149
regulation 124–6, 128–31
    demands for 73, 125, 158, 163, 169,
    171
reproductive technology 39–41, 138,
    151, 170, 178–9
Republican Party 155
respectful fear 7
    raw fear and 8
risk
    analysis and management of 2, 5, 15,
    24–5, 70, 156
    autonomy of 27–8, 71
    aversion and avoidance of 2, 9–10,
    13, 15, 26, 53–4, 113, 153, 159,
    169 *see also* caution

awareness of 8, 25, 56–61, 63
    definition of 25–6
    sociology of 62, 65
risk consciousness 1–6, 9–10, 12–17,
    23–8, 32, 35, 37–8, 70–3, 136–7,
    153–4, 158–9
    consolidation of 106–7, 147
    explanations of 66–7
    influence of the media on 16, 58–60
    literature on 79
risk factors 27–8
'risk society' 63, 65, 71
risk-taking 13, 26, 63, 130, 158
risky activities 12–13, 15, 34
risky products and relationships 38–9,
    46
road rage 32, 47
Roiphe, Kate 83
RSPCA (Royal Society for the
    Prevention of Cruelty to Animals)
    136

safe sex 13, 130, 157–8, 172–3
safety, perceived value of 13–16, 123,
    153
SARS (severe acute respiratory
    syndrome) 30
satanism 79–80, 85, 103, 190
schools
    bullying in 87
    moral values taught in 154
    security 14, 119
science 10, 17, 56, 63–4, 136–9, 143,
    151, 190
self-belief and self-doubt 142–4, 148
self-help groups 74, 142, 177
self-interest 73, 145–6, 167
sex education 143–4, 157
sexual abuse and violence 31, 83, 84,
    85, 88–9, 92, 127
sexual addiction 99
Sexual Addiction Problems, American
    Association on 99
sexual revolution and counter-
    revolution 171–3
shared values 146, 154, 155
Shell 139
Sheppard, Kay 99, 100
Shrader-Frechette, K. 30–1
sibling assault 105

side effects 35–42, 68, 149, 171
Simpson, Mona 83
Singer, E. 58
single mothers 55–6, 75, 76
sleaze, political 187–8
Smiley, Jane 83
Smith, Adam 167
Smith, Roger 184
smoking 158
social attitudes 25–8, 42–3, 66–8, 77, 190, 197–8
social experimentation 70–1, 115
social phobia 47–8, 98, 100
social problems and policy 47, 65, 93, 94, 104
Social Services Inspectorate, British 85
social solidarity and isolation 74, 77, 87, 131, 134–5, 145–50, 154, 169, 177–9 see also fragmentation of society
Social Trends 144
social workers 27, 54–5, 82, 85
Social Workers, British Association of 82
sociology of risk 62, 65
Somerville, Julia 81, 82
Sontag, Susan 34–5
space travel 16–17
speciesism 71, 150
speculation, about future dangers 39–42, 43–6, 66
sperm counts 43–4
sport 34
Stearns, P. N. 7
stoicism 17–18
Stone, Oliver 146
'Stranger Danger' initiative 33, 116–17
strangers, attitudes to 33, 115–21, 124, 131, 133
streetwise children 123–4
students 24, 98, 119, 124–31
  regulation of 124–6, 128–31
students' unions 119, 129–30
subjectivity, diminished role of 70–2, 149–50, 153, 168, 175, 178
suffering, response to 178
Sun 18–19
sunbathing 33, 45–6
Sunday Times, The 59, 116

survival, focus on 28–31, 91–2, 148, 149–50
Sykes, Charles 142, 173

tampons 57–8
Tate, Dr Nick 154
teachers 120
  bullying of 87
technology and technological advance 14, 16–17, 24, 36, 41–2, 60–6, 69–71, 136, 137, 153, 178–9, 190
  see also reproductive technology
television 82–3, 102, 136, 162, 183
teenagers 2, 157
terrorism 4–5, 185, 187
Thatcher, Margaret 108, 147, 157
Time (magazine) 47
Times, The 62, 75
Townswomen's Guilds, National Union of 136
toxic families and parents 46–7, 91, 101
toxic shock syndrome 57–8
trade unions 74, 87, 97, 108–9, 120, 135, 147, 150
traditional values 153–73 passim
travel 26–7
  space travel 16–17
Travis, Alan 191

unemployment 65
United Kingdom 14, 15, 17–19, 30, 32, 33, 48–9, 54–5, 56, 58, 59, 62, 81, 82, 88, 96, 98, 101, 102, 105, 106, 115–17, 119, 121–2, 126, 129, 133, 134, 144–5, 147–8, 154–5, 159, 163, 164–7, 180–1, 183, 185–6, 187–8, 191–2, 193–4, 195–7
United States 14, 16–17, 24, 30–1, 32, 57–8, 65, 80–1, 88, 99, 100, 101, 102, 105, 106, 121, 125–6, 128–9, 133, 134–5, 146, 147, 153–5, 159, 161, 163, 181–3, 184, 185, 186–7
universities 87, 88 see also students
Universities and Colleges Admissions Service 126
University of Cambridge 129
University of Iowa 88
University of Oxford 129
University of Surrey 87

University of Syracuse 128
uranium, depleted 23
Urry, J. 178

vaccinations, of children 179
venous thromboembolism 59
victimhood, culture of 92, 101–8, 149,
    153, 178
Victim's Charter 108
Vidal, John 180
Vines, Reverend Jerry 4
violence 32
    cycle of 92–6
    see also children; continuum of
        violence; domestic violence;
        patients; sexual abuse and violence;
        women
voluntary risks 35
voter apathy 135, 184–6

Walsh, Clive C. 82
wealth, consumer activists 182–3
Webster, Stokely 195
Weinstein, Mark 186
Which? (consumers' organization) 26,
    181, 189, 193–4
women, violence and 84, 87–90, 108,
    119, 171–2, 176 see also feminism
Women's Environmental Network 57
Women's Institutes, National Federation
    of 136

X Files, The 136

Yalding (Kent) 18
young people 6, 164, 186 see also
    children; students; teenagers

Zaire 35
Zedner, L. 104–5